MW00576220

OFFICER'S OATH

Why my vow to defend the Constitution demanded that I sacrifice my career

By

Terry Lakin with Jack Cashill

and David Mercaldo

STEPHANIE THANKS FOR ALL YOU ARE DOING TO SAVE OUR COUNTRY! YOURS IN CHRIST!

TTM/TCM

Paperclip Press®

Officer's Oath

Published by:
Paperclip Press.
1603 Belvue Drive
Forest Hill, MD 21050
paperclippress.com

ISBN 978-0-578-08664-4
Library of Congress Control Number: 2012939370

Copyright ©2012, 2014, 2016 by Terry Lakin and the Terry Lakin Action Fund

Printed in the United States of America

By Terry Lakin with Jack Cashill
and David Mercaldo
Marco Ciavolino, Managing Editor
Current News Photography by Marco Ciavolino
Copyedited by Rita Samols
Draft composition and production by Enktesis, LLC / enktesis.com

Related Sites:
TerryLakinActionFund.com
SafeguardOurConstitution.org
OfficersOath.com

1. Constitutional Law, 2. Presidential Eligibility, 3. Voting

First Edition July 5, 2012
First Edition Update July 12, 2012
Second Edition May, 2014
Second Edition, Minor Edits, July 2016
LAKIN-OfficersOath-20140512-Color-PPP-v37

About the Contributors

Terry Lakin

Lieutenant Colonel Lakin received military orders in late February 2011 for deployment to Afghanistan, including a requirement that he provide "copies of his birth certificate." Lt. Col. Lakin is prepared to provide a certified copy of his certification of vital record that lists his birth hospital, physician's name and other key information. He has provided this document for many other required processes, such as his commissioning into the military as an officer, his security clearance and his marriage license. He is not only the highest-ranking active-duty officer to go public over this controversy, he is also the first active-duty officer to do so. Terry was court-martialed for his pursuit of confirmation of Barack Obama's eligibility to act as commander of our armed services.

Jack Cashill

Within the last decade Jack has written six books of non-fiction: First Strike, Ron Brown's Body, Hoodwinked, Sucker Punch, What's the Matter with California, *and* Deconstructing Obama. *Three of his books have cracked Amazon's top ten list. Jack has produced a score of documentaries for regional PBS and national cable channels, including the Emmy Award–winning* The Royal Years. *Jack has a Ph.D. in American Studies from Purdue University, has taught media and literature at Purdue and at Kansas City area universities, and served as a Fulbright professor in France.*

David Mercaldo

David Mercaldo, who holds a PhD in childhood neurological behavior, is a prolific writer on such topics as education, politics, finance and drama, and travels nationwide as a motivational speaker to schools, colleges, civic organizations and business groups. This educator, playwright and author has given us such acclaimed works as Ferry *(as in Staten Island),* Seamstress, *and now a children's book,* Little Boy Boo *(the adventures of a Yorkshire terrier who thought he was a boy).*

Marco Ciavolino

Marco Ciavolino, who holds a ThM, was engaged by the original law firm to provide technology support for the court-martial. He has continued to support Terry's case by overseeing the websites, communications, and the book. He has been working in general marketing-communications since 1984 and has provided a wide range of services to his clients including design, project management, application development, technology research, event management, logistics, web development, photography, radio and video (live and recorded), and campaign management for Republican candidates.

Dedication

Dedication

No story of hardship can be told without thanking the people who have stayed true to the storyteller throughout his ordeal.

Thank You, Jesus, for coming into my heart when asked, for forgiving all sins, past, present and future. Thank you for providing a goal for me to reach in my life and supporting me through my wrong turns, setbacks and hardships. Thank You too for letting me enjoy the fruits of honest hard work, letting me be part of a happy family, and giving me the ability to help and assist others in need as I try to follow in Your footsteps.

Thank you, my wonderful wife, Pilaiporn, for enduring your own hardships yet willingly sharing my burdens and accepting my shortcomings. You have enabled us to emerge through this ordeal stronger and closer, and now all the richer with Jesus as the third person in our covenant.

Thank you to my mother, father, brothers, family and friends. All of you have had a part in influencing my life for the better. I truly have been blessed to have such loving and dedicated parents, such loyal brothers, and such close friends. You have helped to form my belief system and have shared in the successes and joys of my life as well as its hardships.

Like Christianity, the family reveals its truest value only when a member is confronted with adversity. All too many people have no positive family ties and refuse to seek evidence of the Creator. My prayers go out to those people. I pray that they may find their way to the Lord, that they may become the anchor for a morally grounded family or group of friends of their own, and that they in turn find their way to help their neighborhoods, churches and communities. It is through such voluntary associations that our country became great. Our Founders knew their value, and it is up to us to prevent their erosion.

What is the purpose of this book? I have hoped to tell my story, share my opinions, describe my journey to Christ, and relate my continuing education in our country's history and in its wonderful Christian Founders. My greatest hope is that some who read this story will ask for Jesus Christ to be their Savior. I hope others will read, learn and truly make efforts to restore our country to the values embodied in our Constitution: freedom, self-reliance, strong families, churches and communities, and empowered states with limited federal government.

I am certain that I and the many people involved in this book will be attacked by those who wish to deny that our Constitution and country are in peril. Although I am not optimistic, I hope these critics will honestly and reflectively address the simplest of questions: Why has the question of constitutional eligibility persisted? Why has the truth not been accessible? Why has our nation become a nation where many in our government appear to be above the law? Transparency and truth are the solutions to the divisive issues that plague this country.

There are so many people who have helped support and protect me, and I wish I could name you all. But for present purposes, Jack Cashill, thank you for your assistance with this book and your mentorship in life views; David Mercaldo, for taking on the task of interviewing so many fine people who care about this issue; and Marco Ciavolino, thanks for your outstanding technical assistance, your friendship, and your guidance in so many areas. And thanks to all the other Christians and Constitutional Patriots who have believed in me throughout.

The truth matters. The Constitution matters.

Peace in His Name,

Terry

෨

OFFICER'S OATH

Why my vow to defend the Constitution demanded that I sacrifice my career

Table of Contents

Prologue

In July of 2010 a friend called and asked me if I wanted to take on an interesting project, one that would challenge the office of the President of the United States.

Who, I asked, was going to head up this project? He briefly explained the facts of Lt. Col. Terry Lakin's case and his decision to disobey a direct order, to force a court-martial. The plan was that the court-martial would allow for a modicum of discovery and investigation that might bring some resolution to the already growing concerns about Barack Obama's constitutional eligibility to be president.

So, after a few phone calls with Paul Jensen and Margaret "Ducky" Hemenway, we began the project. First we built the Safeguard Our Constitution website. This would form the foundation for Terry's communications. A few days later I traveled to Washington, D.C., to meet Terry, Paul, and Ducky for the first time at a private club in downtown Washington.

After a few introductions we taped Terry's first statement. Originally, we had intended to produce something very edgy, with shifts and cuts. But once I met Terry and heard him speak the script that we had worked on, it was very clear that we needed to just let him speak directly to the camera. In that first video, Terry stated clearly what he was about to do. Within weeks the video had been viewed by upwards of 300,000 people on YouTube.

Over the next few months the case grew in complexity and frustration. It was clear, early on, that the military courts were simply not going to allow for any discovery. The twists and turns of that experience are the core of the story, so we'll leave it to Terry to fill in those details.

A few weeks before the court-martial and highly probable conviction, Terry and his brother approached me and asked me to serve as the administrative trustee for a family trust that would raise money for Terry's family. It would also fund the communication of Terry's message and help protect him from further actions and perhaps another court-martial.

Why another court-martial? Even though Terry was stripped of his income, benefits, pension, and authority, he was still under the Uniform Code of Military Justice (UCMJ) until discharged. This meant he had to continue under his oath as an officer. An aggressive or ideological JAG could interpret any activity on Terry's part as 'conduct unbecoming an officer' and possibly send him back to jail.

Starting the trust was like starting any other business. We had to open a post office box and set up bookkeeping, bank accounts, and more. We needed a logo, a website, an e-mail address, and social media pages. Shortly after we began the Terry Lakin Action Fund, Terry was convicted and sent to prison.

During the five and a half months Terry was in prison, and subsequently, we received a steady stream of encouraging e-mails and letters. Yes, we had some hate mail and some very abusive phone calls also, but they were few and far between. And yes, Terry, his life, the websites, his mailings, and just about everything else about him (and me a bit as well) have been dissected and dismembered by a couple of the active 'Obot' sites. 'Obots' are devotees who are fixated on Obama without regard to Obama's behavior in the birth certificate area and other areas.

The two websites, two Facebook sites, Twitter site, YouTube account, and various support sites have logged more than a million visitors. The two Facebook sites had more than 3,000 friends between them. Terry received thousands of e-mail messages. They almost all say the same thing: *Thank you for standing up for our Constitution when no one else can or will.*

After the release of the purported long-form birth certificate on April 27, 2011, contributions dropped dramatically. The trust then had to drop back to maintaining only basic communications and supporting the Lakins as funds allowed.

This book fell within the scope of my responsibilities. It was my desire that it tell Terry's story well. However, the story is much bigger than Terry's personal experiences, and the country needs to know the principles behind Terry's decision and the broad range and scope of his influence.

To that end we invited several of those who have continued the work to contribute essays covering various related topics. You will find their insights in the second section of the book.

We then engaged an author, David Mercaldo, to interview key people who contributed to Terry's case intellectually or emotionally. You'll find their stories in the third section of the book.

The Constitution was not created by accident. It was not a frivolous effort. Some seem to think a bunch of guys were sitting around a pub one night and said, "Hey, let's start a country." The founding of our country was anything but that.

Our Constitution, Bill of Rights, Declaration of Independence, and other founding documents came out of thousands of years of struggle, death and dialogue, debate and discussion, bravery and boldness. They were the most precise expression of a form of government that finally abandoned the concept of a sovereign monarchy in favor of government by the people, for the people.

The basis of this form of government is the value of the individual endowed with unalienable rights (rights that cannot be revoked under any circumstances). It is on this basis that we formed representative government (not a democracy). We elect individuals to manage our affairs locally, statewide, and nationally, assuming they will manage according to constitutional law, which enabled them to be elected in the first place.

Any elected official or appointee who flagrantly refuses to comply with the Constitution by commission or omission must be called to account.

That is all Terry asked for: simple compliance with the Constitution. As of the date of this prologue neither Obama, nor his staff, nor any of the sitting members of Congress have been willing to do what Terry did.

The Constitution is demanding. It demands that we learn it and protect it.

And what is the reader to take from this work?

- First, hopefully, a deepened appreciation for a man who took seriously his oath to protect and defend the Constitution of the United States, an extraordinary document that came out of millennia of physical and intellectual struggles.
- Second, an awareness of the effect that one man or woman can have when they stand up for what is right. Terry's huge personal sacrifice has provided the motivation for many others. Read the vignettes of some of them in the third part of this book.

- Third, the conviction that we must all work to defend what makes this country great and good and bring it back to its senses.
- And finally, the desire to get involved in the political process at any level.

Teach your children, teach others, and participate in the work of running this great country.

&

Wednesday, August 20, 2014

We now find ourselves five years past the beginning of this issue. A few continue the effort with diligence. Every Senator and Congressman and numerous elected officials have been informed, notified, and visited. Yet not one will even ask for a simple hearing to get the facts straight.

What do they have to lose? If they prove that Obama is qualified they end the issue. If they find he is not, they save the Republic. Yet month after month Congress will focus on a number of significant and insignificant issues. We have seen full up hearings organized within hours. Still this issue, the one of Constitutional integrity and the authority of the office of the President, goes unattended to and is carelessly discarded.

Court after court continue to dismiss many legitimate cases. Our elected officials claim they have more important work to do than to focus on a piece of paper. And Obama has skillfully avoided the issue with persistence so that he has convinced hundreds of well-educated leaders and millions of citizens that it really does not matter.

Early in the project we would get barraged with foul-mouthed calls and emails. Many said, "It's not that important. Leave Obama alone. It just doesn't matter" We would ask them, if you are so willing to give up this very clear part of the constitution what will you give up next? Freedom of religion, speech, right to bear arms, freedom from frivolous search and seizure?

Well, it does matter. And it should matter to every United States citizen. It should matter to you.

Marco Ciavolino
Administrative Trustee for the Terry Lakin Action Fund

&

1. 27 April 2011

"Lakin, come over here, come over here!" said one of the ch'mos.[1]
"You've gotta see this."

I was staying in the Joint Regional Correctional Facility at Fort Leavenworth, Kansas, a prison in all but name. At that moment I was about to leave my cell, a windowless, 14 x 7 model of Army efficiency: two steel bunks, two steel half lockers, a combined steel sink and commode, and a sheet metal desk with a sheet metal seat that doubled as a step for the upper bunk.

Until I went to prison I had no idea how much I would come to appreciate luxuries like plastic and porcelain.

Looking back, I am sure it had to be the early evening when the ch'mo alerted me. I was on my way to outdoor rec at the time, and rec followed our early supper. Thank God for rec! Although less than an hour long, it helped me keep in shape and keep my sanity. I usually did some running

---

[1] Ch'mo is prison shorthand for a child molester.

and sprints around the fifth-mile track, and power walking when I could do no more.

I had started running when I was stationed in Honduras in 1994–95. I ran around the airfield; there wasn't much else healthy to do there. Later, in Germany and Bosnia, I confess to slacking off some. In Germany, in those rare moments when I wasn't serving the troops, it was often too cold. In Bosnia, it was too hot, and I am not referring to the weather. There were land mines planted all over the place. One wrong step off the beaten path, and your running career could be over quickly and permanently. Sometimes we would even find land mines *in* the path. Luckily for us, these mines had lost their reliability over the years, so it was not quite as hot as it once was.

It wasn't until I was sent to Hawaii that I got serious about running and swimming. I did some mini-triathlons there and ran the famous Honolulu Marathon. In Hawaii I was attached to the 25th Infantry Division (Light). In 2003, the Division deployed overseas, part of it heading for Iraq, the rest, me included, to Afghanistan.

My division was based at Kandahar Airfield. There we renovated most of the "Talibans' Last Stand," a hardened concrete airfield hangar with a big hole in the roof from a JDAM guided bomb. My bunk for several months was against the plywood wall on the interior edge of the blast damage. In October of that year, our unit made a hasty move to Shindand Airfield to quell the Herat riots. We then set up Regional Command–West and were responsible for providing security for a large area of the country.

Very generously, the Honolulu Marathon officials sent us all the equipment we needed to keep the race going. Later that year, 200 of us ran the Honolulu Marathon, but thanks to Honolulu's generosity and the Army's support, we ran our Honolulu Marathon in Afghanistan. The unit at Salerno hosted it.

If "Salerno" does not sound like a name you would expect to find in Afghanistan, there is a reason why. It was named for the beachhead in Sicily where the 505th Parachute Infantry Regiment dropped in on 14 September 1943.

My physician assistant (PA) and I trained for the marathon while we were at Shindand. He was a little better runner than I and much more of a running enthusiast. We made the arrangements to get our area medically covered and then flew together on a C-130 supply flight to Kandahar. From there, a couple of Chinook helos took a group of us to Salerno.

My PA was a good friend with a great backstory. He and his brother fled Hungary when it was still Communist and made their way to a refugee camp and eventually to the United States. Here, he became a naturalized citizen and a very successful PA and officer in the U. S. Army.

To get back and forth between bases, the runners were able to hitch rides on a few Chinooks and a C-130. At the start of the race, a few Harriers did a fly-by, and a B-2 dropped some flares to let the Taliban know we were not to be messed with. If I don't get a chance to say it later, I want to thank now all those people who did so much to support our troops wherever we went.

Now, back to prison. On 27 April 2011, I was being held in the minimum-security quarters at Leavenworth. I had recently been moved there from medium security because I had only a few weeks left of my sentence. More on this later.

This particular cellblock had two levels of twenty cells, ten on each side, and a common area in the middle. There were two TVs in that common area. The ch'mo directed me to the one on which President Barack Obama was speaking. We watched an extended clip from a press conference he had given that morning. I was at my prison job when the press conference aired, and there had been little warning that it was coming, so I had missed it.

Although some of the words I heard I won't forget, I can't claim to remember them all, so I have gone back and watched the video. Let me share portions of it with you.

> OBAMA: As many of you have been briefed, we provided additional information today about the site of my birth. Now, this issue has been going on for two, two and a half years now. I think it started during the campaign. And I have to say that over the last two and a half years I have watched with bemusement, I've been puzzled at the degree to which this thing just kept on going. We've had every official in Hawaii, Democrat and Republican, every news outlet that has investigated this, confirm that, yes, in fact, I was born in Hawaii, August 4, 1961, in Kapiolani Hospital.

"Every official in Hawaii"? I guess the president did not consult with Tim Adams. During the 2008 election cycle Adams served as senior elections clerk for the City and County of Honolulu. He saw enough shenanigans there that in September 2008 he resigned and headed back to graduate school in his native Kentucky.

In 2011, shortly after my release from Leavenworth, Adams posted his masters thesis from Western Kentucky University. It was titled "Discourse and Conflict: the President Barack H. Obama Birth Certificate Controversy and the New Media."

In his thesis Adams tells the story of what happened to him when in 2010 he innocently went public with what he knew about the famed birth certificate. "There is no hospital record of his birth in Honolulu," he said in a June 2010 radio interview and repeated in his thesis, "and the Hawaii Department of Health told us in the Elections Office that there was no birth certificate."

"From all I have seen," Adams continued in the interview, "Obama has lied about being born in a hospital in Hawaii. It simply didn't happen."

If you don't know about Adams, there is a reason why. Within a week of his one radio interview on the subject, tech-savvy Obama fans launched "phishing" attacks against Adams by digging their way into his personal data. The functionaries who represented Western Kentucky University were verbally abused, threatened with violence, and charged with institutional racism. Adams' contacts at WKU were told in no uncertain terms that his Adams was a Nazi. And MSNBC's Keith Olbermann publicly named Adams the "Third-Worst Person in the World."

Adams, who is anything but a conservative politically, was stunned. Although his WKU superiors did not boot him, they put him under a gag order until he graduated. If other Hawaiian officials needed a warning, the abuse of Tim Adams served it up on a platter. As of this writing, no official in Hawaii has made a serious effort to look into Obama's birth certificate, and those who said they did have not been able to keep their stories straight.

"Bemusement" was another word in Obama's presentation that struck me way wrong at the time. Obama said he had watched "with bemusement." Did he watch "with bemusement," I wondered, when I kissed my wife and three children good-bye and headed off for five months at Fort Leavenworth?

> OBAMA: Now, normally I would not comment on something like this, but . . . during that entire week the dominant news story wasn't about these huge, monumental choices that we're going to have to make as a nation. It was about my birth certificate. And that was true on most of the news outlets as well.
>
> And so I just want to make a larger point here. We've got some enormous challenges out there. We're going to have to make a series of very difficult decisions about how we invest in our future but also get a hold of our deficit and our debt—how do we do that in a balanced way.
>
> And this is going to generate huge and serious debates, important debates. And there are going to be some fierce disagreements—and that's good. That's how democracy is supposed to work. And I am confident that the American people and America's political leaders can come together in a bipartisan way and solve these problems. We always have.
>
> But we're not going to be able to do it if we are distracted. We're not going to be able to do it if we spend time vilifying each other. We're not going to be able to do it if we just make stuff up and pretend that facts are not facts. We're not going to be able to solve our problems if we get distracted by sideshows and carnival barkers.

"Carnival barkers"? That was the phrase that stung most. I suppose the president was referring to Donald Trump, who had publicly challenged the president's nativity story, but I thought he might very well have been referring to me as well. If I was not a carnival barker, I must have been part of the "sideshow." I must admit I was not a very big part of it. From the beginning the mainstream media had little interest in what I was doing, and the president probably less.

> PRESIDENT: I know that there's going to be a segment of people for which, no matter what we put out, this issue will not be put to rest. But I'm speaking to the vast majority of the American people, as well as to the press. We do not have time for this kind of silliness. We've got big problems to solve.

And I'm confident we can solve them, but we're going to have to focus on them—not on this. Thanks very much, everybody.

"Silliness"? Is that what all my efforts amounted to, court-martial and imprisonment included? You might think that at this point I was totally deflated, but I wasn't. I was a little disappointed, but more confused than disappointed. I hoped his birth certificate was for real, but I was skeptical. "Trust but verify," President Reagan had said.

My release date was 13 May 2011. The Jerome Corsi book *Where's the Birth Certificate?* was scheduled to come out days later. I had been listening to Trump, and apparently the president had been listening too. My suspicion was that the pressure was mounting. I figured the president had to say something, but what he said did not convince me. My fellow inmates knew what I was in Leavenworth for, and they said out loud pretty much what I felt. I should add that Obama has few fans in the U.S. Army, even in its prisons. Say what you will about prisoners, they develop an even healthier respect for freedom than most of the rest of us. "If this is a sideshow," said one prisoner, "Obama is the one who caused it." I was heartened. Most of them got it. Most of them were sympathetic. Most of them respected me for the stand I had taken. The ch'mos too. Before judging too harshly, please be aware that a certain percentage of all prisoners are falsely accused.

One of them asked how I felt. "Relieved," I said. "I'm glad it's finally out."

"That should help you," he said. "Don't you think they'll drop the charges now?"

"I doubt it," I said. "You know how the Army works."

"One question, Terry."

"Shoot."

"All you were asking for was a birth certificate, correct? If Obama had nothing to hide, how come he didn't release it a long time ago?"

I guess what they say is right: no one knows a con job better than a convict.

2. Are You Still Free?

It is a long drive from my home in Woodbine, Maryland, west of Baltimore, to the Aberdeen Proving Grounds (APG) on the eastern edge of that same state. Given where it eventually led me, namely prison, some people would say "too long." That "some" would come to include people very close to me, including my parents.

During those years of President Obama's rise, I was commuting from Woodbine to APG. Depending on traffic, and there was always lots of it, the trip could take as long as two hours each way. I filled that time as best I could with audiobooks and talk radio.

I think it was Socrates who said, "The unexamined life is not worth living." I don't know what he said about the examined life, but I can tell you from my own experience that it is no picnic either.

It was tough to leave Woodbine each morning. We have a nice home in a wonderful subdivision in a great little community, twenty minutes from what my wife Pili likes to call "civilization." More than the house, of course, it was my family that I hated to leave behind.

Before I left in the morning, I took great care to give each of my three sleeping children a small kiss and whisper, "I love you so much." My military and medical careers have taught me to appreciate each moment with my family, as those moments can be drawn short unexpectedly.

I met Pili in medical school in 1993 at what was then called the UHS–COM, the University of Heath Sciences–College of Osteopathic Medicine. We just called it U-SCUM. Today, it is called Kansas City University of Medicine and Biosciences. We were carrying our microscopes to histology lab and I offered to help with her case, which to a tiny girl like Pili must have seemed like a small piano. I thought at the time, and forgive me for thinking in such limiting terms, "A pretty Asian girl with a Southern accent. Does life get any better?"

Pili, of course, proved to be much more than that, and the better I got to know her the more I appreciated her wisdom and her strength. Believe me, I could not have endured what I have gone through without her support. And forgive me again, but if you have seen Pili you know that she is little, she is Asian, she still has a bit of a Southern accent, and she is much prettier than I deserve.

Pili was born in Thailand. Her father was a doctor, her mother a nurse. Much to my good fortune, her parents brought Pili to the United States to live when she was seven years old. Happily for me, too, she decided to follow in her father's footsteps or else we would not have met.

After medical school, we each finagled an internship in Denver, I at Fitzsimmons Army Medical Center in nearby Aurora and she at Presbyterian–Saint Luke's. It was during that year in Colorado that we married, first at my family's Congregational church in Greeley and later at a Buddhist monastery in Denver.

Our first child, Holly, was born at Fort Bragg in 1999. Our first son, Andrew, was born at Tripler Army Medical Center in Hawaii in 2002—and yes, we can validate that in about a half-dozen ways. On the last day of 2007, our second son, Jackson, was born at National Navy Medical Center in Bethesda, the same campus where I studied for my masters in public health and did a second residency in occupational and environmental medicine. Pili lovingly put her career as an internal medicine physician on hold to raise our three children. I know they will appreciate this later on. I appreciate it right now.

Tough as it was to leave home each morning, as an officer in the world's greatest military, I had my duty. That duty is summed up in the officer's oath:

> I, Terrence Lee Lakin, do solemnly swear that I will support and defend the Constitution of the United States against all enemies, foreign and domestic, that I will bear true faith and allegiance to the same; that I take this obligation freely, without any mental reservation or purpose of evasion; and that I will well and faithfully discharge the duties of the office upon which I am about to enter; So help me God.

The "God" part matters. It is not just a word on a page. In Psalm 15, David asks the Lord, "Who may live on your holy mountain?" David learns that the mountain-dweller "keeps an oath even when it hurts, and does not change his mind." Before my ordeal was through, I would identify with David, not just the David of the Psalms, but David as in David versus Goliath. In fact, when meeting with two congressional staffers later, they raised the Goliath image. They joked that I was confronting not just one Goliath but a dozen or so of them. Scary thought!

I will come back to this point, but the reader needs to know the difference between the oath taken by officers in all seven of the uniformed services and that taken by enlisted personnel. If you review the oaths you will easily see the issue: *The oath taken by officers does not include any provision to obey orders; while enlisted personnel are bound by the Uniform Code of Military Justice to obey lawful orders, officers in the service of the United States are bound by this oath to disobey any order that violates the Constitution of the United States.*

Needless to say, that understanding of the officer's oath, once I accepted its implications, would change my life.

From August 2007 to June 2009, as a lieutenant colonel in the United States Army, I served as Program Manager for Occupational Medicine at Aberdeen Proving Grounds. In this capacity, I supervised a staff of five and consulted on occupational medicine issues throughout the world. These included battlefield exposure to chemical and biological weapons and the health and wellness of workers who handled these materials.

My medical studies, especially in public health, showed how often in the past flawed or biased medical research led to false results. So I learned how important it was to probe, to sort out the valid from the invalid, to seek out the truth.

And yet the more attention I paid to things political, the more I began to wonder why the major media had abandoned their skepticism on many issues, especially on anything having to do with Barack Obama. I was astonished at their lack of interest and lack of scrutiny, and the media's willingness to ignore any of the facts.

I would often come home at night and check out on the Internet what I had heard that day on talk radio. I would do the same on weekends. I took nothing for granted. I adopted an informal "50 percent" rule: if only half of what I was hearing on talk radio was true, it was appalling.

I was reading books as well to give me a better grounding, and hats off here to Mark Levin. Listening to him was an education in itself. I finished reading his book *Liberty and Tyranny* when I finally had a chance to catch up on my reading—in prison.

The more I learned, the clearer I could see that my subscription to the *Washington Post* was not my best investment. In the run-up to the 2008 election, I wrote the *Post* a couple of critical letters asking why its reporting was so biased. Three weeks before the election, I had had enough and sent the following e-mail to *Post* ombudsman Deborah Howell canceling my subscription:

> Ms. Howell,
>
> I read with an open mind your column on 12 October 2008. I perceived your attempt to defend your paper as being unbiased, weak as it was. . . . Then I look at your front page today, 13 October 2008. Great headline about Obama, and low on the front page you have a crappy old picture of John and Cindy McCain with a story that has as much quality news as I would expect from a middle-schooler.
>
> I have been an independent and still am. But I am totally against your paper and the mainstream media in your lack of vetting our candidates. Why would you not have any stories on the ACORN investigation? Why do you refuse to look at alliances that Obama could have with William Ayers,

ACORN, etc.? Sean Hannity is correct, "Journalism in America is dead." You prove it. My support is going to McCain, Republicans and Reagan Conservative ideals.

Terry Lakin
Proud Veteran and current Soldier

Given my military status, this letter was not for publication. Although Ms. Howell wrote back denying any bias, a few weeks later she had an apparent change of heart. Here is what she wrote in the *Post* after her newspaper helped elect Barack Obama president.

The *Post* provided a lot of good campaign coverage, but readers have been consistently critical of the lack of probing issues coverage and what they saw as a tilt toward Democrat Barack Obama. My surveys, which ended on Election Day, show that they are right on both counts.

Howell quit the *Post* a month later. "Some of us think we're just a little more special than some of the folks we want to buy the paper or read us online," she wrote in her farewell column. Amen to that, sister! In the next few years, I would learn firsthand just how special these people thought they were.

At work, many of my colleagues had the same concerns I did. We were scared about the direction in which our country was headed. We were especially worried after the election when the new president began to treat the Constitution as if it was just a list of suggestions.

One of my supervisors, as much a mentor as a friend, was as concerned as I was. Together, we went to one of the first Tea Parties, this one in Washington outside the White House on 15 April 2009. We were a little late getting started, but we had good conversations on the trip down, all day for that matter, on things we rarely discussed in depth.

One subject was integrity. When we walked around Washington looking for the site of the rally, we saw any number of federal buildings inscribed with calls for truth and justice. One inscription at the Supreme Court seemed to capture my feelings perfectly: "Justice the Guardian of Liberty." We had to ask ourselves whether we were honoring the wishes of the Founders, and the honest answer was no.

Once at the rally, we hung in the back. As active military, we avoid direct involvement in the political process and attended the rally only because it was our day off. Although it was cold and rainy, there were many people there and much to see, including quite a few people dressed in colonial garb. Some were warning not about the tyranny of the British but the near tyranny of institutions like the Federal Reserve. At the time I did not know much about their issues, but I respect their opinions now.

I was most touched when we joined a group at the fence of the White House. People were taking turns speaking through a battery-powered bullhorn. I remember in particular one middle-aged Hispanic woman warning of the dangers of socialism. I suspect that she had seen enough of it where she came from.

Then a handsome young guy took hold of the bullhorn. He was wearing a leather duster, as was his pretty wife, and he had his toddler on his back in a carrier. He spoke up, said he was military, recently returned from deployment, and was extremely worried about what the future held for his child. He said there was no need for hateful rhetoric, but there was no reason not to ask questions about our commander in chief. One of those questions centered on Obama's eligibility to be president.

I had hoped to hear Alan Keyes, and we managed to catch the tail end of his speech. From what I heard that day and what I have seen in the video of his speech, the former ambassador and presidential candidate did not disappoint. I know no one who speaks so eloquently on the subject that was coming to matter to me almost as much as my family: the Constitution I swore to support and defend in my officer's oath.

"Are you still free?" Keyes asked the crowd. "Do you still have the courage to maintain your freedom?" He did not mince words, and those words have reached my heart.

"If you have come together here today to give me an affirmative response," Keyes continued, "and then go home and reject your responsibility, then you might as well not have come."

I would go home, but I would not reject my responsibility.

&

3. Never Give Up

In the movies, at least, it is the restless hippie child who rebels against his straight-arrow conservative parents. In my real-life family, it is kind of the other way around.

Although I have loving parents, and their first priority has always been to support me, I think it would have been easier on them emotionally if I'd had a drug or alcohol problem than a problem with the constitutional fitness of my commander in chief.

My father, Franklin Pierce Lakin, is one of the rare Americans to be named, at least indirectly, after the fourteenth president of the United States, Franklin Pierce. The fact that his mother's maiden name was "Pierce" may have had more to do with his naming than that Franklin Pierce was a Democrat, like my father and probably his father too.

Dad grew up in Santa Fe, New Mexico, a time and place when Democrats saw military service as an honorable pursuit. A bright kid—his mother taught Spanish and business at his high school—he graduated a year early and promptly enlisted in the U.S. Marine Corps after a friend convinced him that it was better to volunteer than get drafted.

The Marines did not scare him. When he was one of the youngest and smallest players on his high school football team, he never shied from tackling guys twice his size. Now he was ready to tackle the Marines.

Soon enough, he found himself on the way to an undeclared but very hot war in Korea, where he served in the 1st Division, 1st Marine Regiment under legendary Lieutenant General Burwell "Chesty" Puller. Puller would retire in 1955 as the most-decorated Marine in American history, with five Navy Crosses to his credit.

Back then, a high school degree was about the academic equivalent of an MBA today. Always a smart guy, Dad advanced quickly to become a buck sergeant, but when his superiors discovered he could type—his mother taught typing too—they pulled him back to the rear.

Although Dad was not happy about the move, a week later his unit suffered 60 percent casualties. Dad would sometimes reminisce about typing casualty reports for his own buddies. Being a REMF (Rear Echelon Motherf—) has its advantages, but I could see the emotional toll it had taken when Dad told us these stories. The guilt, however, was balanced by the knowledge that he might not have had us three kids had he served on the front lines.

We would reminisce whenever we visited a veterans memorial built about ten years ago in a nearby park. In the middle of the memorial stands a statue of Private Joe Martinez, the first Coloradan to be awarded the Medal of Honor during World War II. My parents donated to the building fund, so they are listed as donors. In addition to donors, there are lists of county residents who have served in each U.S. conflict. Dad is listed for serving in Korea. My brother is listed for serving in Desert Storm and Panama, and I am listed for Bosnia—the memorial has not yet been updated to include Afghanistan. My brothers and I often visit the memorial with my dad, he in a wheelchair. There we speak of war, the cost of it, the devastation, the honor. No family in America respects military service more than my own.

In 2002, almost exactly fifty years after my father served, I found myself stationed in the Korean DMZ at Camp Stanton, within miles of where my father had served. I still have the pictures he gave me of his days in that area. The obvious difference between then and now is that where I saw forests he saw scarred, naked hillsides.

Back in the States postwar, dad enrolled at the University of Northern Colorado in Greeley to study education. He soon enough spotted an incredibly strong, unique young lady also in the teaching program named Donna Lee Dhority, my mom. It was from her side of the family that I got the "Lee" in Terry Lee Lakin.

Although a few years younger than the world-traveling veteran, Donna had lived a harder life. Her parents divorced when she was seven and her sister thirteen. They were raised, for the most part, by their father and his new wife, a stepmother straight out of the Brothers Grimm, an angry woman who resented the little girls who got between her and her husband. That life could have turned mom inward and hard, but it seemed to have had the opposite effect. No one I know is more giving.

Mom worked as a waitress to put herself through school. Dad, probably not by chance, happened to be eating at the establishment where she worked. As the story goes, when the time came to leave a tip, he pulled out a twenty, ripped it in half, and promised the other half only if she would see him again.

The trick worked; soon enough, Frank and Donna were married. While they continued their educations, they lived together as resident assistants overseeing a student dorm. Thus began a long and fruitful relationship between my parents and the university.

Upon graduation, dad took a job as a high school teacher and wrestling coach. Always ambitious, he went on to get his doctorate in education. He would spend most of his professional life at the University of Northern Colorado, eventually working his way up to become Vice President of Academic Affairs.

I remember our house being full on a regular basis with people from the university and the community. In part, it was my father's role to host such gatherings, but I suspect it had as much to do with my mother's welcoming nature.

I remember meeting many of these people, including General Benjamin Davis, the first black general in the United State Air Force.

I was less impressed that he was the first of anything—what did I know about civil rights?—than that he was a general with a cool little Datsun 240Z. He even took me for a ride to the local convenience store.

It was in Greeley that I came of age, the third of three boys in a nurturing, supportive family. Mom stayed home to take care of us. She was a natural caretaker. When her father died, she was good enough to take care of the mean old stepmother, by now an odd, reclusive woman who smoked like a chimney.

From as early as I can remember, Mom involved herself in the community, helping out at a clinic for migrant workers and at a day care center for their children. She was also involved with the Salvation Army and the United Way, as was Dad.

Mom and Dad came from that generation when liberal Democrats, at least some of them, didn't just talk the talk, they walked the walk. A few years ago, in fact, my parents were honored with the Leann Anderson Community Care Award for their extra efforts to benefit the community. The contributions my parents have made and continue to make to life in Greeley have become too numerous for even their boys to keep track of.

Although I was too young to remember, I have been told that over Mom's objections, Dad accepted an invitation to meet with the Black Panthers when he was dean of students. They apparently were so surprised he showed up that they had no agenda to discuss when he got there.

More recently, Dad launched a "Unity House" on the UNC campus. The students accepted into the program were to develop projects to build multicultural harmony. This enterprise grew out of my father's frustration with the students and faculty who did little but gripe about racial and cultural problems on campus.

Politics had never been an issue between us because I was never very political. As I became more engaged, I grew aware of how different were our sources of information. I knew theirs—how can you avoid them? You walk through an airport, and it is CNN all the time. Walk by a rack of newspaper boxes, and you get their headline spin. Open your AOL or Yahoo account, and you find out instantly what terrible thing Sarah Palin or the Tea Party was alleged to have done that day.

The problem was, and this would become more of a problem as time went on, my folks were not hearing what I was hearing or seeing what I was seeing. And by not getting my media, they were not "getting" me.

Worse, their media had changed, gotten more biased by the year, and they had not noticed. These same media led them to believe that it was my sources that were biased, hateful even, and they had only my word to the contrary. On occasion, I would forward to them studies showing how biased the media could be even with simple facts like identifying the party of Republicans who had gone bad and concealing the party label of wayward Democrats. They would inevitably try to explain the bias away. Mom and Dad did not love me any less because of this; they just did not understand where I was coming from.

This, of course, was all a long way down the road. When I was five, my family moved to the home I would grow up in, the cheapest house in the best neighborhood my parents could afford. It was a new subdivision, surrounded, as I remember it, by cornfields. Like so many American childhoods we don't hear about, mine was free of deprivation, free of abuse, free of marital strife.

Our family lived and taught a great work ethic. I don't recall anyone in our family either not working or working on some project. In our new house, my older brothers took on a paper route for the *Denver Post*. They had one of the largest routes in Greeley.

The three of us would deliver the daily paper on our bikes. My brothers had larger bags to carry the load, and I tagged along to cover the outlying homes and the apartment buildings. Sunday delivery was a family project. Once we received the inside sections on Saturday night, we turned the garage into a full assembly line as we put the comics, the classifieds, and the other miscellaneous sections together.

Early Sunday we received the front-page news section and stuffed the pre-assembled innards into it. Together, we would load all 160 to 180 papers into our Oldsmobile Vista Cruiser with a 455 cubic inch V-8 Rocket engine, better known as a "Woody" for its wooden side panels.

The papers would fill the entire back of the car. Dad would drive, Mom would navigate and locate the houses. I sat in the backseat, compiling a list of apartment numbers. When we got to an apartment or condo, I would run up and drop the papers off.

My brothers sat on the back tailgate and tossed papers out both sides or ran up to the newspaper box if there was one. Today, parents could get arrested for not having them wear seat belts, but that was a simpler and freer time.

As I remember it, we would finish our Sunday deliveries near dawn and be treated to breakfast at the Village Inn for a job well done. We now joke that the cost of the gas and breakfast surely surpassed the few pennies per paper we were making.

We three boys never understood until years later the sacrifice our parents made to help us with this job. And the paper route was only one of many jobs we boys did together or our whole family did collectively.

In thinking back about the course of my recent life, I cannot trace my decisions, which seem crazy to some people, to any early need to rebel. Just the opposite. I always wanted to do well. I wanted to get good grades. I never wanted to disappoint my parents in anything. Rebellion, if that is what it is, has not at all come easily to me.

As Mom reminds me, though, even as a little kid I was usually the one who took care of other people. I must have learned it watching her. In the first grade, we had a little blind girl in our class. For whatever reason, I took it upon myself to help her find her coat and boots at recess. By the time we were ready to go out, the other kids would be coming back in. The teacher, bless her heart, would let the two of us stay out longer. This being Northern Colorado, where below-zero temperatures are not uncommon, I am not sure she was doing us a great favor.

I was always the one to volunteer to push our wheelchair-bound classmates too. As much as I liked football and dodge ball and the like, I always figured they could wait a little while. Of course, none of this explains why I would spend five months in a military prison, but it might help explain why I became a doctor. As to the prison part, I do confess to being a little hardheaded, especially when I think I'm right.

The family joke is that when I was about four, I got into an unlikely fracas with dad over the fate of my spinach at dinner. Like most moms of that era—maybe they watched too much "Popeye"—my mother insisted on serving us spinach. I was the rare kid who actually liked spinach. What I did not like was that the spinach juice leaked onto the mashed potatoes. When you are a kid, this kind of stuff matters.

To prevent the contamination of my potatoes, I slurped my spinach juice off the plate. My dad spotted me and told me to stop. I tried again. He caught me again. I tried a third time, and he shoved my face into the mashed potatoes. When I inhaled the hot mashed potatoes up my nose, I went berserk, going after my dad with a fork, never a smart thing to do to a wrestling coach whose weight class is about 150 pounds higher than your own.

All three of us wrestled, by the way. My older brother, Greg, about six years my senior, got off to a slow start. Small for his age and asthmatic as a boy, he was nonetheless a great natural athlete who blossomed in high school. If he had not broken his arm, he could have been a leading quarterback in our high school conference. At six-foot-one and 225 pounds, he did become a great collegiate rugby player who might have gone international had he not injured his knee.

What an unusual career Greg has had. He was a biology major at UNC and also a police reservist. He liked the police work better than the biology, so he joined the Greeley Police Department out of college. What he really wanted, though, was to join the FBI. Knowing they preferred lawyers, Greg went to law school and graduated, but then failed the FBI physical because of his rugby injury, a meniscus tear in his knee.

Extremely disappointed, Greg headed to Hawaii, where he served as a prosecutor first on Maui then on the big island. On the Greeley PD, he had gotten tired of arresting the same people. In Hawaii, he got tired of prosecuting the same people.

After a while, biology wasn't looking so bad after all. So Greg gave up the law and went back to medical school. Today, he is a family physician in Wichita and the most supportive member of my family by a long shot. In fact, he holds the family together.

My other brother is three years older than I; he was a senior in high school when I was a freshman. He was quieter than the rest of us, more studious, more technical, a good student and athlete, a great wrestler. He toughed it out at the Coast Guard Academy after high school and then went on to a long and successful career in the Coast Guard.

Unfortunately, my choices have been incredibly difficult on him too. He has the mind-set of my parents, and I have had some very tough discussions with him. We haven't kissed and made up yet. I am hopeful, but I think it will take several years. I only hope that my actions do not in some way tarnish his career.

I followed in his footsteps in high school. I made the varsity wrestling team as a freshman, when he was a star senior. But to make the varsity as a starter, I had to scale down from 125 pounds to wrestle in the 105-pound class. I was the skinny little dude wrestling a lot of fully grown guys with big arms and bad attitudes. I was outclassed as a freshman. I got beat up quite a bit, left a few pints of my own blood on the mat, and lost two-thirds of my matches.

I have played a lot of sports, but none is as taxing as wrestling. You have to discipline yourself to make weight. You go out there alone. You have to drill down deep and get mentally tough. The sport helps you develop internal drive, a drive that my father and older brothers helped instill in me: "Do your best and never give up." If you don't develop it, you get your face rubbed into the mat on a regular basis.

I drilled down. By junior year I made it to the state championships. I was the only one on my team to do so. In my senior year, I played football as a 165-pound pulling guard and wrestled as a 145-pounder. I made it back to the state tournament again. I never did win, but I got there and gave the guys who placed all that they could handle. Losing can toughen you up in ways that winning cannot. I didn't win my court-martial either, but I got there, and that really toughened me up.

4. *You Knew My Path*

I would like to tell you that going to church on Sunday was as important to me as going to wrestling matches or football games on Saturday, but I cannot say that truthfully.

I had important things to do on Sunday mornings, like delivering newspapers on the most ambitious route in town. And although my parents wanted us to be regular churchgoers, except for the can't-miss days like Christmas and Easter, we never quite were. My brothers and I were masters of finding excuses.

The only church I knew was the First Congregational in Greeley. My folks are still very active members. First Congregational is part of the United Church of Christ covenant. Trinity Church in Chicago is a United Church of Christ church as well. If you remember, that was the church of President Obama's hate-preaching pastor, Jeremiah Wright.

The UCC gives its member churches a lot of leeway. No central authority imposes any doctrine or form of worship on its members. The UCC sees Christ alone as the Head of the church and seeks a balance in the faithful between "accountability to the apostolic faith" on the one hand and "freedom of conscience" on the other.

I am perfectly okay with this theoretically, but sometimes indifferent paperboys like me and crazy-talking pastors like Wright could use a little more accountability and a little less freedom.

I did, however, regularly attend church during my confirmation years. I became a junior deacon and helped out as best I could, ushering, doing Scripture readings, monitoring the sound system and the like. My deeply charitable parents were always engaged too, as active in the church as they were in the community.

I am grateful that I had the grounding I did. Although admittedly incomplete, the Christian values I learned at home and in church sustained me during the years I was drifting and served as a base when I needed a foundation the most. Even at my most wayward, I never stopped believing in the Ten Commandments.

I do not mean to preach here. My high school wrestling coach, who was like an adopted brother to us, became a born-again Christian after I graduated from high school. Once he found Jesus, he felt a passionate need to share what he found. I can now understand why. But his strategy for sharing was too aggressive for a bunch of go-as-you-please Christians like my family. Without meaning to, he pushed us away.

In light of this experience, I will try to avoid sounding like an evangelist, but there is no understanding the path I took without understanding the role that my maturing Christian faith played in it.

Although I did well on the Academic College Test in my junior year of high school and assumed I would go to college, I had no real idea what direction I wanted to take. I was thinking of going to Boulder to the University of Colorado, but my father knew enough about me and about higher education to encourage me to go to a smaller school.

My father and I finally compromised: the first two years at Colorado College, a private liberal arts school in Colorado Springs with about 2,000 students, and the final two at Colorado State University in Fort Collins. In retrospect, I am sure he knew he had outsmarted me, knowing that once I was exposed to the high-quality instruction at Colorado College, I would not want to go any-where else.

By the way, the college's alumni include Dick Cheney's wife, Lynne, and his daughters, Liz and Mary. Liz and I were in the same class. I wish I could tell you that I dated her, but unlike some memoir writers, I feel obliged to tell the truth. In any case, I think it will be a while before the Colorado College alumni start bragging about my going to school there.

Colorado College may be best known for its "block plan." When I attended, the school year was divided into nine blocks, and students took one intensive class per block, each block worth three-and-a-half semester credit hours.

The first class I chose upon arriving was physical anthropology, which I took for two consecutive blocks, about seven weeks. The class was pure, undiluted Darwinism, science presented as gospel. In this class, other possibilities for a purposeful life chain did not even surface.

In my high school biology classes, at which I excelled, Darwin was also a given. His theory was not at all open to debate even though some of the teachers were regular churchgoers who, if they saw the obvious contradictions, did not share them.

If a student raised an alternative explanation in class, that alternative was dismissed as stuff best reserved for Sunday school and not addressed. I recall the textbooks having very small sections addressing Creationism, always in the negative, but I do not recall the subject of Intelligent Design being addressed at all. The term was probably not yet even in play.

Next to my freshman dorm at Colorado College was, and still is, a gorgeous eighty-year-old Romanesque church called Shove Memorial Chapel. The college was founded with the support of the Congregational church, and in the past, students were required to attend daily religious services. By the time I got there those days were long gone, but the chapel remained. Except for award presentations and the like, I never went.

Why should I? In my anthropology class I was learning that life on earth was created by random events and without purpose. Man, I was told, emerged by accident through natural selection after an endless series of unplanned mutations. In my science classes, I heard much the same thing. We were allegedly approaching the discovery of the smallest particle and would soon have a grand unifying equation for all life. Who needed God?

Looking back, I feel cheated. We never even asked what was the spark to life, let alone the spark to consciousness, love, and empathy. We never questioned how these intangibles could be explained by natural selection. This is an incredible subject, one that should have been examined from all sides and debated. It wasn't. As science majors, we were fed Darwinism like so much pabulum, and we consumed it without ever questioning its content.

My "luck of the draw" freshman dorm roommate was a likable guy, but he seemed out of place in the generally rowdy atmosphere of our dorm. He tried to express his Christian beliefs to me, even the principles of Intelligent Design. Once, he contacted a family friend of his, a NASA astronaut, who sent me some of his writings on the question. Unfortunately, I dismissed all of this at the time, thinking science held all the answers.

The way I figured it, the way many of us did, was this: what was the point of going to church, even a beautiful one like Shove, if the universe was unplanned and all life was accidental? More and more I was coming to see Christianity as a crutch for the weak-minded. Once the professors removed God from the equation, they felt free to substitute their own faith in reason and science, at least whatever science could be shaped to support their worldview.

The second "block" I took proved to be much more useful in ways that I never would have anticipated. This was a course in cultural anthropology. One of our assignments was to do what the teacher called an "ethnography." This is basically just a study of a culture and the recording of what you find.

When we think of an ethnographic study, we usually expect the subject to be some primitive tribe of half-naked bow-hunters living in some remote backwater. My professor, for instance, had a keen interest in the Yanomami, a scantily clad slash-and-burn culture deep in the Amazon. As a freshman at Colorado College, I did not exactly have access to people like the Yanomami.

Although many of my fellow students went off in search of the exotic, I thought I would study people whose careers I might want to follow myself. So I ended up hanging out with the emergency medical technicians at an ambulance company in Colorado Springs. I spent a lot of time with these guys.

Though their work could be very stressful, they were always completely professional on the job. But after work, as I learned, they knew how to have fun. On occasion, they could get pretty primitive themselves—in a sophisticated way. They showed me, for instance, how to snort Jack Daniel's, proving that if push came to shove, inhalation could be an alternate means of administering medication

The EMTs took me under their wings, and I began to see for the first time just how rewarding this kind of work could be. I wrote a thirty-page report on the group, but what I learned about these guys, including their wonderfully morbid sense of humor, could not be reduced to a report.

Looking back, I can see that it was this experience that inspired me to go into medicine. While still at Colorado College, I enrolled in an EMT course at Pike's Peak Community College, about an hour down the road.

My most memorable instructor was a classic, Vietnam-trained medic turned hippie, and he insisted we know our stuff. Another instructor was so well known for her emergency medical skills, everyone called her the "Trauma Momma."

Along with the other assistants, they taught to a level well above what the curriculum required. I discovered that I loved the stuff and had a gift for it. At the end of my sophomore year, I became certified as an EMT.

While still going to college, I volunteered part-time with the very guys I had been studying. What I learned in doing the work, in being part of a team like this, was how gratifying it could be to know you have the knowledge and skill to make a difference in a crucial part of person's life.

My fellow students might be finding their rewards in acing a test or winning an intramural basketball game, but for me, it was in pulling a person out of an overturned car or arriving at the scene of a shooting or stabbing even before the police got there.

Although some medical people I know do get carried away with the rush that comes with the job, most find the deep inner satisfaction that comes with doing good in the most basic way. This feeling never gets old.

We often had hard decisions to make, and it was always a relief to make them right. I would have a lot of hard decisions down the road. I am not sure I made them all correctly, but thanks in part to my EMT training, I was not afraid to make them.

Toward the end of my sophomore year, an unusual opportunity presented itself. My whole family—mother, father, two brothers, and I—were going to tour Europe for several weeks, together, in one car.

A trip like this can be stressful for any group of people, but you also can learn a lot. You watch the way your parents interact and the dynamics of your family. I had the chance to have some serious one-on-ones with my dad over a beer or two, and I got to see things I never saw before. A lot of effort goes into holding a family together.

As for myself, I got the chance to drive the family around. I enjoyed it particularly because of the 'exotic' Audi 100 we'd rented. As cool as it was, however, this being 1985, the car did not have a GPS.

In one memorable moment while I was driving in eastern Italy, I took a wrong turn, ended up going through a long tunnel, and found I had led us into communist Yugoslavia. Since we were there, we figured, "Why not?" and stayed overnight in a little hotel on the shady side of the Iron Curtain.

I did not need my newfound knowledge of cultural anthropology to tell me that was a place I did not want to live. No one was happy there. That was obvious. At breakfast next morning, we looked around and all we saw were these sad people. It was then that we agreed, "Let's get out of Dodge."

What is weird is that I remember the experience as though it were in black and white. There had to be some color there, I'm sure. I just don't remember it. Color or no, in less than a day I learned all I needed to know about the great socialist experiment.

When I was in Austria, I invested my savings in a good rope for a new hobby I had picked up from my college and EMT buddies, rock climbing. Soon after coming back, I decided to try it out with some friends at the Garden of the Gods, a public park and rock climbing attraction in Colorado Springs.

I went with my good pals, Tom Walsh and Rob Griggs. What I learned the hard way was that a good rope does not compensate for a lack of skill, strength and practice. In fact, only Rob's desperate barehanded grab of my safety rope kept me from falling to my death or something very close to it. From then on, I had a much greater appreciation for the process of risk evaluation and management, a major component of occupational medicine.

After my sophomore year I decided to take a year off to work as an EMT. The plan was good, but the job market was not. I could not catch on as an EMT anywhere, and I ended up back in Greeley working as a 911 dispatcher. The transition was easy because my brother Greg worked as a police officer just down the hallway in the Greeley city complex and showed me the bureaucratic ropes.

Although my critics on the left may disagree, I have always been responsible, and my superiors noticed. Soon enough, they made me an ad hoc supervisor on the 11 p.m. to 7 a.m. shift. I developed a lot of respect for people who work the night shift. Many of those jobs are essential, but working those hours can throw your life out of whack quicker than you can say, "Boy, I need another cup of coffee."

After a year, I was back at Colorado College. By now, I knew the path I wanted to follow and began studying biology and other sciences. Although I was a good student, Colorado College was filled with good students, all looking for those elusive A's. I wish I could say that A's were all I got, but I can't. The chemistry classes, organic and analytical, were struggles, and the liberal arts and other non-science classes did not seem serious to me.

I did reasonably well on my medical college admission test, the MCAT— and unlike the current president, I am willing to share my test scores—but my overall B average did not exactly make me a medical school's first-round draft pick. My adviser, in fact, was downright discouraging.

This is where my wrestling experience came in handy. Getting rejection letters was like getting cross-faced by a brawny senior and having my nose rubbed in my own blood. I had two choices. I could quit trying or I could keep on fighting. I had learned my lesson well from my father and brothers: "Never give up." I wasn't about to. I decided to take off as long as it took to improve my chances. I looked for a job and, to build up my résumé, enrolled in some additional course work.

Once again, EMT jobs proved tough to come by. I finally accepted a job at a beef packing plant, where I served as a nurse on the night shift, 11 p.m. to 7 a.m. once again. Nights seemed to be my destiny.

This was a big plant. I was one of more than twenty people on its medical staff. The workforce slaughtered 400 cattle each hour, which meant a lot of tough and dangerous work. I saw lacerations aplenty and burns from steam cleaning and chemicals. These were some hardworking, blue-collar people—black, white, but mostly Hispanic. You could not help but respect them. I took a Spanish class after my shift to keep up. This was in addition to courses in genetics, pharmacology and human anatomy.

I was also encouraged to go on the floor, observe the processes, and advise on safety practices. The plant also had an innovative health and wellness center. Only in the movies do business owners not care about the health and welfare of their employees. It was a lot of responsibility for a young guy, but I ate it up. These experiences would help me as I moved into occupational medicine.

I made some valuable friends there too. Several were volunteer firefighters. These guys worked forty or more hours a week and then volunteered more hours off-duty to help others in need. They convinced me that I could make a contribution, so I signed up for the Western Hills Fire Department. I received some incredible training, and although I never arrived early enough at a scene to be nozzle man, I got to be a hose man on several fires.

I never left a fire until all duties were complete. Many volunteers would fade back and leave shortly after paramedics took over the patients. I remained to contribute, even driving the ambulance to the hospital several times so the EMT team could work on critical patients in the back.

I met a lot of great people at the plant. One particularly impressive guy was following the same career track I was. He had been a petroleum engineer but was now applying for medical school. He was seven years older. I figured if he could stick it out, so could I.

Our perseverance paid off. The following year we both had a few acceptances. I chose to attend the Osteopathic College in Kansas City, in part at least because I could drive there in a day from Colorado.

On the East Coast, 600 miles is forever. In this part of the world, however, Denver and Kansas City are virtual neighbors. There is nothing in between them but a lot of open space and eight hours on cruise control. I turned in my aging four-wheel-drive mini-Blazer for a totally un-cool Voyager mini-van that drives better on the highway and holds a lot more stuff. I loaded it up, and headed east.

There was no way I was going to let my parents pay for my medical education; they had spent enough getting me through college. A few years earlier, when I had been prepping for my MCAT, a recruiter came to our class and explained the military's medical scholarship program. If I accepted, the U.S. Army would pay for my books and tuition and provide a stipend. I, in turn, would be obligated for four years of service.

On the potential downside, the danger quotient was high in the military. On the upside, the adventure quotient was high as well. I enjoyed the action and camaraderie of the EMT and firefighting teams. This sounded like a good deal all around, and I was all gung ho for it. Then too, all of this seemed necessary training for an imagined "Lakin Brothers' Rescue Team," a high-adventure A-Team my brothers and I had been scheming and dreaming about for years.

On August 20, 1989, I was sworn in to the United States Army. A little over two months later, on 9 November 1989, the Berlin Wall came down.

Just about that same time, on the very first day of class, I took another oath. This one was written about 2500 years ago by a doctor named Hippocrates. It is amazing how much sense it makes even today. The modern version of the Hippocratic Oath that we swore is not a whole lot different from the original one:

> I swear by Apollo the healer, Asclepius, Hygieia, and Panacea, and I take to witness all the gods, all the goddesses, to keep according to my ability and my judgment, the following Oath and agreement:

> To consider dear to me, as my parents, him who taught me this art, to live in common with him and, if necessary, to share my goods with him; To look upon his children as my own brothers, to teach them this art.

> I will prescribe regimens for the good of my patients according to my ability and my judgment and never do harm to anyone.

> I will not give a lethal drug to anyone if I am asked nor will I advise such a plan; and similarly I will not give a woman a pessary to cause an abortion.

> But I will preserve the purity of my life and my arts.

> I will not cut for stone even for patients in whom the disease is manifest; I will leave this operation to be performed by practitioners, specialists in this art.

> In every house where I come I will enter only for the good of my patients, keeping myself far from all intentional ill-doing and all seduction and especially from the pleasures of love with women or with men, be they free or slaves.
>
> All that may come to my knowledge in the exercise of my profession or in daily commerce with men, which ought not to be spread abroad, I will keep secret and will never reveal.
>
> If I keep this oath faithfully, may I enjoy my life and practice my art, respected by all men and in all times; but if I swerve from it or violate it, may the reverse be my lot.

Unfortunately, some modern versions sidestep the prohibitions against abortion and assisted suicide, but the osteopathic oath I swore kept them. It read, "I will give no drugs for deadly purposes to any person, though it be asked of me." In my book, this covers both abortion and assisted suicide.

On the plus side, all versions treat the oath as something sacred and inviolable. It is not a series of recommendations; it is a vow. In the original version, if you violate your oath, you wish harm upon yourself.

Ours was one of the largest classes to go through this medical school, about 125 in all. Just wearing the white lab coat to class made us feel as if we were part of a very special heritage. On the first day, the president of the college came to talk to us about that heritage and about our schedule as well. As I interpreted my schedule, it allowed about thirty minutes every day to sleep. Being a B student in college, I studied extra hard and was gratified to discover that I could compete.

As a classmate, Pili helped me greatly. She was one of the nicest, most grounded girls I had ever met. I just enjoyed being around her. We started dating before Thanksgiving that first year. I have to confess that Pili tried to break up with me when she went home. In fact, we "broke up" before any number of holidays. The breakups never lasted, though; we would be back together again pronto.

A lot of our dates were study dates. On other dates, we worked out together. Pretty romantic, huh? With little time to stay in shape, I had even less time—or so I told myself--to think about my faith. We were all locked into medical science overdrive. Besides, I still thought Christianity was a crutch. I was convinced that organized religion in general led to wars and strife. In fact, the subject of faith rarely came up when we were with friends.

The one person who kept the idea of Christianity before me was the fellow who sat next to me in class, Randy Legasse. Unfortunately, Randy is no longer with us. He tried to dodge a deer that ran in front of his car a few years ago and died trying.

When he was here, though, Randy made his presence felt. The alphabet put us close to each other physically; Randy's faith brought us close in other ways. He didn't preach his faith; he lived it. I think even today of his selfless example. He had had a traumatic family life growing up, was a barber for many years in a small town, and struggled through a few of the classes. Yet he was an anchor of support in his faith as well as in study groups, where he helped several students struggling more than he was. At every step along my life's path, there has appeared a person like Randy.

Pili was a Buddhist, not a serious ceremonial Buddhist, but she knew the philosophy. I dabbled in it, even tried some meditation. One of my brothers had been on a spiritual quest and had become a practicing Zen Buddhist. He may still be. Although we talked a little about his quest and about "life energy" and such things, I did not have much time for that either.

Years later, when I was faced with my prison ordeal, he would tell me that his God would not encourage me to go through with it. He lost me there. I did not understand this. I was under the impression that when you swear an oath "so help me, God," the God you are swearing to expects you to keep it. Isn't that the whole point of an oath?

As I came to discover, God even provides encouragement for those who have made the kinds of decisions I have been compelled to make. Imagine how the words of Psalm 142 sound to a man who has found himself in prison for doing what he knows to be the right and just thing.

> I cry with my voice to the Lord.
> With my voice, I ask the Lord for mercy.
> I pour out my complaint before him.
> I tell him my troubles.
> When my spirit was overwhelmed within me,
> you knew my path.
> In the way in which I walk,

they have hidden a snare for me.
Look on my right, and see;
for there is no one who is concerned for me.
Refuge has fled from me.
No one cares for my soul.
I cried to you, Lord.
I said, "You are my refuge,
my portion in the land of the living."
Listen to my cry,
for I am in desperate need.
deliver me from my persecutors,
For they are stronger than me.
Bring my soul out of prison,
that I may give thanks to your name.
The righteous will surround me,
for you will be good to me.

From Hebrew Names Version Bible, HNV

But these prayers were way down the road. When I was in medical school, I wasn't worried about my soul; I was worried about my grades. That did not make me a bad person. It just made me an incomplete one.

5. *Something to Hide*

I don't really remember when I first heard questions raised about Barack Obama's eligibility to be president of the United States, but it might have been the Philip Berg case.

In August 2008, Berg filed a complaint in federal district court challenging Obama's eligibility. I am not sure what to make of Berg, but he does not exactly fit anyone's profile of a "birther," the derogatory name for people investigating Obama's eligibility.

First off, Berg is a Democrat and has the résumé to prove it. He served as chairman of the Democratic Party in Montgomery County, Pennsylvania, and was once a member of the Democratic State Committee. He also served as deputy attorney general of Pennsylvania. And before anyone accuses him of being a racist, you should know that he is a paid life member of the NAACP. As you might guess, he was a supporter of Hillary Clinton in the 2008 election.

In his suit, Berg claimed that Obama was not a "natural born citizen" of the United States. This term, which comes directly from the United States

Constitution, takes some explaining. It is often misunderstood or deliberately twisted. Section 1 of Article II of the Constitution reads as follows:

> No person except a natural born Citizen, or a Citizen of the United States, at the time of the Adoption of this Constitution, shall be eligible to the Office of President; neither shall any Person be eligible to that Office who shall not have attained to the Age of thirty-five Years, and been fourteen Years a Resident within the United States.

The Constitution does not define the term "natural born," but there is a pretty substantial historical record of what the Founding Fathers meant by the term. Basically, they wanted to assure that no future commander in chief would have divided loyalties.

The problem is that this definition has never fully been tested. There is no official body that determines whether a presidential candidate meets the definition. So Berg's court case seemed to me a reasonable approach.

We know that if a person is born overseas of foreign parents, that person is clearly not eligible to be president. The Austria-born Arnold Schwarzenegger could serve as governor of California once he was naturalized as a citizen, but he could never serve as president of the United States. That much is clear.

Many of the delegates to the Constitutional Convention served in the first Congress, which passed the Naturalization Act of 1790. In this act, they defined "natural born citizen" to include "children of citizens of the United States that may be born beyond the sea, or out of the limits of the United States." These Founders were less concerned that a child be born in the United States than that he or she be born to two parents of undivided loyalty.

John McCain was born in Panama. There is no doubt that his parents were loyal citizens. His father, who would later become an admiral in the U.S. Navy, was stationed there. Still, in 2008 McCain had to jump through all kind of hoops, including a hearing in the U.S. Senate, to confirm his eligibility.

Some activist Democrats were hoping to prove that McCain was born in a civilian hospital off the naval base. They thought that if they proved this, they could disqualify him or at least raise enough doubts that people would vote against him. They could not. McCain was able to confirm that he was born on the base, and the Senate passed a resolution in March 2008 affirming that McCain was constitutionally eligible to run for president.

You have to go back and look at the media coverage from early 2008 to see who the original "birthers" were. On 28 February of that year, the *New York Times* ran a big story with the headline "McCain's Canal Zone Birth Prompts Queries About Whether That Rules Him Out." The next day NBC reporter Pete Williams posted a story headlined "McCain's Citizenship Called into Question." This story went on for months. If I remember right, even a *New York Times* editorial observed that if McCain were elected, there would be litigation about his eligibility.

The deeper I got into my research, the more I wondered why it was okay, even patriotic, to question the citizenship of a man who had served in the military and spent five and a half years in a POW camp, but it was not okay, was even racist, to question the eligibility of a guy who was unwilling to produce his birth certificate.

Let me deal with the "racist" stuff first. If any other prominent African-American had run for president, no one would have thought to question his eligibility. No one did when Jesse Jackson ran or Al Sharpton or Alan Keyes.

We have no doubt that these men were born in the United States. Their parents were, too, and their parents' parents, probably going back hundreds of years.

The United States Constitution allowed Congress to ban the importation of slaves as early as 1808, and on January 1, 1808, Congress did just that. Although some slave traders violated the ban, the great majority of African-Americans can trace their ancestry back more than 200 years.

Barack Obama cannot, at least not on his father's side. Obama Sr., who was born in Kenya, was a British citizen when he came to Hawaii in 1959. We know from his history and his INS (Immigration and Naturalization Service) documents that he had no intention of ever becoming an American citizen.

If the president was born in the United States, he would still have been a dual British-American citizen at birth. In 1963, when Kenya became independent, young Barry Obama automatically became a citizen of Kenya, and he remained a citizen of Kenya until he turned 21 in 1982. At that point, he had to choose between Kenya and the United States, and he apparently chose the United States.

Let's go back to the Constitution that I am sworn to uphold and defend. The first sentence of the Fourteenth Amendment reads as follows: "All persons born or naturalized in the United States, and subject to the jurisdiction thereof, are citizens of the United States and of the State wherein they reside."

Obama supporters insist that the Fourteenth amendment makes anyone born in the United States a "natural born citizen." But the two senators who wrote this amendment felt otherwise. They included the phrase "subject to the jurisdiction" to exclude the children of foreigners who claimed allegiance to another country. Supreme Court rulings have upheld this interpretation.

What this means is that even if Barack Obama was born in Hawaii, his status as a "natural born citizen" is not a given. The same question hangs over the head of the Republican governor of Louisiana, Bobby Jindal. His parents were citizens of India in the United States on visas when he was born in Baton Rouge in 1971.

No one doubts that Jindal was born in the United States, but what is not clear is whether he is a "natural born citizen" under the law. Jindal, however, has already released his birth certificate. If he chooses to run for president, his eligibility will have to be determined much as McCain's was. And Obama's was not.

Now, if Obama was born outside the United States, say in Kenya, he would not have been considered a United States citizen at birth, let alone a "natural born" citizen.

For a person born outside the United States to be a citizen at birth, at least one parent who is a U.S. citizen must have lived in the United States for at least ten years, five of those years after the age of fourteen. Obama's mother was eighteen when he was born, so she did not meet that requirement. Neither, obviously, did Barack Obama Sr.

In other words, if Obama were born in the United States the courts would have had to determine if he was "natural born," and no one knows how they would have ruled. If he were born outside the United States, the courts would almost certainly have ruled against him.

Now, you may be thinking, "Didn't Obama post his birth certificate online in the summer of 2008? Didn't it show that he was born in Honolulu on August 4, 1961?" As you might expect, there is a story here too.

In June 2008 a group of Hillary Clinton supporters known as PUMA— People United Means Action—began spreading the rumor that Obama was born in Kenya. They demanded that Obama produce his birth certificate, as John McCain had to do. They hoped to prove Obama was born outside the United States. By this time, there was no other way Hillary was going to get the nomination.

Bizarrely, the first outfit to respond was the leftist, Obama-supporting Web journal Daily Kos. On 12 June 2008, its editors posted an official-looking item entitled "Certification of Live Birth."

This document listed the date of Obama's birth, the time, the island, the city, the parents, and the parents' races, but it did not list the hospital or the doctor who delivered the baby. It bore no signatures and no seal, and for no good reason, the certificate number was blacked out.

Daily Kos did not report how it came up with the document. When challenged, publisher Markos Moulitsas simply said, "I asked the campaign." Moulitsas never explained in what form the Obama campaign sent the document and why the campaign did not simply post the document itself, as it would do a few days later on its "Fight the Smears" website. Soon afterward, a campaign spokesman confirmed that this was Senator Obama's "birth certificate."

Even if legitimate, this short-form certification was not a birth certificate. The long-form birth certificate lists the hospital and the doctor and includes signatures of the doctor and the mother, but for the media the short-form Certification of Live Birth was enough.

Just a few days before Obama released his alleged long-form birth certificate on 27 April 2011, George Stephanopoulos was waving the short-form document in Republican presidential candidate Michelle Bachmann's face, claiming it was the official birth certificate. The media refused to learn.

Obama supporters also pointed to the announcements in two Honolulu newspapers confirming Obama's birth. They both read as follows: "Mr. and Mrs. Barack H. Obama, 6085 Kalanianaole Hwy, son, August 4."

There is no denying these newspaper announcements, but all they prove is that someone registered Obama's birth in Hawaii, likely his mother's parents. If Obama was born elsewhere, there were many advantages to his being registered in Hawaii, U.S. citizenship first and foremost.

At the time, a family member could submit a statement to the Hawaii Department of Health that the baby was born in Hawaii but outside a hospital. Once the baby was registered, the newspapers automatically printed the announcement. This certainly does not prove Obama was born outside the state, but it does not prove he was born there either.

I approach things skeptically, as a scientist does. I do not rush to judgment. I was absorbing this information and processing it. All along, my gut was telling me there was something wrong. I failed to see why a candidate for president of the United States could not be more forthcoming.

All my training—medical, military, and general life experiences—have taught me to weigh the benefits against the risks. In a decision as important as choosing the president, there is no excuse for not weighing the risks.

Then, too, there were complications beyond where Obama was born. When he was three or four years old, his mother married an Indonesian national named Lolo Soetero. At age six, Obama and his mother joined Soetoro in Indonesia, where Obama registered at St. Francis of Assisi School in Jakarta as Barry Soetoro, an Indonesian citizen and a Muslim. Because Obama will not release his records, we do not know if Soetoro adopted him and whether he officially became a citizen of Indonesia.

What I did not understand, and still don't, is why Obama did not just come forward with his key documents and be done with it. Instead, he ordered all of his important records to be kept under seal.

These include his long-form birth certificate, his adoption records if any, his kindergarten and Punahou Elementary School records from Hawaii, his Occidental College records, his State Department passport and travel records, his Columbia University records, his college thesis, his financial aid records, his Harvard Law School records, his medical records, his Chicago law practice records, his Illinois State Senate records, and all of his grades and standardized test scores.

Although I did not see it then, I have since seen an account in the *New York Times* from October 2007. At the time Obama was an announced candidate for president, but an underdog. Hillary was expected to win the nomination pretty easily. The *Times*, which favored Obama, hoped to do a puff piece on his New York years, but Obama would not cooperate.

A shocked *Times* reporter wrote, "He declined repeated requests to talk about his New York years, release his Columbia transcript or identify even a single fellow student, co-worker, roommate or friend from those years." Obama stonewalled the reporter, but the *Times* refused to ask why an underdog would not welcome favorable press from the *New York Times*.

In August 2010, when Obama was complaining about corporations that conceal their political donations, he actually said, "The only people who don't want to disclose the truth are people with something to hide."

I have seen this video clip more often than I care to admit. The first time I saw it, I was looking down the road at a prison sentence and I almost fell out of my chair. It still shocks me to watch it.

It is with utter dismay that I constantly read statements like this: "In spite of overwhelming evidence to the contrary, birthers still won't accept Obama's eligibility." These claims appear almost daily in the press. Let us be very clear on this. The Obama camp has presented exactly two pieces of evidence, both of which are digital scans of alleged official documents.

Neither would be legal in a court proceeding. Against Obama's position is a growing body of evidence, facts, documents, and more that challenge Obama's eligibility. Most recently, Arizona Sheriff Joe Arpaio's cold case posse concluded that both the proffered birth certificate and Obama's selective service card were likely forgeries. So tell me: Who has something to hide? It would seem to be President Obama, and sooner or later the voters of this country are going to make it clear that his stonewalling cannot continue.

&

6. Of Paramount Importance

On 31 December 2008, attorneys Philip Berg and John Hemenway brought suit in District of Columbia Court on behalf of Gregory Hollister, a retired U.S. Air Force colonel, in a complicated case that came to be known as *Hollister v. Soetoro et al.*

Berg had lost his own case, *Berg v. Obama*, due to what is called a lack of legal standing. In other words, the judge ruled that Berg would suffer no personal harm even if Obama had been ineligible to serve as president. I think Berg would disagree.

Berg and Hemenway were of the opinion that although Hollister had retired from the Air Force in 1998 he was subject to recall due to his participation in the Individual Ready Reserve. This was one of the many cases challenging the president's eligibility. I was not aware of it when filed, but it would come to have a major impact on my life both directly and indirectly.

In the early months of 2009 I was growing more and more interested in the question of President Obama's eligibility. As with Col. Hollister, the issue affected me more than most citizens because I was subject to Obama's direct orders as commander in chief. Being on active duty, I was even more affected than Col. Hollister.

Asking around, I became aware of one of the more powerful rights under the Uniform Code of Military Justice (UCMJ). It is called Article 138. Not many of my colleagues knew about it, and none had ever resorted to it. Few had used it anywhere in the military.

According to Article 138, "Any member of the armed forces who believes himself (or herself) wronged by his (or her) commanding officer" may ask for redress. If refused, the soldier can lodge a complaint, and a superior officer must "examine into the complaint." This right, I learned, extends to anyone subject to the UCMJ.

Each branch of the service has its own style for handling complaints and forwarding them through the chain of command. I made an effort to find out as much about the Army style as I could. My question was whether I could file an article 138 against my commander in chief.

I discussed the subject with some of my peers, and they did not know anything about it. I talked to the company commander, and although sympathetic, he lacked the experience or knowledge to offer any assistance. "Submit what you want," he told me. "Maybe you can talk to Legal Assistance, but whatever you submit, I'll have to take it to JAG to get some response."

During this period, I talked to an attorney who was a high-level military adviser. He said he could not help me either. When I persisted, he offered me some scary advice. "Don't complain," he said. "People disappear or have car accidents." People disappear or have car accidents? What was *that* all about?

There were two women in my office who were very knowledgeable about procedural matters. They sympathized with my concerns—many I encountered in the military did—but they, too, warned me not to continue. I asked them, "Since when do you get in trouble for doing the right thing?" Looking back, I know I was a *little* naïve, but it was a naïveté rooted in my expectation that others would see just how right and just was my cause.

"A *little* naïve?" I can almost hear Pili laughing. Thank God for Pili. She was supportive throughout. At the time we thought that the worst outcome would be early retirement and maybe I would owe the Army money for bonuses I had received. None of this worried her. To Pili and me, it was pretty simple: someone had to prove Obama's eligibility.

Without intending to, Pili's parents reinforced my convictions. Some time down the road, my mother-in-law, a naturalized citizen, attempted to talk me out of my pursuit. "The little people like us don't have a chance," she told me. "It is the big people in the government that will always win." She was speaking innocently out her experience, but her words struck me hard. That was perhaps Thailand's government she was thinking about, but not ours, not the country I was serving, not the country whose Constitution I was protecting. Or so I told myself.

In June 2009, I attended an Army Intermediate-Level Education (ILE) program at Fort Dix in New Jersey. ILE is the equivalent course to the Command and General Staff College, a nine-month course at Fort Leavenworth, but with a selective enrollment. All officers are required to complete CGSC or ILE to continue to be promoted.

The ILE that I enrolled in was largely with reserve officers. Phase 1 lasted two weeks at Fort Dix, Phase 2 required one weekend a month for six months, and Phase 3 would be another two weeks at Fort Dix. As a lieutenant colonel I was one of the highest-ranking officers in the class, including most of the instructors.

Phase 1 consisted of maybe ten groups of ten to twelve officers, arranged in small-group instruction. In this group I was the "class leader" because of rank, but the instructors ran the class. My job was to relay administrative information or help with accountability.

Ironically, many of our case studies and discussions centered around leadership conflicts in combat, interpretations of the rules of engagement, and questions about detainee search-and-seizure scenarios that had occurred during our global war on terror—or, in the newspeak of the Obama White House, "man-made disasters" and "overseas contingency operation." We were learning how to curtail some dubious practices, which was good, but we were sometimes sacrificing security for political correctness, which was not.

Most of the others in my class were reserve officers from captain to major in rank. In casual conversations, I told them about Article 138 and sought information wherever I could find it. I explained that there were valid questions about the president's eligibility that had not been addressed. It was clear to me that Obama was not coming clean on anything, and I felt uneasy that we were trusting our national security to someone we knew so little about.

Fortunately, there were four lawyers in our group. One was Tim Griffin from the Reserve Component Command JAG, a U.S. Attorney from Arkansas who knew his way around Republican politics. JAG, as you probably know, is shorthand for the Judge Advocate General's Corps. (Mr. President, "corps" is pronounced "core," not "corpse.") The Army JAG Corps is made up of lawyer-officers who provide legal services to the Army at all levels of command.

What you may not know is that General George Washington founded the U.S. Army JAG Corps a year before the Declaration of Independence was signed. The weird thing is that we know more about the first few years of Washington's life than we do about Obama's.

I felt comfortable working with Griffin. During the first week I shared my concerns about serving under a questionable commander in chief. He gave me two bits of advice, one discouraging, one encouraging. On the downside, he told me that Article 138 did not apply to the president.

On the upside, Griffin referred me to an extraordinary woman who would play a major role in the events that unfolded over the next two years. Her name is Margaret Hemenway. Everyone in Washington knows her as "Ducky." I called her that night. (Griffin, by the way, was elected to Congress in 2010.)

Ducky began her D.C. career at NASA in the Office of Legislative and Intergovernmental Affairs. She served in the Department of Defense as a liaison to the Bush White House. She worked for former House Speaker Denny Hastert, Senator Bob Smith of New Hampshire, and ultimately Senator Jon Kyl of Arizona.

Ducky knew all about the eligibility issue through her father-in-law, the attorney I mentioned in the first paragraph of this chapter, John Hemenway. She knew better than I did that the opposition was prepared to play hardball.

When the *Hollister v. Soetoro* case first came before the court, Clinton-appointee Judge James Robertson dismissed it with an insult, saying, "The issue of the president's citizenship was raised, vetted, blogged, texted, twittered, and otherwise massaged by America's vigilant citizenry during

Mr. Obama's two-year campaign for the presidency." "Twittered"? If the judge wanted to appear hip, he should have at least gotten the terminology right and used "tweeted."

Continuing to abuse Hollister and his attorneys, Judge Robertson wrote, "Even in its relatively short life the case has excited the blogosphere and the conspiracy theorists. The right thing to do is to bring it to an early end." He then demanded to know why the attorneys shouldn't be penalized financially for daring to question Obama's eligibility through the courts.

The judge was messing with the wrong guy. The 82-year-old former infantry lieutenant had faced harder challenges, much harder. As Hemenway reminded Robertson, he had been slotted for the invasion of mainland Japan. "But for President Truman's use of nuclear weapons to end the war," wrote Hemenway, "this would have transpired. The legality of orders in and out of combat is of paramount importance."

As Hemenway pointed out, Hollister deserved better too. As a retired colonel, he was subject to recall. "Plaintiff's concern is how an order received from Obama is to be regarded. Would it be a legal order which he must obey or an illegal order which he must disobey?"

Hemenway wasn't through. He challenged Robertson's argument that Obama "had been properly vetted." Just the opposite was true. Hemenway pulled no punches:

> It is sad to read this court's use of material from the Internet to imply that the issues in the numerous lawsuits filed have been resolved by the "twittering and blogging" to determine that the litigants are invoking "conspiracy theorists." It suggests that the intellectual capacity of this court focused on the issues in the instant suit at a very low level, perhaps for political purposes, such as to win attention from the highest authority when a seat on the Supreme Court of the United States becomes vacant.

Ouch! Hemenway further criticized Robertson for threatening him with the defendants' costs, especially since Obama could have ended "this political chicanery" by simply displaying "his actual birth certificate."

Instead, said Hemenway, "ranks of attorneys" had been hired to block access to all records that would shed light on Obama's citizenship status.

Obama had never himself come clean. The only proof his supporters presented, Hemenway added, was a meaningless Certification of Live Birth posted on a number of friendly websites.

Hemenway called Robertson's threatened sanctions "a device to deprive the undersigned attorney of his civil rights and the right to due process." He added fearlessly, "Without even a hearing or access to discovery being granted to defend against the charges, such a sanction would be a veritable lynching."

While this was going on, Ducky weighed in with supporting articles of her own. In one she nicely summed up the weakness in Robertson's understanding of the case:

> Sadly, the American people depend upon a vetting process for national candidates which evidently is, truly and astonishingly, non-existent. Instead of actual verification of genuine documents to determine citizenship by some impartial board or committee, the vetting process appears to have become subjugated in the case of Mr. Obama to competing campaigns or partisan websites, a flawed Internet phenomenon which Judge Robertson referenced as Twittering and blogging.

Robertson was obviously stung by Hemenway's fierce rebuttal. He conceded in his response that Hemenway was "82 years old and takes considerable and justified pride in his patriotic public service and his status as a Rhodes Scholar." He waived the threat of financial sanctions.

But Team Obama was not yet through. A few days after Robertson's response, Hemenway received a letter from Robert Bauer, then an attorney with the power firm of Perkins Coie. The April 2009 letter begins, "I represent President Barack Obama and Vice President Joseph Biden." That is enough to intimidate right there.

After some explanatory rehashing, the letter closes with a threat: "Should you decline to withdraw this frivolous appeal, please be informed that we intend to pursue sanctions, including costs, expenses, and attorneys' fees, pursuant to Federal Rule of Appellate Procedure 38 and D.C. Circuit Rule 38."

When the "we" includes the president and the vice president of the United States, you get a sense that the judicial playing field is not exactly level. It wasn't. At the end of the day, the U.S. Court of Appeals upheld the dismissal of Hollister's suit and the reprimand of veteran Hemenway. What I took away from the suit was this: voters now had "no standing." Federal judges accepted tweeting as evidence. And members of the military did not have a meaningful way to question potentially illegal orders. Was this really the United States that I had signed up to serve? As for Robert Bauer, he was appointed White House counsel in November 2009. By this time, I was paying close attention.

7. *Grounding in Good Sense*

In looking back on how I came to do what I did, I see that my e-mail exchanges during this period are as good a guide to my thought process as any. I was corresponding with "Ducky" Hemenway and a California attorney ally of hers named Paul Jensen. Both would help guide me down the path I followed and catch more than a fair share of abuse for their troubles.

I am editing all these e-mails down to their critical nub and clarifying some abbreviations, but they are otherwise unchanged. This first e-mail comes from Jensen to Ducky on 10 June 2009, in response to a question by Ducky:

> First, [Terry] doesn't have any redress under UCMJ article 138. JAG was right to end that matter. The President is not a "uniformed officer" subject to court martial and in fact has been held by the courts not to be a member of the armed forces. Moreover, all the UCMJ provides is that the chain of command take appropriate measures—e.g., the reporting soldier can never be heard to second-guess the response to his report.

Furthermore, as I read the law Obama IS qualified to serve EVEN if born in Kenya or Indonesia or on the moon, because as I wrote you before, the law was amended a few years back to give retroactive citizenship to anyone born abroad with at least one parent who was a U.S. citizen, and this change passed the Senate . A senator may request unanimous consent, with [Senator Robert C. Smith] not objecting. That makes the question devolve to "natural born" citizen versus "foreign born" citizen, and as I recall the best thinking is that litigation on that distinction would not likely be successful.

Still, some cases that are "not likely" to succeed should still be brought, and I DO think this would be one. . . . In such a suit, I would name the plaintiff fictitiously as "John Doe", but sooner or later his name would get out, and at that point his career would be over, period. He has to know that already, but he really needs to hear this: his career will be over if he sues, win, lose or draw.

Jensen and Ducky both worked for Senator Smith, which is how they came to know each other. As Jensen got deeper into the law on this subject, he came to see that where Obama was born *did* matter because his mother, although an American citizen, had not lived in America for the necessary number of years to qualify for that exemption. He sent Ducky an e-mail with this information, and Ducky forwarded it to me that same day.

Terry—Here's from my good friend & former Senate colleague— just to show you a legal opinion on this topic! Paul is very smart and a solid conservative—others have been dealing with trying to delve into Blackstone, etc. for definition of "natural born" but of course we don't even know if Obama is a naturalized U.S. citizen or what he is! We don't know if he legally changed his name from Barry Soetoro to Barack Obama—the guy is a cypher and deliberately so.

Please read this & mull this over—and would you like to speak directly to Paul? I also mentioned you to my father-in-law and he thinks it would be a shame to give up 17 years of military service to stick your neck out too far when it may not be necessary for you to do so—with Rush Limbaugh mentioning [the eligibility issue] today for the 1st time on his radio program, let's give it a bit more time to see what the fall-out from his comments are—I don't want you to fall on your sword if we can reach our objectives (full disclosure by Obama) by other means.

As you can see, neither Jensen nor Ducky was eager to make me the sacrificial lamb in this case. I responded to Ducky later that same day.

I guess I am in a better position than others to risk the career-ending move. I have a good income, a four-year contract (3 1/2 years left) for medical bonuses, in the zone for Colonel this fall. It would be pretty unusual for them to revoke my contract, and being passed over would mean retiring as O5, or losing retirement, the worst case. I feel I am still young and marketable for employment as a physician. [It might] set me back a lot of years financially, but not insurmountable. There may even be better opportunities for me outside the military. [It is] worth more to stick to my principles.

"Losing retirement, the worst case"? Little did I know! I e-mailed Ducky again on 16 June after speaking on the phone with Jensen.

Paul and I had a good talk late last week. I discussed more with my wife too this past weekend. I am still as resolute as ever to do the right thing, or add to what pressure I could for others to do the right thing and solve this issue.

I would hope to not garner any attention and remain anonymous, but will deal with it if it is not possible. Let me know if there is anything to do or more info you would like from me.

On 8 July, Ducky came out to our house in Maryland. She is one of those slender, high-energy, professional-looking staffer types you see in Washington. She is very well read and well networked, the ultimate multi-tasker and a force to be reckoned with.

Later, after my deployment orders came through, Ducky took me up to the Rayburn House Office Building and everyone recognized her. It was really amazing. I think she can reach everyone on the right side of the aisle in Washington with no more than two phone calls. On that first meeting, Ducky impressed both Pili and me with her knowledge and her sincerity. She e-mailed me the next day.

Terry—thanks for such a nice evening—your family is lovely—I will call Paul today and discuss options with him—and let him know you're inclined to push ahead, still reserving a legal option

down the road. I can see why you like being out in Howard
County with some room and wildlife (not the same kind of wildlife we have in & around DC!).

Later that same day, 9 July, I responded.

Kids liked you, and said you can come over any time. I discussed
the Birth Certificate with another friend. She said there is an Army
reg that says I can be relieved "on the spot" for saying defamatory
things about the commander in chief. After explaining I am trying
not to do that, but that my issue is the Constitution, she recommended (I think) Special Judge Advocate's office. . . . She said
that if they decline then I am justified in going civilian lawsuit
route.

So, was it Queen's Hospital or Kapiolani Hospital? The *Berg v. Obama*
ruling needs to be looked at again, doesn't it? Snopes was not accurate? Is
Twitter a higher-level authority than Snopes? Wow!

Forgive my sarcasm here, but I am referring to a 7 July article on *World
Net Daily,* the online publication at the forefront of the eligibility issue. Up
until January 2009, the Obama-friendly websites, including Snopes and
Obama's own campaign website, had been listing Honolulu's Queens
Hospital as the site of Obama's birth.

I was aware that Snopes was just a husband-wife team with no special
training. I had also seen photos of the Factcheck.org "investigators," the
ones who photographed the early Certification of Live Birth. They looked
like a couple of college interns booted from their parents' basement. Yet
these apparently were the "experts" doing the heavy lifting for the media.

On 24 January 2009, Obama sent a letter to Kapiolani Hospital claiming
that Kapiolani was "the place of my birth." Once WND pointed out the
switch, the websites began scrubbing all their previous references to
Queens Hospital.

Yet no matter how many times Snopes and others change their story, the
editors at these websites feel free to mock those of us who are just trying
to get at the truth. Go figure.

Let me give you another example of an unreliable story. In his weekly address from the White House on the day before Father's Day in 2011, President Obama repeated the tale about his early years that he first floated in
his 1995 memoir, *Dreams from My Father.*

"I grew up without my father around," Obama said at the very beginning of his Father's Day address. "He left when I was two years old." Obama said the same thing in a *People* magazine Father's Day essay early in the week: his father, Barack Obama Sr., left the family when he was two.

This is important because Obama built his candidacy around the story of the happy little multicultural family. He started his Democratic Convention speeches in both 2004 and 2008 with the story. Up to and through the 2008 election every mainstream story about Obama, including a few book-length biographies, simply repeated this tale.

The only problem is that it isn't true. As we know now, and as some people on the right knew well before the 2008 election, there never was an Obama family. According to the records of the University of Washington in Seattle, Obama's mother was enrolled there within weeks of his reported birth in August 1961.

All accounts back up those records. She had the baby with her, but Barack Sr. stayed behind in Hawaii. He left for Harvard before Obama and his mother returned to Hawaii in 1962.

Three months before Father's Day in 2011, Obama Sr.'s INS records were made public. The mainstream media did report that he had been thrown out of Harvard on moral grounds, but none of them reported the real bombshell.

An INS document from August 1961 states that just weeks after the birth, the baby was "living with mother" and she was living "with her parents." The baby's father, Obama Sr., was reported to be living at a separate address. In other words, there never was an Obama family. The documents relied on the testimony of Obama Sr., but even he acknowledged that Obama's mother was on the verge of leaving for Washington State.

It hurts to say this, but Obama lied to America's children on Father's Day. Why? He can get away with it, that's why. The same media who mock us as "birthers" refuse to learn *anything* about Obama's birth. If Obama lied about the first two years of his life, as we can prove, why should we believe him about the year leading up to his birth?

In May 2011 *New York Times* reporter Janny Scott came out with her book on Obama's mother, Ann Dunham. The book is called *A Singular Woman*. Scott spent three years researching Dunham's life.

Do you know what Scott tells us about the six months leading up to Obama's birth, the only event in Dunham's life that made her worth a book? Nothing. Not one word. Dunham finishes her first semester at the University of Hawaii at the end of January 1961. Then the baby is born in August 1961. If anything happened in between, we don't know about it.

On February 2, 1961, Scott tells us that Obama's parents "reportedly" got married on Maui, but that is all we know about the wedding. Scott is the *New York Times* reporter, the official biographer; she cannot use the word "reportedly" on something as significant as the marriage. From 2 February to 4 August is a blank page. Nothing. No photos from this period either.

As to the birth itself, Scott tells us nothing that was not listed on the short-form Certification of Live Birth, plus she tells us Obama was born in the now-agreed-upon "Kapiolani Hospital." There are no baby pictures, no tales of worried grandparents or a frantic trip to the hospital, not a single thing about the birth except when and where the *alleged* birth took place.

In June 2011, Sally Jacobs of the *Boston Globe* came out with her book on Barack Obama Sr., *The Other Barack*. Like Scott, she leaves a massive hole in the Dunham biography: not one word on Dunham's whereabouts from the marriage, "apparently" a quiet civil service, to the birth.

To Jacobs' credit, her book opens well. The first two sentences read, "Every man who has served as president of the United States had parents who lived out their lives upon American soil. Barack H. Obama did not." Yes, media, that is what makes Obama the subject of scrutiny, not his race.

Although no one in the major media would tell the truth about Obama's origins, Scott did expose one significant Obama lie. In his 2008 campaign, as well as in his drive to pass his version of health care reform, Obama repeatedly claimed that his mother spent the last months of her life "arguing with insurance companies because they're saying that [her uterine cancer] may be a pre-existing condition and they don't have to pay her treatment."

As Scott pointed out, Dunham had comprehensive health coverage through her employer. All she had to pay were the deductibles. She did, in fact, try to get her disability insurer to cover those but failed. And that small-potatoes dispute became the stuff of ObamaCare legend.

On 13 July 2009, I heard again from Jensen:

> I caution you against false optimism; just because you have a right-eous cause doesn't mean that you will succeed in court, and I have

spent the last 20 years bringing only winning cases to court. I frankly never bring a case that I expect to lose, and this is what separates me from [others]. I have a busy and successful trial practice here in California, and if I take your case it is not merely because I believe in it but because I believe it can win!

I wrote back to Jensen on 16 July.

Thanks for my monthly "grounding in good sense." My desire to do something remains strong and I need the occasional good counsel to keep me in check. I read your note several days ago, and just have not had the time to reply and express how much I value your wisdom and advice.

After months of asking questions and getting no answers, it was refreshing to talk to someone who had some. In September we picked up the thread once again in what I affectionately came to call my "monthly smackdown." I asked Jensen:

Do I have a case for Breach of Contract with the Army? Signing my Oath of Office seems like it is implied that both parties agree to make the contract achievable. I feel my contract of the Oath is not possible because no one in my chain of command—per my Article 138 and Congressional Complaint—can provide me good info about BHO's eligibility.

I have crossed the line of thinking that I could remain neutral on the political level arguments—that I could drive on with duty if eligibility is proven, but even if that could happen now, I feel little desire to serve under political and military leadership that has not been more diligent and so partisan.

I am wondering how my current Commander would handle the situation if I just stopped wearing my uniform and performing military duties. I'll still show up, work hard, perform my duties as Chief of Primary Care at the Pentagon Clinic. I would just not be doing it in uniform.

Jensen was not exactly thrilled with my ideas and did not hesitate to tell me:

As to your question on breach of contract assume that it could be proved that [Obama] was ineligible, there can be no doubt that he IS serving pursuant to law. That of course begs the question of whether his FURTHER service would be according to law, but in a contract case, the court would have no personal jurisdiction over Obama, and since your case would lie in the Court of Claims, the reach of that court's jurisdiction would not extend to a determination of the president's eligibility to serve, so the court would lack subject matter jurisdiction. I just see no reasonable chance that the Court of Claims would grant you money damages.

As to your question about just showing up to serve but refusing to wear the uniform, and to perform "military duties," I can immediately think of several provisions of the UCMJ that would support a court martial: Article 91, insubordination; Article 92, refusal to obey a lawful order; and of course the catch-all, Article 133, CUBO [conduct unbecoming an officer.] Among others I haven't mentioned, these could subject you IF CONVICTED to significant imprisonment. You would have a defense, of course, that the orders were not lawful, and in any event, you were excused from performance by the ineligibility of Obama to serve. IF you won, that would be monumental. If you lost you would serve a long stretch in the stockade. Considering the likely composition of the court, I cannot suggest that any lawyer, even one as brilliant as I, could save you from being convicted. So, I urge you NOT to follow that course!

Speaking of smackdowns, about this time a judge in Georgia handed the attorney Orley Taitz a pretty brutal one in a federal court. The case was known as *Rhodes v. McDonald*. Captain Connie Rhodes, like me a U.S. Army physician, had retained Taitz to help prevent her deployment to Iraq. In requesting a restraining order, Taitz argued that Rhodes's deployment was illegal because of the questions surrounding Obama's eligibility. On 16 September, federal judge Clay Land rejected the motion. Did he ever. Said Land:

A spurious claim questioning the President's constitutional legitimacy may be protected by the First Amendment, but a Court's placement of its imprimatur upon a claim that is so lacking in factual support that it is frivolous would undoubtedly disserve the public interest.

Land commented that Rhodes did not seem to have any "conscientious objections" to taking orders from Obama as long as she was "permitted to remain on American soil." Land then scolded Taitz for using military officers as pawns to pursue her own agenda. As I say, it wasn't pretty. On 16 September, the day of Land's decision, I shared my thoughts with Jensen and Ducky:

> Sigh! I see the result and supporting argument, but the biased tone is appalling to me. Is that usual? I think I am in much better position than Captain Rhodes—17 years service, deployed to Bosnia under Clinton and Afghanistan under Bush.
>
> I think I have exhausted my military options. I submitted Article 138 asking for someone in my chain of command to release a statement that I was not violating my oath of office or to advise me as to my proper course to address this. I was denied any recourse by my unit Commander and never offered counseling by Legal Affairs despite my asking. I submitted Congressionals and both Senators took little/no action. My congressman Zach Wamp did submit it to DA Legislative Affairs, who sent it back to my old unit Commander, who submitted the same reply.

Jensen had some questions about Taitz's approach that were relevant to our going forward and some good advice for all of us:

> I agree with the court, though, that Orly was seeking to reverse the burden of proof. The PLAINTIFF always has the burden of proof, and the Hawaiian document creates a presumption that he was born there, not vice versa. That presumption can be rebutted, but only by admissible evidence.
>
> You are correct that your facts are better than Captain Rhodes's . . . but even on your facts, the abstention doctrine is a serious impediment. Coupled with the standing issue which will likely determine the outcome in Rodearmel[2], I just don't see any basis at this juncture for optimism that you could pre-

---

[2] *Rodearmel v. Clinton* (No. 09-171) – Hillary Clinton is constitutionally ineligible to serve as Secretary of State due to the "emoluments" clause

vail in court. . . . The negative turn of events this week convinces me that we need to look to a different mechanism than the courts for redress of our grievance.

I think one reason I felt defensive about these other plaintiffs and their attorneys is that I had gotten to meet John Hemenway, Ducky's father-in-law. As you recall, the judge in the Hollister case insulted Hemenway with his foolish "Twitter" remarks.

Sharp as a tack at 80-something, John is a pretty formidable fellow. So is his son David, Ducky's husband and an attorney himself. David is a big burly guy who is not afraid to speak his mind. He got his law degree at the historically black Howard University. I suspect he stood his ground there too. You get the sense that if Ducky does the talking, David provides the muscle.

We met at John's home in an older established neighborhood within the Beltway. Ducky's mother-in-law, an elegant Southern lady now struggling with Alzheimer's, was there as well. When you meet these people, the ones on the front line of the battle for constitutional justice, you lose patience with the small-minded people who make fun of them.

By November 2009, I was also losing patience with the chain of command and faith in the commander in chief. As a result, my desire to continue my military service was slipping away. That November, I sent a letter withdrawing from my ongoing ILE program. What this meant was that, barring the unforeseen, I was abandoning any chance of future advancement. The letter, edited for relevance, sums up my feelings at the time:

> A little over a year ago I was volunteering to deploy again, but currently my thoughts are that if I am ordered to deploy, I may consider refusing. It sure seems like our elected leaders no longer have use for the Constitution. My oath as an officer to "support and defend the Constitution" is losing meaning. I feel compelled to stand up and "bear true faith and allegiance" in what manner I can within the military system, and likely having little recourse, it would be time for me to exit the service. One way I have tried to stand up is by submitting an Article 138, UCMJ Complaint of Wrongs against Commanders. I submitted a complaint over 6 months ago that was turned back by my Company Commander stating I had no recourse. I decided to submit another Article 138 Complaint directed at

General Casey, the Army Chief of Staff. I will attach a copy for your review along with some supporting articles. I know—"great, more reading"—but it is not required :) I only attach for your understanding and education if you like.

Very Respectfully, Terry Lakin, DO, MPH, LTC, MC

With this letter, the die was officially cast.

&

8. Take Some Responsibility

The Pentagon is a city unto itself.

Army brass broke ground for the building in September 1941 and, under wartime pressure, opened it just sixteen months later. Today, that would be a good pace for a neighborhood Applebee's, but the Pentagon is not exactly an Applebee's. It is the largest office building in the world.

On any given day about 26,000 people show up to work there, and starting in July 2009 my job was to take care of them.

My commute was a monster. If I left my Maryland home by 0530 hours, I could usually get to work in an hour. There was no good time to leave at the end of the day. The drive home would take two hours no matter when I headed out. So I usually left by 1900 hours in the hope that I could see the kids before they went to bed.

Other than the commute, I loved the work at the Pentagon health clinic, where I was assigned. In my seventeen-year military career, it was one of my favorite postings. When I got there, however, things were pretty chaotic. The physicians were having a hard time relating to Lt. Col. Christine Edwards, the deputy commander for clinical operations.

One major problem was that Edwards was a dietitian, not a physician. She needed help managing the docs and welcomed me into the morning clinical command meetings. The administrative tasks she assigned me, however, did not help with what the clinic needed most: an actual provider to see patients, respond to internal emergency calls, assist the walk-in provider during busy times, and take up issues the patient advocate needed help with. In other words, the clinic needed a real, honest-to-God multitasking doctor, and that was me.

I loved feeling that I could do it all. Besides, the administrative tasks could always wait until the evening, after the patients had been taken care of. That's the way I like to roll.

I liked the challenge of it all. I have always been something of a problem solver, and, as the saying goes, I play well with others. I was happy to run interference for Edwards with the physicians to help get her credibility back. We quickly made some good progress.

I have always felt it best to lead by example, and that is much easier to do when you like your work. I loved mine. I worked hard at it, too. I was one of the first ones there in the morning and the last to leave at night. In addition to the administrative duties, I worked directly with patients and filled in wherever there was a shortfall. I made a point of never turning anyone away.

I also helped with urgent care. This work reminded me of my EMT days. With many thousands of people working there regularly, and thousands of others visiting, rarely a day went by that we did not have an emergency or two.

When we did, I would head out with our first-responding "runner" medics. We had to literally run because our golf cart could not negotiate some of the elevators and corridors. My colleagues had trained well and knew the layout of this massive building. By accompanying them, I could assess their work. Usually, within seconds, I could tell if the medics could address a problem themselves. If they could, I let them do their duties as if I were not there. My presence could be a little intimidating, but they got accustomed to it and did well. There is nothing like a team response to an emergency to develop a rapport with your co-workers.

Through the end of 2009 and the beginning of 2010, all went smoothly. I continued to monitor the eligibility issue. I spoke regularly with Jensen and Ducky. And I plowed away at my job. As much as I loved my work, I loved the weekends more. Our kids were turning into real people right in front of my eyes. Holly was ten now, Andrew seven, and Jackson three.

As a physician, I was keeping an especially careful eye on ObamaCare, Obama's health care reform plan. There was much about the bill as proposed that bothered me, but what bothered me even more was the way Obama was demonizing doctors to slam this bill down our throats.

I particularly remember a comment President Obama made at a New Hampshire town hall meeting. I looked up the quote. This is what he said about the treatment of diabetes:

> Right now if we paid a family—if a family care physician works with his or her patient to help them lose weight, modify diet, monitors whether they're taking their medications in a timely fashion, they might get reimbursed a pittance. But if that same diabetic ends up getting their foot amputated, that's $30,000, $40,000, $50,000—immediately the surgeon is reimbursed.

Here is the message Obama wanted people to walk away with: doctors would rather amputate your foot than treat your diabetes because they will make more money and get paid more quickly. As a doctor, I was personally offended by this message.

Obama's comments on tonsillectomies were just as ill advised and along the same insulting line. In a June 2009 press conference he argued that if a child with a bad sore throat sees a doctor, "The doctor may look at the reimbursement system and say to himself, 'You know what? I make a lot more money if I take this kid's tonsils out.'"

Obama had been pounding on this anti-doctor, anti-freedom theme since he first started running for president. This would have been bad enough if he knew what he was talking about, but he clearly did not. Let me share one more Obama quote that caught my attention, this one from a town hall meeting in Virginia:

> Everybody knows that it makes no sense that you send a kid to the emergency room for a treatable illness like asthma. They end up taking up a hospital bed. It costs, when, if you, they just gave, you gave them treatment early and they got

some treatment, and a, a breathalyzer . . . or inhalator, not a breathalyzer.

No, Mr. President, a breathalyzer is something police give to suspected drunk drivers. An inhalator is not the right word either. I think the word Obama was searching for is "inhaler." We all make mistakes, but this was the man who wanted to take the health care system, one-sixth of the American economy, and put it under his personal control. Not only did he get the words wrong, but he also showed a complete lack of understanding of the way American medicine works.

Until asthma care went "green," inhalers cost only about $15. That is about the cost of a twelve-pack of beer. What parent in America would choose a twelve-pack over an inhaler for an asthmatic child? If you can find such a parent, we should put that person in jail, not build a health care system around his criminal neglect. Even an environmentally friendly inhaler—were inhalers really destroying the planet?—costs only about $30.

Thank God Sarah Palin has never said anything as stupid as Obama's breathalyzer quote! It would have made the evening news and been the grist of the late-night comedy mill for the next half-century. But since Obama said it, people like my parents never got to hear it. People like my parents, and I am talking here about two-thirds of all Americans, know very little about what Obama has been doing to this country.

I got a sense of this on 20 March 2010, when I took my son Andrew down to see the anti-ObamaCare rally on Capitol Hill. We made a day of it. We went to lunch, then we stopped by the Capitol. Along the way, I got to tell him what a great country this is and why his daddy was fighting to preserve it.

At the Capitol, we visited the U.S. Senate chambers. There, an Obama-friendly senator was holding forth in front of just about no one except maybe the TV cameras. He was carrying on about how one of his elderly constituents could not get a half-million-dollar lung transplant because he had no supplementary insurance to cover it.

I was tempted to yell out, "Maybe if this guy wasn't smoking, he wouldn't have lung cancer. Maybe he could have spent the cigarette money on health insurance. Maybe people should take some responsibility for their lives." As I told Andrew, "This is not a good way to run a government."

We did not see much of the Capitol Hill rally, but I saw enough to know that it was like several of the other Tea Party rallies I had attended. This one was spirited but peaceful, free of profanity and vulgarity, and much neater than rallies staged by the left, even those for environmental causes.

That night and over the weekend, however, I began to see news reports that protestors shouted racial insults at black Democratic congressmen and spit on them. Here is one of the first headlines that came across the wire, this one from the liberal McClatchy Newspapers: "Tea Party protestors scream 'nigger' at black congressmen."

By Sunday morning, March 21, House Minority Leader John Boehner, R-Ohio, was calling the actions of the Capitol Hill protestors "reprehensible." He had fallen for the trap set by the liberal media. If it were not for those dang video cameras that are everywhere now, we never would have known the truth.

As more and more videos were posted online, it became clear that not a single person had shouted a racial slur, and no one had spit on anyone. Conservative media mogul Andrew Breitbart offered $100,000 to anyone who could produce a video with a racial epithet of any kind. He had no takers.

The whole story was a scam, but it worked. Millions of Americans, including my parents, were led to believe that Tea Party people were a bunch of racist lunatics. Why else would they oppose ObamaCare? As Keith Olbermann summed up the episode, "If racism is not the whole of the Tea Party, it is in its heart."

I will be honest. I did not vote for Barack Obama, but like many people I felt some pride that America had elected a black man and some hope that race would no longer be a dividing issue of this country. But I was dreaming. Obama and his allies have used race to turn his political base against anyone who questions the president or his agenda.

Unfortunately, this would come to include me and my supporters.

&

9. The Constitution Matters

As 2010 rolled around, my attorney Paul Jensen and I had given up the idea of a lawsuit, but I knew all along there was one thing that could shake up the status quo: an RFO, request for orders, and one finally came down in early February 2010. I got the word from Lt. Col. Edwards that my name was on the short list for deployment. It looked as if I was heading back to Afghanistan.

This was troubling news for both Edwards and me. Edwards had come to rely on my ability to solve any issue related to medical care. She did not want to lose me. "You have deployed a couple of times already," she told me. "We'll get you out of this." But I had a better feel for the Army than Edwards did. "I'll believe it when I see it," I told her.

I had learned to be skeptical in Bosnia. There, whenever my Apache Battalion Commander would hear new rumors of our redeployment home, he would say, "Don't buy any of these wolf tickets until you actually see the official orders." This proved to be good advice.

There was no easy exit. In mid-March the deployment orders came down. I was to report to a new unit, which was part of the 101st Airborne Division. We were to muster at Fort Campbell in Kentucky and from there it would be a few weeks of training and then, "Hello, Afghanistan!"

If I told you I was of two minds on my decision to deploy, I would be undercounting the number of "minds" involved. On the one hand, the assignment sounded interesting. I called the people at the unit in Kentucky to ask what they needed from me. I liked them immediately. They were gung ho to have me, and I thought it would be a great unit to work for. I looked forward to seeing Afghanistan again, checking out the towns I knew, and monitoring the progress.

On the other hand, I had been growing in my resolve for the last year or more. I had finally decided it would be wrong for me to accept orders that ultimately came from a commander in chief who refused to confirm his eligibility for office. During this time, I was hoping that President Obama would come clean, would show his birth certificate, would save me from taking a step I did not want to take.

I wish I were Sergeant Rock, the World War II comic book hero, so I could laugh in the face of danger and spit in the enemy's eye. Or if I had been a constitutional scholar or a military historian, I could have answered my own questions and resolved my own issues. But being none of the above, I was torn.

Somewhere along the way, Jensen alerted me to the one provision in the Uniform Code of Military Justice that led me to think I could make a difference. It is known as Article 32. I'll cite just the opening paragraph so you can see why it intrigued us:

> No charge or specification may be referred to a general court-martial for trial until a thorough and impartial investigation of all the matters set forth therein has been made. This investigation shall include inquiry as to the truth of the matter set forth in the charges, consideration of the form of charges, and recommendation as to the disposition which should be made of the case in the interest of justice and discipline.

By refusing to deploy I was inviting a court-martial. That much I knew. But if the investigation into my refusal would "include inquiry as to the truth of the matter," a court-martial might very well provide the means to test the truth: Is Barack Obama constitutionally eligible to serve as president of the United States?

It was not an easy decision. For insight, I did a lot of Bible reading. Ducky put me in touch with her friends, Gordon and June Smith, and they were very helpful in offering me counsel and religious guidance. I paid attention at church more. I listened closely to the personal testimonies of my fellow church members. Some were extraordinary. Every service touched my heart.

Communion meant more to me than it ever had before. It meant more to Pili as well. She and all three kids were baptized; three-year-old Jack did his cutest best to follow the lead of his big sister and brother.

One time at church, I remember fixing on an image of Jesus on one of the stained glass windows. It was one of those profound, tearful moments. There is scene in the Garden of Gethsemane where Jesus is praying for enlightenment on the eve of his crucifixion. "Father," Jesus prays, "all things are possible to You. Take this cup away from me, but not what I will but what You will."

I don't mean to compare myself to Jesus. My point is that in Jesus' life we all can find eternal wisdom if we look. Here He was, a man dreading what He faced but knowing He had to do it. If Jesus could pray for strength and guidance, so could I. I just needed to know that the path I took would be the right one.

I prayed, too, for a miracle. I prayed that somehow, somewhere, someone would resolve all the eligibility issues around Obama and I could accept my assignment with a clear conscience. Deep down, though, I knew that was not going to happen.

At this time, too, Andrew, Holly, and I were taking a karate class together. The kids were making great progress, Andrew especially. The lessons we learned there about restraint and discipline and courage strengthened my will and helped the kids understand my motives.

At the clinic, Lt. Col. Edwards never quite understood. I tried to explain my thinking, but she just did not wish to get it. She had more than enough going on, professionally and personally. Closing her eyes and ears, turning her head away and saying she did not want to be involved was her way of coping.

Still, Edwards knew this issue was not about to go away. She cared for me as an officer and a doctor. We were starting to see light at end of tunnel in our effort to straighten out the clinic. She wanted to keep me, but I think she thought I was angling for a way out of deployment. No, I tried to tell her, that wasn't it.

One morning on the way to work, I was listening to popular radio host Fred Grandy on Washington's powerful AM station WMAL. He said something that struck hard at the time: "Once you throw down, you can't throw up."

What Grandy meant was once you take a stand, you can't just stand down when the going gets tough. For the last year I had taken a stand. It was not all that public; only a few people really knew. But I knew. What would I tell myself? What would I tell Pili? "I only *sort of* mean all those things I said"? No, that is not who I am.

At the time, I was getting ready to take a few days off to prepare for an up-coming military acupuncture course. I was trying to tidy up a bunch of my administrative tasks and had been reviewing labs and notes for my patients for the previous day or two. I remember sitting at my desk about 1700 hours this one particular evening. The clinic locked up at 1600 hours, and almost everyone who worked there was out the door at 1601.

I was hoping to finish up my work and head home by 1900 hours to see the kids before bedtime, but then I got a call from a panicked young Army cadet who was in a masters program at a Virginia college. This cadet had just spent the last several weeks trying to get a flight physical in order to attend flight training. He had been put off by several other flight medicine clinics before finally getting an appointment at the Fort Meade, Maryland, clinic.

The cadet showed up at the clinic, did everything he was asked, and at the end of it was told that he had not actually gotten a formal flight physical; the clinic did not have anyone qualified to complete one. Now the cadet was up against the wall. He had to have his flight physical done and stamped with approval by the review officer at Fort Rucker, Alabama, by close of business the next day.

Somebody had given him my name and told him that if anybody in the area could get it done, I was the guy. So he called me at 1730 hours. I tried at first to put him off, but it was evident that this soldier was being given the bureaucratic runaround. If there was anyone in the Army who could identify with that, I was that guy too.

The cadet needed to see me as soon as we opened the clinic doors the next morning. I agreed. We would complete his physical exam and anything else that needed to be done and then we would try and get his physical approved by Fort Rucker.

He faxed me his paperwork, and it all had to be processed pronto. I realized now that I had no choice but to spend the night in my office. I had done it a few times before, sleeping on the cold, hard exam table, getting in a few hours of sleep but basically working the whole night and taking a shower in one of the restrooms down the hall.

Later that night, at about 1930 hours, I had a conference call with Paul Jensen and Ducky Hemenway. According to Jensen, this was the last chance for me to make a decision. I had been holding off for a long time, and he needed to know my intentions—now. If I refused deployment, he would be on a flight the next day or two to get the ball rolling.

This was it. Was I going to disobey deployment orders and take a stand, or was I going to call it all off? During this very tense call, I was going through a risk assessment, weighing the pros and cons. I was also saying silent prayers in search of guidance. I told Jensen I would get back to him.

Later than evening, as I was looking at my orders sitting on the desk, the last line jumped out at me: "bring five (5) copies of your birth certificate." I had read the orders several times and had glossed over a detail that had previously seemed routine, but this time I felt like Wile E. Coyote getting smacked by an anvil. I needed a birth certificate to deploy, but the president did not need one to order my deployment? This was nuts.

The realization seemed altogether providential. I decided right then: If not me, who? If not now, when? Over the previous several months, I recalled many times that there seemed to be other signs of what I thought were divine guidance. I may have just been looking for validation everywhere, but I was finding it more often than chance would dictate. Now I had found the mother of all signs. I was not going to Afghanistan.

The young cadet came in the next morning. It was supposed to be my day off, so I had the time to jump in and walk him through the process. As we were leaving the optometry clinic, a large entourage blocked our exit. This was one of the many VIP tours that came through the clinic, most of which I succeeded in avoiding.

This one featured Secretary of Defense Robert Gates. My clinic commander, who was escorting Gates, panicked when he saw me. I think he was afraid that I would grab Gates by the lapels and demand an answer to the eligibility question. To be honest, the thought did enter my mind, but I was too responsible an officer to undermine my commander in that way.

Gates and I shook hands, had a quick photo op, and I presented the cadet as a future Army aviator to the secretary of defense. Not the average day for a cadet, I can assure you. After his feet finally came to rest back on the ground, the cadet and I went to lunch. He was a sharp young guy, on the way up and soaking it all in; I was likely having my last lunch at the Pentagon as a welcomed member of the U.S. military. To put an Army spin on the old saying, we were two tanks passing in the night.

It was not easy, but we were able to get the cadet's aviation flight physical stamped "approved" by the end of the day. He was enormously grateful. His dreams of a career as an Army medevac pilot would have been delayed for another year, maybe longer. He had a great future ahead of him, a future that depended on our Constitution, a future that I hoped was not slipping away. He had no clue as to what was transpiring in my life at the time, but I hope that somehow in the future he will understand and appreciate it.

On Saturday, 20 March 2010, the press release from SafeguardourConstitution.com went out. I reported to the Pentagon clinic the next morning with dread in my heart, fearful of unknown reactions. I was just finishing up the acupuncture course, and I was soon to begin two weeks of leave before my scheduled report to Fort Campbell.

Our clinic commander had picked a great day to be gone. His absence left the deputy commander of administration (DCA) in charge. He had gotten word of the press release. Passing me in the hallway early in the morning, he told me we needed to have a counseling session later. This began a day of somber military counseling and conversations with Jensen on the phone. I knew there had to be any number of officers and lawyers up the chain getting involved as well.

Despite the emotional turmoil, I continued with my acupuncture training. My mind was elsewhere, but I was trying to hold it together. The instructor, I think, sensed my stress and selected me among just a few other docs in this class of thirty to receive a special treatment called "Internal and External Dragons." The title fit. I was facing both.

The treatment seemed to work. When I went home afterward, I felt calmer, more in tune with my family. The following day, the instructor asked me and the other test subjects about our experiences. I gave an honest testimonial. I told the class I had been under stress, and I told them in general terms why.

I had to leave early that Tuesday for a meeting with my brigade commander, Col. Gordon Roberts. My fellow students and instructors wished me well, not knowing that I was soon to be disobeying orders. The instructor even offered to put small ear acupuncture needles in for the meeting, and I don't think he was kidding. I almost took him up on the offer.

Jensen had flown in for the meeting with Col. Roberts, and he accompanied me to Walter Reed Army Medical Center to see the colonel. Roberts, however, was not available. We met instead with his executive officer, an African-American woman, and informed her of my plans. She was not sympathetic.

I showed her a copy of the letter that I had sent to the White House addressed to President Obama. Paul would let her take notes but not keep it or photocopy it. The meeting was confrontational. At first, she probed to see if I had been flagged or was facing medical or administrative action. In her way of thinking, I might have been doing all of this as some form of retaliation. When this line of inquiry went nowhere, she asked, "And you had no problem with a white President Bush?" Fortunately, you don't much see such racism in the Army.

Later that day, I was given a counseling statement that included comments from this executive officer. According to her, I had said President Obama was not a "native born" citizen, which, of course, I had not said. It seemed too convenient that this misinformation would be written on my counseling statement for me to sign. My experience told me that in signing the document I was only agreeing to the administrative details, but under these unusual circumstances, all bets were off.

Through tears, I wrote that I did not agree with what had been written and that my lawyer would address the executive officer's comments as appropriate. I also received word to report to Col. Roberts at Walter Reed before 1600 hours the next afternoon.

I took the next afternoon off. By this time, Jensen had returned to California. While driving to Walter Reed, I phoned both him and Maj. Matt Kemkes. As the system was set up, the Army had assigned me a military attorney to defend me without cost. In my case that was Kemkes. He advised me to comply with my orders. Jensen more or less agreed, saying he could not ethically advise me not to comply. Even so, it troubled me that I would now have to face the commander without legal counsel, without even an impartial witness. I had crossed the Rubicon and "thrown down" in a big way. For all I knew, I could be placed in custody at meeting's end.

When I got to Walter Reed, I just wasn't ready to see Col. Roberts. There was someone else I needed to talk to instead, and I found Him in the chapel. I read the Bible, asked Him for guidance, and finally headed home after an hour or two. I finished the week working at the Pentagon and began my leave on the following Monday.

A few days later, while I was home on leave, I was able to find a little comic relief. The deputy commander of administration called and said that the command group at Walter Reed had suggested a brain scan. A brain scan? I asked how he, an administrative officer, could justify the need for a high-cost brain scan.

"Well," he said, "some of the physicians were worried this could be a tumor or something that was setting off your behavior. You have been such a great officer up to now." I had no other symptoms: no headaches, no visual problems or memory difficulties. The only symptom seemed to be that I took decisive action after failing to get adequate response to an important constitutional question. Of course, a brain tumor!

About this time, my advisers posted on YouTube a simple three-minute video we had recorded a few days earlier at the Army & Navy Club in D.C. I suppose I was hoping that someone close to the president would see it and understand that there were real-life consequences to the game Obama seemed to be playing with the American people. More realistically, I hoped that those who knew me would understand why I was doing what I was doing. Here are some highlights:

I want you to know the reasons I feel I have no choice but the distasteful one of inviting my own court-martial. For the first time in all my years of service to our great nation, and at great peril to my career and future, I am choosing to disobey what I believe are illegal orders, including an order to deploy to Afghanistan for my second tour of duty there.

I will disobey my orders to deploy because I—and I believe all servicemen and women and the American people—deserve the truth about President Obama's constitutional eligibility to the office of the presidency and the commander in chief.

If he is ineligible, then my orders—and indeed all orders—are illegal because all orders have their origin with the commander in chief as handed down through the chain of command.

Any reasonable person looking critically at the evidence currently in the public domain would have questions about President Obama's claim to be a "natural born citizen." The troubling but compelling information that calls into question Obama's claim . . . has gone unanswered because he refuses to release his original birth certificate dating from 1961 and bearing the signature of the doctor who delivered him. This burden of proof must fall upon the president.

President Obama, I ask you to respect and uphold the Constitution. Be transparent and show your honesty and integrity. Release your original, signed birth certificate, if you have one, thus proving your birth on American soil, and thus assure the American people that you are lawfully eligible to hold the office of the presidency and serve as commander in chief of the Armed Forces.

The constitution matters. The truth matters. I am Lieutenant Colonel Terry Lakin. Thank you for your time, and God bless us and God bless our nation.

By now, nearly a quarter of a million people have seen this video. But then, except on the right side of the blogosphere, the coverage came slowly. The little that appeared in the mainstream press came mainly out of Colorado. A Greeley *Tribune* reporter, for instance, saw fit to seek out my parents and ask their opinion.

Reported the *Tribune*, "Lakin's father, Frank Lakin of Greeley, said he didn't know enough about the situation to comment Thursday afternoon, but he did say his son's video wasn't representative of the family."

"This does not reflect the opinions or the attitude of the family by any means," my father told the reporter. "We're Obama supporters." I think I've mentioned that my parents and I don't exactly see eye to eye on politics.

I read the *Tribune* article online and the comments that followed. Many of the respondents insulted me. That I took in stride. What hurt was the one guy who said he knew Frank Lakin was a socialist, and now he had proof. I wrote an e-mail to the *Tribune* asking them to remove this nonsense. My father was an honorable man, a veteran to boot, and always had the best for the community in mind.

A follow-up article in the *Colorado Independent* magnified the split. The headline read "Birther Army doctor Lakin refuses to deploy, his Greeley family supports Obama." The article by John Tomasic claimed that on the YouTube video, I was "speaking in familiar talk-radio terms."

I would bet that Tomasic and his readers never listen to talk radio, so I do not know how, if there even was a talk-radio language, it would be "familiar" to them. Like so much of the reporting, this was patronizing and dismissive. It would not get any better.

My day of decision was 12 April 2010. That day, a Monday, was a nightmarish blur. I got up early—I had hardly slept—and packed my car as though I were going to be on US Airways Flight 1123 out of Baltimore/Washington International at 0820 hours. I was expected to check in at Fort Campbell, Kentucky, no later than 1500 hours. I headed not to the airport, however, but to the Pentagon. There I took a photo of myself with my bags to prove that I was still willing to deploy if Obama's eligibility could be validated.

I was hoping I would get some e-mail from Jensen or Ducky telling me that new eligibility evidence had come out; if so, I would head out to the airport and make my flight. I would leave the car at the airport and Pili would pick it up later.

The commute to work that day was a torture of self-reflection and second-guessing. I found myself near tears questioning why I had brought this on myself and my family. And yet I knew why I had to do what I said I would do, and I was determined to do it.

Help came from different and unexpected places. After the YouTube video was posted, I started receiving lots of messages, more than I could hope to read. I had been avoiding Facebook, but this morning, at about 0500 hours, as I sat in the parking lot of the Pentagon hoping and praying for new information, I took a look. There was a Facebook friend request from "Patrick Henry."

I did not think fake names were allowed on Facebook, but I accepted the friend request. The info on his wall was humorous and, of course, it contained Henry's greatest speech, best known for that rousing finale, "Give me liberty, or give me death!" Another part of the speech, though, seemed to speak even more directly to my situation:

> They tell us, sir, that we are weak; unable to cope with so formidable an adversary. But when shall we be stronger? Will it be the next week, or the next year? Will it be when we are totally disarmed, and when a British guard shall be stationed in every house? Shall we gather strength by irresolution and inaction? Shall we acquire the means of effectual resistance by lying supinely on our backs and hugging the delusive phantom of hope, until our enemies shall have bound us hand and foot?

Unlike Patrick Henry, I was not risking death or the loss of my entire fortune. I was risking my career and my freedom at the hands of an "enemy" that was, in its own way, trying to help me. And yet what Henry said about "irresolution and inaction" hit home. How would these behaviors make me stronger? How would they inspire others to speak out? How would they encourage the president to come clean with the American people? Irresolution and inaction, I knew, accomplished nothing. It never had.

I arrived at the clinic about 0620 hours and saw Lt. Col. Edwards in the hallway. She was obviously concerned. She had earlier told me that she hoped she wouldn't see me this day, that I would be at the airport instead, but here I was.

"Tell me you are going to be on that plane," she said hopefully.

"Has there been a birth certificate released?" I asked, even more hopefully.

Edwards must have called Lt. Col. William Judd, who soon stopped by my office. Judd asked whether I understood that I had orders to be on the plane. His voice seemed on the verge of cracking; he knew the consequences of what I was doing. Judd relayed the message from brigade headquarters that I was ordered to go to Walter Reed Army Medical Center to see Col. Roberts. He offered to escort me. I declined his offer.

This was all uncharted territory. I had no idea what to do. Halfway to Walter Reed, about a half-hour drive into northwest Washington, I had second thoughts and got on the phone with Jensen. He was reluctant to give the advice he did, but for consistency's sake, he basically advised me and then called Judd and told him that I was not obeying orders from then on, that anything I said from here on in could be used against me.

So I headed home. Pili—God bless her—greeted me with a kiss and a serious hug. Then we put on our game faces for the kids. All along, as best I could, I had been explaining to Holly and Andrew what I was fighting for. This was hard enough to explain to an adult. To a child, it was that much harder, but I wanted them to be prepared. I did not want this experience to be any rougher on them than it had to be.

Next morning I reported to the Pentagon once again. Col. Dale Block stopped by my office. He said he had been told not to talk to me, but he didn't care. He knew I was a good guy and wanted to make sure I knew what I was doing. I replied with what was becoming my mantra: "I think this is an important issue that needs an answer." A big hugger, the colonel laid a good one on me and wished me well. Later that day, I was assigned to Walter Reed.

When I reported to Walter Reed, I was placed in a kind of bureaucratic limbo while my superiors tried to figure out what to do with me. On Thursday I finally did go see Col. Roberts. Roberts was a formidable guy. In Vietnam, on 11 July 1969, he single-handedly wiped out three machine gun nests and saved many fellow soldiers in the process. A few weeks earlier, he had turned nineteen. This was no fluke. He had already been awarded a Silver Star and a Bronze Star. The action in July 1969 won him a Medal of Honor.

At the time, Col. Roberts was the only Medal of Honor winner on active duty in the military, and he was the one guy I had to go see. It was an honor to serve under him, but reporting to him made my mission doubly difficult.

I told Roberts I was remorseful about having to take this stand, but I saw no other way to get to the truth. He was very matter-of-fact in his response. He expressed his regrets and said the decision was up to me, but there was a process that I would have to go through. It began with the colonel reading me rights and me signing a form saying I understood them. I felt hurt and humbled.

I always knew this would be hard. I was just beginning to realize how hard.

❧

10. *The Truth Matters*

On 6 August 2010, in a Fort Belvoir, Virginia, hearing room, I was formally charged by the U.S. Army with "missing movement" and refusing to obey orders.

The four previous months had been an emotional roller coaster, a phrase I found myself using more and more. Col. Roberts had assigned me to Walter Reed in April. I met first with my company commander, Capt. Lance Jelks. He was doing his official duty by executing all the paperwork the military attorneys had carefully crafted. When all was said and done, he had to 'flag' me. This meant no favorable action would be coming my way: no promotions, no training or schools, no awards, no citations.

Jelks told me, though, that he still respected me as a lieutenant colonel and would demand that same respect from the people in his company. He told me, too, that he wished we could have had a beer early on, and maybe he could have talked me through my decision. I think he meant talk me "out of" it.

As he was speaking, I noticed that he had his officer's oath framed and hung on his office wall. It obviously mattered to him. I reminded him that we were obliged to "support and defend" the Constitution, that those words should mean something.

"I see your point," Jelks told me, "but it does not make us the Constitution's enforcers." Jelks is a good guy, and I did not want to argue, but I had to remind him that we in the military were part of the executive branch of government. If *we* did not enforce the Constitution, especially since we had sworn to do so, who would?

His indifference made no sense to me, but additional argument was only going to hurt me. If called upon, he would have to tell the prosecutors about anything I had said, and it certainly would not be used in my defense.

I should mention that Capt. Jelks is an African-American. He never read race into my argument, and I did not read race into his. I do not know an institution that has done a better job in creating an environment where race matters less than the U.S. Army.

At this time, I knew that a court-martial was inevitable, but I had no intention of being a martyr. Our goal was to draw attention to my case in the hope that it would inspire the White House to produce the relevant documents or perhaps get Congress and/or the judiciary to do their jobs.

It could not be good PR for Obama to send a military officer and physician with seventeen years of unblemished service, including several overseas deployments, to the Fort Leavenworth stockade.

That was our plan. We hoped something would surface and the Army would let the matter more or less drop. I did not expect a ticker tape parade, but I hoped they just might let me leave in peace instead of sending me to Leavenworth.

My superiors at Walter Reed treated me decently. The deputy commander for clinical services (DCCS) met with me and assigned me desk duty away from the main buildings, with flexible on-duty hours to accommodate my preparation for trial. I wanted to continue to see patients; that was my best contribution to the Army and to its troops. The DCCS confirmed that my clinical skills were never questioned. It was just that "your convictions are, well, your convictions," so desk duty it was.

My new immediate supervisor really did not know about my situation for weeks. She reviewed my officer record brief and the résumé that I presented to her. She did not see why I was being assigned to her, but she greatly needed the extra help and immediately put me to tasks. When she later learned of my issue, she e-mailed me, "While I don't agree with what you have done, my wishes are with you and your family to get through this."

After much back and forth, I managed to get an office at the occupational medicine clinic and made myself as available as I could. To be honest, I was no longer gung ho about my job. I was no longer the first one in and the last one out. I was doing my time, 0800 to 1600 hours, with an hour off for lunch and an hour here and there for chapel. I also put more than a few hours in on legal research.

I loved my country and the Army no less for my difficulties, but emotionally it could be tough. At Walter Reed, this was especially true because I came in contact with so many wounded warriors. These guys and gals had given their all, and their commander in chief could not be bothered to prove his eligibility. A recruit had to show better documentation just to enlist than Obama had shown to become president.

Ducky had done an excellent job ginning up publicity, but the mainstream media remained indifferent, if not actually hostile. On 7 May 2010, Paul Jensen and I got a taste of that hostility from CNN's Anderson Cooper.

The whole deal was pretty strange. Ducky and Jensen had negotiated with Cooper's producer to make sure the show would be recorded live and in the studio, with no defamatory graphics. The producers agreed, but only after much arm-twisting, a sign of their instinctive bias.

This whole experience was frightening for me. I have never liked being in front of the public. Television is certainly not my element, but I wanted to help as much as I could. Tasks like this one pushed my envelope of safety and comfort, and we lacked the time and resources for media training or mock interviews, but I knew I had to do this.

So on 6 May 2010, Jensen, his son, Ducky, and I took the train up to New York. When we got there, we learned that Cooper had been called out of town to cover a flood somewhere and we were bumped back to the next night. That wasn't terrible. On the following day, I took a couple of long runs through Central Park, which is very pretty in the spring, to do some soul-searching and to calm myself down.

That evening, CNN sent a car for us. It's a little thing, but it makes you feel like a guest. At the studio, the producer continued to treat us as if we mattered. Jensen and I went through makeup and were feeling hopeful about the show, but just as we were getting ready to go on, the producer told us there had been some technical difficulties.

As a result, we would not be sitting with Cooper. He would be in a separate booth, and we were put on some high, uncomfortable stools looking at a blank gray screen with a camera behind it. We could not see Cooper. We just had his voice in our ears. This was unnerving.

I learned later that speaking to a remote camera is the hardest kind of TV to do. I don't doubt it. By keeping himself physically removed from us, Cooper, who is a bit of a wimp, could speak to us in a way he would not dare to do if we were face-to-face. We suspected this was a setup.

Given the likely court-martial to come, there was little I felt free to say. Even if I could have talked more, Jensen is the kind of guy who feels comfortable on center stage. Like most lawyers, he is not shy about offering his opinion.

For whatever reason, Cooper kept repeating what an honorable guy I was. But then again, Marc Antony called Brutus "an honorable man," and he did not mean it either.

The first "question" Cooper asked me was this: "To say there is significant evidence that the president was not born in America is just false." He then stumbled around trying to make a question out of this open-and-shut condemnation. Calling your guest a liar at the very first opportunity struck me as an odd way to create a real dialogue.

"Well, Anderson, let me answer as his lawyer," Jensen responded before being cut off.

"No, no, no," Anderson jumped in. "Excuse me. . . . This is a doctor. This is a man who served his country for eighteen years. I think he can answer a question by himself."

"I think that the lawyer should protect the client from incriminating himself," said Jensen in return. "*You* say it's false. You're not prosecuting this case."

The tone was set. When Cooper got through squabbling with Jensen, he accused me of hiding behind my attorney. Even if I were not shy by nature, I would have had a hard time getting a word in edgewise.

Like most media people, Cooper had only the shallowest understanding of the issue, but his ignorance did not keep him humble. Just the opposite. He came at us like a schoolyard bully, insisting that the short-form "Certification of Live Birth" posted online was Obama's official birth certificate. When Jensen tried to tell him it was just an "abstract" that could be gotten by anyone who registered for it, Cooper cut him off again.

I finally got a word in and tried to tell Cooper why I was pursuing this issue. "This is a constitutional matter," I said more calmly than I felt, "and the truth matters and–," Here, Cooper jumped in and cut me off.

The line of questioning that Cooper pursued was obviously planned in advance. It was designed to make us look stupid, but it revealed how little they knew. Basically, they wanted to know why I had not asked to see the citizenship papers of any of the other officers I had served under, particularly Gen. George Casey, the Army chief of staff at the time.

"You served under General Casey. Where was *he* born?" Cooper blurted out as though it were a "gotcha" question.

Jensen tried to answer that it did not matter where Casey was born or whether he was at least thirty-five years of age. The Constitution makes no demands on the Army chief of staff.

Cooper would not give up. He asked me whether all soldiers from Hawaii were "suspect" if the state provided them with only short-form documents like the one Obama had posted.

It was like talking to a wall, a noisy wall, and in a remote shoot all you get is the noise in your ear. For someone who speaks slowly and measures his words, as I do, it was very difficult to respond.

Cooper knew so little, it was painful, and we hardly had time to set him straight. At one point I think he started to say, "You have to be a citizen to serve in the military," but caught himself and stuttered out the following bit of nonsense: "To serve in the United States Army, citizenship papers have to be brought to bear."

Here is what I would like to have said. More than 4,000 individuals have achieved citizenship through military service. It is a well-established path to citizenship for immigrants, including some who are in the country illegally. Even veterans are eligible to apply for United States citizenship, which means that U.S. military personnel don't have to be citizens in order to serve. Heck, green card holders even have to sign up for the draft.

In fact, some of the best medics I worked with—from Poland, Hungary, Mexico, and elsewhere—were holders of green cards, not citizens. Or take the case of General John Shalikashvili, who was appointed chairman of the Joint Chiefs of Staff the same year I joined the Army, 1993.

Shalikashvili's father fought in the Polish army and spent World War II in a prisoner-of-war camp. Shalikashvili did not come to the United States until he was sixteen. He learned to speak English watching John Wayne movies. He became a citizen a month before he was drafted, not that his citizenship status mattered to the draft board.

Not a single one of these 4,000 new citizens, however, could ever become president of the United States, not even Shalikashvili. As I explained earlier, it is not enough for a candidate to have been born in the United States. He must also be a "natural born citizen." This is a very specific category, and it applies only to the president and vice-president.

When Cooper accused me of grandstanding, I explained that I had quietly explored all avenues I could for more than a year, "asking and begging my leadership for guidance in how to address this issue." I told him that refusing to deploy was the only way left I knew to draw attention to the issue. Frustrated at getting nowhere, Cooper finally asked me, "Why is it this issue?"

"It is a fundamental clause of the Constitution," I answered, "and my oath of office is to the Constitution, and I believe we need truth on this issue."

The real issue, Jensen elaborated, "is why hasn't the president released his original birth certificate if it exists. This could be over tonight. Tonight."

The resulting coverage was predictable. The leftist Huffington Post declared, "Anderson Cooper Slams 'Birther' Army Officer for Hiding Behind His Attorney." On the conservative blogs, the headlines ran along the lines of "Out-of-control Anderson Cooper Interviews Lt. Col. Lakin." For most of the media, including much of the conservative media, the mystery of Obama's eligibility wasn't newsworthy at all.

I remember seeing the *Tribune* in Greeley, Colorado, at the time. On the front page was my story intentionally juxtaposed with pictures of two reservist brothers enlisting. On the one hand, it made me feel horrible that these young guys were signing on and I was not going to be there to take care of them. On the other hand, since they were enlisted men, I felt all the more responsibility to ensure that orders are lawful and coming from a duly appropriate source, namely a commander in chief who has validated his constitutional eligibility.

We never did meet Cooper. The producer escorted us out, as friendly as he had been when he'd escorted us in. I guess calling people liars and fools is business as usual on CNN.

To say the least, I was not happy with the way the show went. I felt sick in my gut for days wondering how these "journalists" could care so little about the truth. The phone calls I got did not help. My parents called saying Cooper was very fair. What? Friends from college called saying I looked good with makeup on. I wasn't sure that was a compliment.

For better or worse, I was learning a good deal about the media, and the lessons had just begun.

&

11. *Doing What Is Right*

To this point, almost nothing had gone as I had hoped. My goal was not to go prison, not to become a martyr to a cause, but to take advantage of military due process to resolve the question of Barack Obama's eligibility to be president of the United States.

My civilian attorney, Paul Jensen, had planned to use what is called an Article 32 hearing, sort of like a military grand jury, to get certain evidence in play. In May, we submitted a memorandum explaining the chain of command, the requirement that the commander in chief be a "natural born" citizen, and my obligation to disobey illegal orders.

To make the case, we requested the testimony of Dr. Chiyome Fukino of the Hawaii Department of Health and all the records of her agency that deal with the president's birth. We had also requested relevant records from Punahou Elementary School, Occidental College, Columbia University and Harvard Law School. Like the birth certificate, these records had all been kept under seal. We did not think our request unreasonable.

I did not care a whit what Obama's grades were. We thought it best to include all the educational documents in the hope that one or more among them would reveal something about Obama's eligibility. As military, I felt I had a right to any information that would determine Obama's "natural born" status.

The Army did not exactly agree with us. In early June, in fact, Lt. Col. Daniel Driscoll[3] turned us down flat. He ruled that all key documents, as well as testimony from the custodians of those documents, would be off-limits. Not surprisingly, Driscoll also rejected our request to have President Obama testify. His reasoning for the decisions was convoluted. He claimed that the requested documents were not relevant to the charges I faced: missing movement, failure to obey orders, and dereliction of duty.

In short, the Army contended that my orders did not come from the president to me, that these were orders from a colonel with the authority to order me to a unit. The Army lost me on the authority question. I had been ordered to a unit preparing to deploy to Afghanistan as part of the "surge" ordered by President Obama. I heard him say as much in his address to West Point in November 2009.

The Army seemed to be taking liberties with the notion of a unified chain of command. My understanding has always been that all officers, especially those ordered to deploy to a foreign-soil combat zone, get their authority from the commander in chief. Retired Lt. Gen. Thomas McInerney made this point in a sworn affidavit submitted upon my behalf. It reads in part:

> The President of the United States, as the Commander in Chief, is the source of all military authority. The Constitution requires the President to be a natural born citizen in order to be eligible to hold office. If he is ineligible under the Constitution to serve in that office, that creates a break in the chain of command of such magnitude that its significance can scarcely be imagined.

But even the general's support could not help me. This was a potato too hot for the Army to take out of the oven, let alone hold.

Once I realized it was impossible for me to present a defense at the Article 32 hearing, originally scheduled for 11 June, I officially waived the proceeding. There was no point in going through with it. We decided to take

---

3
  Driscoll was the investigating officer for the article 32 who denied Terry any kind of discovery at the article 32/grand jury type investigation.

our chances with a general court-martial, not that I had much choice at this point. I faced a potential punishment of four to seven years in the brig.

I was hoping for three years or less. Our savings might be able to sustain Pili and the kids that long, and my loss of medical proficiency would not be fatal. For his part, Maj. Kemkes, my military attorney, did not expect the confinement to last longer than the length of the deployment, but there was no guarantee, especially in a case as unique as this one.

I wish I could tell you that my legal team and I fought with one heart and one mind throughout this process, but that was not the case. Although I pride myself on being a team player—medicine is all about teamwork—I cannot say that I put together a legal team that worked anything like the way a team should work. My failure to do this resulted in the most painful period of my life.

Although Maj. Kemkes was a super smart lawyer, it seemed to me that all the military lawyers gossip among themselves. Kemkes may not have talked about my case, but those following the CAAFlog blog could see that someone was, and that kind of talk could hurt anyone attempting to gain a fair trial.[4] As much as I liked Kemkes, I did not fully trust him to keep my confidences. Nor was the strategy he hoped to pursue in sync with my own thinking. Still, he was always well organized and on top of things.

Paul Jensen, my civilian attorney, was not. That was not his style. The Army allowed a civilian attorney as well as a military one, but the cost was on me. Let me thank here the many donors who made that possible. By June 2010, there were more than 1,200 of you.

From the beginning, Jensen and Kemkes had different agendas. Jensen wanted to get at Obama's eligibility; Kemkes wanted to get me off the hook. These strategies were at odds with each other. In addition, any number of outside attorneys offered advice.

One attorney recommended that I employ the so-called Twinkie Defense. As you might remember, this was the defense used to lessen the sentence of San Francisco Supervisor Dan White, who had assassinated Mayor George Moscone and Supervisor Harvey Milk. White's attorneys argued

---

[4] CAAFlog is blog of The National Institute of Military Justice.

that their client's depression was triggered by eating too much junk food, Twinkies in particular.

Bizarrely enough, the defense actually worked, but then again, that was San Francisco. Who knows what can work there? This was the real world, the U.S. Army, and I was not about to plead insanity or anything like it no matter how successful such a plea might have been. I knew what I was doing. I was doing it of my own free will, and despite what the media might have thought or said, I was not crazy.

Another suggestion was to move my trial to the civilian courts, but this, of course, was not remotely possible. Another helpful soul wanted me to question the judge on her authority or slam Obama's book down on her desk and declare that Obama admits in his autobiography that he is dual citizen, born of a foreign father, and therefore not eligible.

When I thought about the consequences of any of these strategies, I could see Charles Manson getting out of prison before I did.

Ducky Hemenway and I filtered these requests and sent on to Jensen only those that had some merit, but he resented even those. I remember on the Fourth of July that year, while I was at a fireworks display with the kids, Jensen called and exploded on the phone—cannons to left of me, cannons to the right. He wanted to know why I was wasting his time with these opinions.

Jensen was a well-meaning guy, but a difficult one. For a while I thought that might be a virtue. If he was difficult with Kemkes and me, I thought he would be hell on the opposition. But we never got to that point.

The 6 August arraignment at Fort Belvoir, Virginia, showed me how unpleasant this whole process could be. The afternoon before the hearing, Lt. Col. Steven Brodsky of the JAG Corps told Jensen that I had to report hours beforehand to my duty post at Walter Reed so I could be "transported under escort" to Fort Belvoir.

Brodsky wanted me at Walter Reed so he could be sure I would show up at the hearing. Or so he said. Allegedly, he did not want me to embarrass our unit. When Maj. Kemkes protested that an enlisted man facing similar charges would not face the same indignity, Brodsky blew him off. He knew there was zero chance I would miss the hearing. This was about payback, not justice. I had been present for other phone calls between Kemkes and Brodsky. It was obvious, as Kemkes confirmed, that Brodsky and other prosecutors wanted to see me burn in Hell—or someplace very much like it in northeastern Kansas.

Brodsky informed Kemkes that an Army colonel would escort me, and this was non-negotiable. This all struck me as odd. Brodsky was a judge advocate. His job was to prosecute me, not humiliate me. What was he doing deciding how I got to the hearing? This was one of many questions for which I would never get answers.

On the day of the hearing a male sergeant and a female full bird colonel showed up at Walter Reed. They loaded me into a van and off we went. When the van started, the radio came on and incredibly, the first story on the news was of my arraignment. The colonel changed stations pronto.

There were some media present when I arrived at Fort Belvoir and a few supporters. One sweet older lady shook my hand and thanked me profusely, tears welling in her eyes. None of this attention pleased the prosecutors.

We arrived early. While we waited in the small office lobby, Brodsky came traipsing through with an entourage of lower-ranking military lawyers trailing behind him. He pulled the colonel into the hallway and, within earshot of me, told her to keep me from "signing autographs or kissing babies."

Brodsky then said to colonel that if I should try to talk to the media, "just tase him and throw him in the van." She came over and asked me if I'd heard all of this. I had, as I am sure I was meant to. The word somehow got out that I responded with the already famous line "Don't tase me, bro," a comment that worked even better given the name "Brodsky." It was one of the few moments of mirth in a grim proceeding. In truth, although I might have wished I'd said it, that is not how I think, let alone talk.

In fact, I was feeling deeply insecure and out of my element. While I waited, I had a nicely normal conversation with the sergeant, which helped settle me. In situations like this, you're never quite sure who your friends are, and you welcome people who will speak to you without looking over their shoulders.

Jensen was late. Unfortunately, that had become something of a habit. One thing you learn in the military is to be on time, and you come to expect the same of others. Still, it would not have mattered if Jensen had gotten there a day early; he was presenting a case no one wanted to hear.

After the brief *pro forma* hearing, my lawyers asked the colonel if I had permission to speak to the press. Both CNN and NBC had sent camera crews. She brusquely refused and ordered me into the van to be transported back to Walter Reed. I was afraid to talk to anyone lest I get tased, or worse, some civilian just trying to talk to me would get strong-armed by one of security officers that were all too evident.

Jensen arrived late once again at the motion hearing on 27 August. At a later hearing, Colonel Lind, the judge in my case, was openly displeased that Jensen had filed a motion only two days prior to the hearing when he'd had over four weeks to submit it. "I would have to cite delays that are attorney-client privilege" was his quick response, a sharp lawyer trick that shifted the blame to me.

As we awaited Judge Lind's expected rebuke on this ruling, I grilled Jensen on the next step. I wanted his promise that he would submit the appeal in a timely manner. When he resisted this request, I knew I needed another lawyer. The discussion turned into a "Fire me if you're unhappy with me" exchange.

"No," I said, "you quit if you cannot represent me well." I was reluctant to fire Jensen, partly out of loyalty, but also partly because I had no one to take his place.

The hammer came down in a hearing on 2 September. Jensen argued that under U.S.C. Rule 46 I had the right to call any and all witnesses and obtain any evidence in my defense, but Lind wasn't listening. It took her forty minutes to read her ruling on the evidence, but the outcome was clear from the beginning. I would be denied access to Obama's records as well as any testimony from those who control the records.

Lind claimed that the laws I violated were legitimate on their face. My chain of command, she ruled, led up to the Pentagon and no further. She did not think it "relevant" for the military to be considering claims like the one I had made.

Lind, of course, decided much as the federal judges had in the many civil lawsuits over Obama's eligibility. To a person, they had refused the plaintiffs any access to documents that might prove or disprove the president's eligibility. There was a major difference, though. Mine was not a civil lawsuit. I was facing criminal charges, and what the judge told me was to find a new defense. With this ruling she sent me to prison. The only real question now was for how long.

CNN headlined its story on the hearing "Judge removes 'birther' elements from Army doc's court martial." You don't have to be paranoid to read bias—even glee—into that headline. After we went through the motion hearings, I had nothing left. Jensen's strategy was not working; Lind was not allowing evidence into the trial. I needed a new strategy and a new attorney.

It was about this time that I attended a fundraiser for Allen West, who was running for Congress from Florida. West knew something about military justice. While serving as a battalion commander in Taji, Iraq, in August 2003, then Lt. Col. West was overseeing an interrogation of an Iraqi police officer suspected of passing on his insider information about convoy movements. His goal was to set up attacks and IED placements against West's unit. When the guy refused to talk, West fired a round close to his head and the fellow started singing. At the time, West was just short of twenty years of service. That did not matter. He was charged with violating the Uniform Code of Military Justice and was processed through his own Article 32 hearing. At the hearing he admitted what he had done, and he pulled no punches.

When asked if he would do it again, West replied, "If it's about the lives of my men and their safety, I'd go through hell with a gasoline can." As West recounted, the Iraqi police officer cracked and warned of an ambush. West's strategy worked. There were no more ambushes in Taji during the two months he remained in-country before being relieved of his command. No matter. The Army fined him $5,000 for misconduct and assault, but at least allowed him to retire with military honors and full benefits.

During his inspirational talk at the fundraiser, West pointed out several people that he needed to thank. One was Gen. Casey's attaché. Another was Neil Puckett, an attorney and a retired Marine Corps lieutenant colonel. I made a beeline to Puckett. I wanted to see if he might be interested in representing me.

Puckett was a sharp-looking guy, well dressed, cocky, a Harley rider, well organized, totally professional. You knew that he knew what he was doing. We had a great conversation about the case. I suspected right then that he would be my attorney. I sensed something else too. The case would not end well. As sympathetic as Puckett was, he really did not believe in what I was doing.

West was another story. On the way out, he stopped by without prompting and said something to the effect of "You are doing what is right." Coming from a guy like West, that mattered.

&

12. Stay Strong

Even in the middle of the worst ordeal, God provides small graces. The day before my court-martial was to begin, I drove down to Fort Meade, which is about halfway between Baltimore and Washington. My Army training taught me to recon routes and ensure on-time arrival, even if it was to my own demise.

While there, I got a room on the base for my parents to rest up in during the days of the trial. They are both up in years, and my father in particular was not well. I was touched that they had come at all, especially given their political leanings.

Just as I was leaving the desk, I thought I recognized a fellow waiting behind me. I did a slow exit to hear his name as he talked to the clerk; he was who I thought he was. I waited in the small lobby near the desk to introduce myself.

"Commander Kerchner," I burst out, pleased at so unexpected a meeting. A retired U.S. Navy commander, Kerchner had been one of the first military officers to recognize that his officer's oath demanded that he question the eligibility of the president. He had earlier joined in a suit to challenge the president on this issue.

Kerchner had driven down to the court-martial from Pennsylvania with a Vietnam combat veteran friend who shared his passion. We could hardly believe that we had chanced to meet. "I'm pleased to meet you," I said. "I'm honored to meet you," he responded. "I'm here to support you." I was moved that he would say that.

There was a guy within earshot checking in. We were not paranoid, but this guy looked like a juror. (We were right.) So we walked out into the blowing snow, headed across the parking lot to my car, and climbed in. After a few minutes of conversation I knew I wanted more, but it was late in the day, so I asked the guys out to the house for dinner.

"Are you sure?" Kernchner asked. This being the night before the trial, he thought I might want to spend more time with my lawyers. I explained that I was pretty much lawyered out. I repeated how honored my family and I would be to have him visit, and Kerchner responded in kind, telling me that he was the one who was honored. "You're risking everything," he said. "Not me."

At the house we had pizza with Pili and the kids. It was a rewarding experience. No one has schooled himself more thoroughly on the eligibility issue than Kerchner. His background in genealogy adds another dimension. He knew so many details and so much history, the evening was an education unto itself.

On the downside, I had to point out to Kerchner and his friend that the court-martial was pretty much a done deal; he ought not expect any dramatic proof of Obama's eligibility to surface during the trial. I was there only to take my punishment. At this stage, if I were to grandstand, it would only lengthen my sentence. Still, Kerchner's presence lifted my spirits. Our meeting seemed providential. The commander would later write on his blog about our meeting in words that I could have written myself:

> I just thought it was God's hand at work there to put us two to-
> gether, the two most recently prominent figures in the Obama eli-
> gibility saga, he as a defendant, and I as a plaintiff. I thought it
> was really remarkable that this happened. When we talked, we
> both had a kindred soul and understanding that we were answer-
> ing the call to do this. We didn't do it for any other reason but to

stand up for our oaths to the Constitution, and we answered a
higher call. Both of us felt that way. We were like two kindred
souls there; we understood each other; we could look at each other
face-to-face, and we knew we both were standing for the truth and
for the Constitution, so help us, God. We both believe in God and
that what we are doing is right.

Both of my brothers came in for the trial as well. Greg was supportive as
always. He gave me some inspirational material and encouraged me to
"stay strong," just as he had back in my wrestling days. "The Lakins can
get through anything," he reminded me. My other brother and I had a
heart-to-heart, which was not easy since he did not believe in this cause.
Still, that made his being there all the more reassuring.

The evening before the trial I packed a duffel bag, knowing there was an
excellent chance I would not be coming home immediately afterward. Pili
and I had been preparing the kids for this, but no amount of preparation
could be enough. To ease the transition for them, we decided that she
should not attend the trial. Some in the media tried to make a point of this,
but whatever their point was, it told their audience more about them than it
did about us.

My day of reckoning came on the blustery morning of 14 December 2010.
I donned my green Class A's and found my way to the magistrate's courtroom at Fort Meade. The sixty or so seats were full, and more people were
standing around the room. I am sure there are a thousand other places that
my mother and father would rather have been, but I was heartened by their
presence. My brothers' attendance strengthened me as well.

I had read on the blogs about protestors wanting to set up outside the gates.
I did not expect trouble, as my supporters live productive lives and have
no background in community agitation. Nor did I encourage anyone to
come. As much as I appreciated the encouragement of my supporters, I
feared that the trial would disappoint them. I knew that the eligibility issue
would barely be raised; I was not sure they did. Then, too, given the suspicions of my prosecutors, I certainly did not want anyone getting tased on
my behalf.

Still, quite a few supporters showed up. Some I knew, some I did not. The
media would write them all off as "birthers." Hovering around some of my
more prominent supporters were court bailiffs, actually soldiers dressed in
camos. I think the authorities must have told them that constitutionalists

were somehow dangerous. Needless to say, they were not needed. Several Army people were there too, at least a few of them lawyers. For better or worse, mostly worse, about ten or so reporters had shown up. They ran the gamut from NBC National News to the *Greeley Gazette*.

My court-martial was about to begin, Judge Denise Lind presiding. I was scared to death. We were in no way prepared to win. The only question was how badly we would lose. For all that, I put on my best game face. In combat situations you can take actions to occupy yourself even if you can't benefit your situation. Here my options were limited, but I did not want anyone to see me depressed or morose when it came to taking my punishment.

The court-martial began before the jury was seated with what is called a "providence inquiry." Although I was sworn in, I remained seated at the table between my new civilian lawyer, Neil Puckett, and my military lawyer, Maj. Matt Kemkes. This phase of the trial dealt with the charges that I was pleading guilty to, the failure to follow orders.

We had been talking for a few weeks about the disobedience issue. In fact, I probably should have followed all orders other than the order to deploy as part of the 30,000-man surge, which came directly from the president. Only the president can order a foreign deployment. But neither Paul Jensen nor I understood military law as well as we should have, and the decision not to obey orders set up numerous violations. These the Army heaped on to add more potential jail time. Puckett hoped that by admitting guilt here I could show the jury that I was accepting responsibility for what I had done and was remorseful for it. We chose not to plead guilty on the "missing movement" charge, however, because an innocent plea on this charge left a door open for appeal.

As we proceeded, Judge Lind had to satisfy herself that I knew what I was pleading guilty to. The trial counsel for the Army, Captain Philip O'Beirne, came prepared. A cool customer, he casually drank from a water bottle while he cut me to shreds. To tell the truth, he outclassed both my attorneys. Never satisfied with my answers, he peppered me with questions that for some procedural reason had to be filtered by Judge Lind and reworded. All the while my attorneys, one on either side of me, whispered advice. This was two hours of pure nightmare.

During this phase, the question of whether Jensen had provided adequate legal advice kept coming up. At one point Judge Lind asked Puckett if he was okay with this line of attack. He said he welcomed it and would likely be raising the issue himself. As part of his strategy to win sympathy, he wanted me to look like a clueless victim of Jensen's bad advice.

Here is where Puckett and I were working at cross-purposes. Regardless of what kind of advice Jensen had given me, I always knew what I was doing and said as much. After all, I was under oath. If oaths did not matter, what was I doing here?

Under the judge's questioning, I accepted responsibility for my actions. "I understand that it was my decision, and I made the wrong choice," I told Judge Lind. I repeated myself later. "I had to make a choice. I chose incorrectly." Many people, both friend and foe, would misunderstand my meaning, some, I think, intentionally. Knowing what I knew in December 2010, I did choose incorrectly. I would not have pursued a path that could end only in failure. As I have said, I had no interest in being a martyr.

But did I choose incorrectly in challenging the president's eligibility? I did not. Did I choose incorrectly in risking my career to get at the truth? I did not. Did I choose incorrectly by refusing to deploy to Afghanistan? Given what I know now, yes I did. This strategy did not produce the kind of information that I hoped it would. Was it worth the sacrifice? Yes, it was.

At the end of the providence inquiry, Judge Lind announced her findings on the four Article 92 specifications to which I had pleaded guilty. There were no surprises here, but the pain and agony of this whole process made me wonder if pleading innocent and serving more time would have been a better option. In any case, my guilty pleas were accepted. It was then that the jury took their seats—five men, three women, all lieutenant colonels or colonels—and my prosecutors went enthusiastically to work.

One of O'Beirne's assistants took the lead. He made the point that the 32nd Cavalry, 101st Airborne Division deployed to Afghanistan—Forward Operating Base Bostick, to be precise—without its surgeon. The surgeon was right here in court, and that would be me.

In his opening, Puckett said he agreed with 90 percent of what the prosecutor had just laid out, but that it was irrelevant. This evidence all spoke to the order violations, to which I had already pleaded guilty, not the missing-movement charge.

Puckett chose a narrow line of attack, namely that no one had specifically ordered me to be on US Airways Flight 1123 on 12 April 2010. This strategy was not without some merit, but I am sure that my supporters had to feel let down. The whole proceeding dealt not with the president's eligibility but with orders that I be on a particular plane at a particular time. Not too heroic.

The government called six witnesses. The first three did not make much impact. O'Beirne was establishing what I was supposed to have done on that day, and Puckett kept repeating the question of whether the witness had specifically ordered me to be on US Airways Flight 1123. This was not great courtroom drama in anyone's book.

The mood changed with the fourth Army witness, Col. Gordon Roberts. Here he was, the only Medal of Honor winner on active duty, and it was just my fate to cross his path at the most critical moment of my life. As I said, he is an impressive guy. In the courtroom he somehow seemed more impressive still. I am sure it was not lost on the jurors that the courthouse was located on Roberts Avenue.

Roberts was respectful. He said that he had asked to see me back in March for any number of reasons. One was that he worried whether I was suffering from post-traumatic stress disorder as a result of my previous deployment to Afghanistan. In fact, all of his concerns seemed to be about my welfare. Did I understand the consequences of my actions on my career and on my family? Did I get good legal advice along the way? His background as a social worker was on full display.

When it came Puckett's turn to cross-examine Col. Roberts, he began by telling Roberts how honored he was to speak with him. I would probably have done the same. Puckett, though, did something I probably would not have done. He made a point of reminding Roberts that he was not the lawyer whose advice Roberts had questioned. I do not know if Puckett was establishing this for his benefit or mine.

O'Beirne also used Roberts to identify the doctor who took my place in the deployment to Afghanistan. His name was Maj. Dobson, and his wife's testimony would help seal my fate. In the cross-examination, Puckett asked the now familiar "Did you order him to be onboard flight 1123 from BWI?" "I did not," Roberts replied "Did you direct anyone else to do so?" Puckett continued. "I did not," said Roberts.

Next up was my scheduling supervisor, Lt. Col. Edwards, the deputy commander for clinical operations at the Pentagon's health clinic. This was tough too. We were close work buddies. We both always gave 100 percent effort to the clinic and to our patients, often at the expense of our families. This was not the case with everyone at the clinic, and we respected each other's contribution. Everyone could see that she was upset and sorry this was happening, but her testimony was damning nonetheless.

Yes, Edwards told the court, she hoped she would not see me at the Pentagon on 12 April—she wanted me to be on the plane—but there I was. So she called Col. Roberts to ask what she should do and Roberts told her it was my duty to get on that plane and go to Fort Campbell. She then testified that she told me my duty was to get on the plane. After that, she called Roberts back to tell him she had relayed his order.

Here we were. A clearly sympathetic female supervisor was telling the court that she did what the most respected man on the planet had told her to do. Observers have commented, rightly I think, that Edwards caught Puckett by surprise and that he had no ammunition ready for any kind of counter-offensive. There is, as you might expect, a story here.

At the outset, the prosecutors told my attorneys that they were not going to put Edwards on the stand, but that they were making her available to us if we would like her to testify. My answer was "Great." Edwards, if anyone, could tell how hard I worked for the clinic and how she counted on me to resolve any issue that came up.

Honestly, I did not recall her telling me to "get my butt on that plane" in the hallway, as she stated. She could have. It was an emotionally charged day, and I was not taking notes. During recess after her testimony, Puckett was upset. He wanted to know why I did not warn him. I could only shake my head mutely, but inside I was screaming, "Why did O'Beirne know what she was going to say, but you did not? Why did you not question her before the trial?"

This was likely a brilliant maneuver by Capt. O'Beirne, and he clearly outfoxed us. I am not a lawyer, but I felt that our defense was about as good as Custer's at Little Big Horn and our chances of survival no better. We were cooked in every way, and the worst was yet to come.

&

13. Crossing the Line

I entered the courtroom on 15 December 2010 knowing that I would leave it at the end of the day in chains. I was not being defeatist, merely realistic.

On day two we made our case for what is called "extenuation and mitigation." I had previously given Paul Jensen a list of fourteen character witnesses—civilian and military, officers and enlisted, supervisors and supervised, male and female, black and white—we might have called to help soften the blow. But given the shift in attorneys and strategies, we had summoned only two and those we scarcely briefed.

Col. Monty Willoughby was my unit's executive officer, who became commander after the tragic loss of our original commander and other troops in an aircraft mishap in the Afghan mountains. We had an excellent relationship. In fact, as ranking physician, I shared a room with him while deployed to Afghanistan. What is more, he counted on my medical input early in all mission planning, an added dimension that lesser commanders ignore. After Afghanistan, we continued to correspond and always knew what each other was doing. When last he stopped to visit wounded troops at Walter Reed, I had the privilege of escorting him around the area and driving him to the airport.

It was obvious that Monty been through a lot in the six years since we'd worked together. With no preparation, he could not specifically recall all the extra efforts that had made me stand out to him at the time. A little more due diligence by my defense team could have helped jog the colonel's memory. Still, he did his best. He told the court how I had been the squadron's lead flight surgeon and that he rated my duty performance as exceptional. He shared as many of my accomplishments there as he could remember.

On cross-examination, however, the trial counsel got Col. Willoughby to acknowledge that I had joined the squadron several months before deployment, and that this training made me a more effective flight surgeon. The point here was that my replacement would not be as well trained as I was.

Willoughby agreed with counsel, too, that I performed my duties well in part at least because I had done what I was told to do. When pressed, Willoughby conceded, "It's critical for leaders of all levels to obey orders unless they are unlawful." My supporters applauded at the "unless they are unlawful" comment. The judge shushed them.

The second and final witness in my defense was Timothy Mayhack, now a civilian in North Pole, Alaska. He had been a CW3 helicopter pilot during my Afghanistan deployment. On the stand, he talked about his unusual background: he served in the Navy, worked for Harley-Davidson, went to nursing school, took a job as a medevac pilot, and finally returned to active duty, this time in the Army. He deployed to Bosnia, and after additional medical training and supervisory assignments, he went on to Afghanistan.

We shared a northeast Colorado origin and grew close in Afghanistan. Mayhack told the court I was one of the top flight surgeons he knew and that I had worked tirelessly treating both soldiers and Afghans.

Not surprisingly, Capt. O'Beirne took Mayhack to task on cross-examination. As with Willoughby, O'Beirne tried to force Mayhack to acknowledge the importance of following orders, but Mayhack was not about to roll over. We had talked regularly over the last few years. The issues that concerned me also concerned him.

O'Beirne chose to open that can of worms over Puckett's objection, directly asking Mayhack what his feelings were about my beliefs. Mayhack answered that since the court had already convicted me, he didn't see where his thoughts had any bearing. O'Beirne prodded. "Over the phone, you said you thought his crimes were an act of patriotism."

"I may have said that," Mayhack answered. O'Beirne pressed further. "You think the president's eligibility to be president is an open question."

"Yes, I do," said Mayhack, and with that, my supporters broke into applause. To this point, the trial had given them little to cheer about. The judge, of course, responded sharply with "Members of the gallery!" They restrained themselves.

O'Beirne continued, "Do you believe the president has a duty to prove he's president before officers have a duty to obey orders?"

"I think those officers on active duty should be compelled to question," said Mayhack. I could see he was turning red. He felt he had been ambushed. Still, he wasn't backing down. "I don't know if the commander in chief is eligible or not. No one in this room does." To me and my supporters Mayhack's suspicions seemed altogether justified. To O'Beirne and the jurors, they just seemed crazy, and Mayhack's testimony suggested a worrisome spread into the military rank and file. This plague had to be nipped in the bud.

After Mayhack, it was my turn to take the stand. This phase of the trial is called the "unsworn statement." I would have preferred to do it in writing. I have no gift for public speaking, but Puckett thought it best to be done as a question-and-answer session between us. He was incredibly confident that he was going to lead me through questioning exactly as he wanted—no script, no preparation. He had told me I needed to trust him to guide me on the fly.

By this stage I was just along for the ride, trying to get through the best I could, wanting to take my punishment like a man. I put all my faith in Puckett's hands because his were the only hands there. There was no practice, no trial runs. Puckett thought it best to "surprise me" on the stand; he boasted as much in his blog. Did he ever.

It all began innocently enough. I talked about where I was born and where I had gone to school. I talked about my parents and pointed them out. I talked about meeting Pili and marrying her. I talked about family practice, which I described as my "true love." This was all easy enough.

I told the court about Honduras, where I served as a flight surgeon. I have a talent for quick diagnosis and saved two lives that way. You never forget that. I was happy to share the experience. From Honduras I went to Germany and from Germany I went to Bosnia and after that on to Afghanistan. It should have been apparent to the jury that I was a physician who preferred deployment to hanging out in the stateside hospitals.

Then Puckett flashed a picture on the wall of me with my three kids. I had no problem telling how much I loved them. Even if the photo seemed like a ploy, the jurors knew I was sincere.

We then moved on to the evolution of my discontent. I had no problem talking about this. I told the court how, during the 2008 campaign, Senator McCain was obliged to provide a birth certificate with the doctor's name and hospital's name, but no one asked Senator Obama for anything despite questions that were arising about his origins. I'd had an open mind about it, but I was skeptical. I wanted answers.

When Puckett asked why I was so interested in this issue, I told him and the court that we all should be. I was concerned that the Constitution wasn't being followed, and I took my oath as an officer to protect and defend the Constitution seriously.

Puckett led me through a discussion of the various steps I had taken within the military to get these issues addressed, all without resolution. I told the court about the letters I sent to two senators and a congressman and the inadequate responses I had received from all of them. At the Pentagon I had filed a second Article 138, but this came to naught as well.

Finally, I had gone to Capitol Hill for face-to-face meetings with a congressman and other high-level staffers. They told me, yes, the issue was a concern, but in the face of constant media ridicule, there was nothing they could do.

As government employees, these congressional staffers had also taken an oath to support and defend the Constitution, and that oath says nothing about a "media ridicule exemption." Any one of them could have done what I was doing, and at least one of them had tried. This fellow later told me that he had begun his efforts even before he'd heard of my case. As he pushed his quest up the supervisory chain, however, his supervisor told him point-blank that he would be fired quickly and that nothing would change other than his no longer having a job.

When the deployment order came, I told the jury how at least one congressional staffer had advised me to go to Afghanistan and raise the issue while there. This I thought a much worse option. A combat zone is no place to introduce any idea that distracts from the mission at hand. I had been there. I knew.

Once deployed, I would have bonded with the unit, the commander, and the troops. I would have been responsible for their well-being. I would have followed these guys to hell and back and not thought to question combat orders. Garrison duty back home is another story. There, to ask a question about the constitutional legitimacy of the commander in chief seemed altogether appropriate.

Puckett then asked what I felt to be a fair question. "You thought if the commander in chief wasn't eligible, you thought your deployment order might retroactively be considered an illegal order." I agreed.

Puckett's tone began to shift when he raised the question of my hiring Paul Jensen. I sensed something coming, but I wasn't quite sure what. I testified about receiving my deployment orders. At the bottom of the orders it said I had to bring my birth certificate. "I thought, there's an issue here," I said, and with that my supporters laughed, then applauded. The judge admonished them again: "Members of the gallery!"

I then told how I chose not to deploy. On my own, I had told the command that I would deploy if the president showed he was eligible to be my commander in chief. Puckett then asked whose "fault" it was that I had done and said these things. Fault? Responsibility, yes, absolutely, but fault, no.

Oddly, Puckett asked if I had used the deployment orders as a way to focus attention on the issue. I could not deny that. Nor could I deny that many people were urging me to stick to my guns, "including enlisted members and officer members." The look from Puckett said maybe that last bit of info would not help me with the jury.

When the questioning turned to Col. Roberts, I readily admitted what I thought was a mistake, namely my failure to meet with him when first ordered. Again Puckett brought Jensen into this equation, wanting, I think, to make me look like the victim of his bad advice. But I would not compromise and throw Paul under the bus.

As the questioning progressed, Puckett's tone became increasingly harsh and his voice increasingly loud. I'd had no idea he would do this. He was trying to rattle me, make me break. Now he was all but yelling at me.

"When you failed to go to BWI, did you know you were crossing a line?" Yes, of course I knew. "Did you know there would be consequences?" I most certainly did. I had lost out on a promotion to colonel, I told the jury, because I had to weigh what the risks were for our Constitution. Risking my career and confinement, I explained, was a small order compared to what the Founding Fathers had risked.

Puckett next asked a useful question: "What would have happened if you'd been invited to General Casey's office and the process was explained to you, that as long as the president is in office, he carries its full weight and authority?"

I told the court that I would have valued that input. I had been begging for that input, but no one had offered that information. What I had done instead was make a last-ditch effort to uphold Army values by challenging this issue in garrison, which I considered much less disruptive than questioning it from the battlefield.

I was candid with the court. I explained that I was not a conscientious objector and would deploy tomorrow. I had sought out every bit of information I could and came up short. The Army apparently could not answer my questions. When Puckett asked "Would you do this again?" I had to answer "No." I explained that I had better information now. If nothing else, my actions had taught me the limits of the process.

Turning to the panel, Puckett asked, "Why should these good people let you keep your job?" I told them I wanted to serve. I had talents the Army could use, particularly on the battlefield. I did not know of anyone else who had my range of skills, which included family medicine, occupational medicine, acupuncture, and flight surgeon experience.

Now Puckett turned on me in full fury. He sounded more like the prosecutor than the prosecutor did. He referred to the picture of my family on the wall and all but shouted, "People are saying you invited this court-martial. How do you feel? Are you proud of that?"

"That little three-year-old," he continued. "How would that little three-year-old feel about visiting you in jail on Christmas Day, if you're even close enough for your family to see you?"

Puckett had done what he set out to do. He brought me to the verge of tears, but I couldn't quite cry. I was cried out. "I've cried about this so many times," I told the court. "I've cried for a year. I can't believe this is happening in this country."

Puckett wouldn't let up. "If these good people send you to jail, those beautiful people will have to live with the image of seeing you through bars or through Plexiglas."

"I wish I'd gotten more assistance," I answered. "I wish I'd gotten better guidance." Fearing how this answer sounded and wanting to put the responsibility back on me, Puckett asked scornfully, "It is the Army's fault?" When I whispered no, he shouted, "It's all your fault." That did not exactly sound like a question to me.

Puckett continued to badger me, forcing if not apologies from me, at least regret at the decisions I had made, especially in regard to Col. Roberts. These moments were long and excruciating. Puckett was right. If my previous steps had all led to this self-defeating mess of a trial, I should never have taken them. In fact, if the military had made it impossible to uphold a sacred oath, I would have left years ago or never joined in the first place. I started the process looking for clarity. I ended up with the opposite.

It was so hard to address the jury members and not look at the paintings on the wall behind them. As fate would have it, these were portraits of various Founding Fathers, and I wondered what they would be thinking. I strongly suspected they would be seeking the truth, about Obama's citizenship status, about his Connecticut Social Security number (there is no reason why Obama would have a Connecticut number), about the multitude of unanswered questions surrounding this man. Here, however, to emphasize the real issues would likely have resulted in a reprimand from the judge and a harsher sentence from the jury. How, I wondered, had our country descended to this level of apathy?

"I'm extremely sorry for everything that's become of this," I told the panel in conclusion. "It's a unique situation. This never happened before. As a military member, I was wrong for pushing this issue."

That said, the defense rested. Although the summaries and sentencing appeals were yet to come, my life as a free man had been reduced to hours.

ℓℓ

14. Duty, Honor, Country

The prosecution held its trump card for the mitigation phase of the trial. These were the Dobsons, two married Army physicians who suffered most directly from my refusal to deploy. Maj. Craig Dobson, a pediatric cardiologist, deployed in my stead. This, he argued, interfered with his cardiology board exams, but it was his wife whose testimony sealed my fate.

She told the court how they had been planning to start a family, but that I had ruined their plans. When she started crying on the stand, I could hear that final nail being pounded into my coffin.

In his final summary O'Beirne would make the case that I had caused the Dobsons to suffer and, worse, had never apologized to them for it. I knew, however, that the Dobsons had led a blessed life by military standards. Both had spent their entire careers in the D.C. area. I am sure their medical training was similar in hours and commitment to my wife's and mine, but at least they were in the same country.

By contrast, in my first five years of service Pili and I spent about two years together, given our grueling internships and my subsequent postings to Honduras, Germany and Bosnia. Later, after we started a family, I spent a year in Afghanistan and left Pili with the kids. As much as I appreciated the Dobsons' service, it seemed small beer compared to what my wife had sacrificed and what she was about to sacrifice in the months ahead.

Still, I wanted to call the Dobsons and apologize, but I feared that I would be charged with improper communication. Maj. Kemkes advised against it. He reassured me that any attempt by the prosecutors to use the Dobsons would backfire, given my own record on deployments. He also confirmed that Dobson knew he was next to deploy and had his bags packed once he heard I was not going.

That all sounded good before the trial, but once the Dobsons testified, we could not offer an alternative explanation without making me look more heartless. As much as the Army preaches equality, a crying woman deprived of motherhood transcends the codebook.

It was now time for the two attorneys to present their final summations. O'Beirne's argument was painful, but I expected that. Puckett's was even more hurtful, which caught me by surprise.

O'Beirne led off, and he was a hell of a performer. As harsh as he was, he at least depicted me as the master of my own fate, a willing participant in a political cause that I advanced at the Army's expense. He played the video from a few months back in which I explained why I was doing what I was doing. And although he did so to make me look bad, at least the video introduced into the court proceedings the reason why I was there. I would have preferred that we introduce this evidence and build our case upon it. I wanted to remind the court that we officers had sworn an oath to the U.S. Constitution and that I had taken every conceivable step to investigate my concerns without an adequate response from anyone in the military or in Congress.

This we could not do. The procedure, as laid out in previous hearings, was that I could not bring up my motives. Judge Lind would strike any attempt to do so. The prosecutors held all the cards and could do as they desired.

According to O'Beirne, I was not sorry about the spectacle I'd created. I showed no remorse. I did not recognize the person O'Beirne was talking about, but it never slowed him down. He even recited a lengthy passage from General Douglas MacArthur's "duty, honor, country" speech, and a wonderful speech it is. O'Beirne began mid-speech. The soldier's mission is "to win our wars. Everything else in your professional career is but corollary to this vital dedication."

O'Beirne seemed to emphasize passages like "Others will debate the controversial issues, national and international, which divide men's minds" and "Let civilian voices argue the merits or demerits of our processes of government."

Although O'Beirne read the following passage as an indictment of me, I think he missed the larger point MacArthur was making. Yes, the speech warned the military against political involvement, but it also laid out the political problems of the day. Those problems sounded familiar:

> Whether our strength is being sapped by deficit financing indulged in too long, by federal paternalism grown too mighty, by power groups grown too arrogant, by politics grown too corrupt, by crime grown too rampant, by morals grown too low, by taxes grown too high, by extremists grown too violent; whether our personal liberties are as firm and complete as they should be, these great national problems are not for your professional participation or military solution. Your guidepost stands out like a tenfold beacon in the night: Duty, Honor, Country.

The problems MacArthur cited had all grown worse in the nearly fifty years since he had given that speech. Somehow, although I was meant to feel the opposite, I sensed that MacArthur was a kindred spirit and would understand what I had done—maybe not approve, but understand.

O'Beirne thought otherwise. He continued on an odd tack, detailing the suffering undergone by the Dobsons in my place. Given his all-out commitment to winning wars and the terrible suffering he had seen, I suspect MacArthur would have had a hard time sympathizing with a couple whose plans to start a family were being pushed back a few months by the husband's first deployment.

All of this was taking place in front of those portraits of the Founding Fathers. I could not help wondering what they would think of this or what they might say. I had hoped that perhaps Puckett would invoke some of their quotes to offset O'Beirne's, but that was not to be.

O'Beirne wrapped up his denunciation with the recommendation that I should serve no fewer than twenty-four months in prison—two days for every day my unit spent in Afghanistan without me. And yes, of course I should be dismissed from the service.

"That was a really good speech," said Puckett to O'Beirne as he began his summation. "I enjoyed it." Puckett added that it must have been written before I gave my statement because its characterization of me was inaccurate. According to Puckett, I was not the driver of my own destiny. I was "simple." I was "facile." I was "one of the most naïve gentlemen you ever met." Although I understood what Puckett was trying to do, I preferred listening to O'Beirne.

To be fair, Puckett did capture the heart of my mission and asked the jurors to understand it. After all, he said, how could there be a greater display of patriotism than a willingness to sacrifice a military career for what I believed was the higher cause of the Constitution. But there was not enough of this argument.

During our many conversations, it had become clear to me that Puckett did not believe in my issue. He would end each discussion with his legal conclusion that according to the Constitution, once Obama was sworn in, he was the president. He could be a hippopotamus, and yet he was the president. This always killed the discussion. But I don't think our Constitution meant for people to have loyalty to a hippo, let alone be ordered into harm's way by one. That's why the Constitution has stringent requirements for citizenship for the president and establishes the procedure if the president-elect fails to qualify for office. But neither Puckett nor any of the mainstream media nor Congress—nor the Supreme Court—for that matter, would address the issue.

Instead, Puckett led the jury through an extended medical metaphor. In it, I had a cancerous obsession that was eating away at me, and I sought a cure. That search led me to Paul Jensen, who was not a specialist but offered treatment anyhow. I went along despite the adverse side effects, said Puckett, because I was so obsessed and so naïve.

"What's different between now and March?" said Puckett in a self-congratulatory burst. "He got a new doctor. That doctor educated him about cancer from the molecular level up. He's convinced now he doesn't have cancer. He realizes he was wrong—wrong to follow the advice of Doctor Jensen."

In his argument for clemency, Puckett called my actions "crazy." He said of me, "He saw a mirage. That's all it was, just a mirage." He argued not only against confinement, but also against dismissal. "He's ready to be used as the Army would use him." Incarceration, Puckett suggested, would not be a particularly good use.

With that, Puckett left the courthouse for a scheduled flight to Italy. There he was to serve as counsel in still another military case, this one involving the Navy. I had approved his departure. By this time, I had grown used to being abandoned by people in authority, from Congress on down. Although I did not fully agree with his tactics, Puckett did what he thought was best, and he did so presumably in good faith. Now it was left to the eight officers on the jury to decide my fate.

They took much longer than anyone anticipated. To me, that suggested at least some sympathy among them. The deliberations started at about 1100 hours and did not end until nearly 1600 hours. When the jurors returned with the verdict, there were still about a half-dozen supporters in the room as well as my parents and brothers, who sat behind me.

As he promised, bless his heart, my father stood while the verdict was read: total forfeiture of my pay and accrued pension, confinement for six months and dismissal from service. No one in the courtroom reacted. My immediate sensation was relief: the sentence could have been several years. Judge Lind thanked the jurors, who quickly departed, and she adjourned the trial. Although it had lasted less than two days, it seemed like an eternity. With one unreality behind me, a new one was about to unfold.

Maj. Kemkes had already done the paperwork to process my confinement. This allowed me twenty minutes or so with my parents and brothers. It was a little tearful, but Mom and Dad were pretty strong. We had known, more or less, what the outcome would be.

My folks promised to do what they could for Pili and the kids, and we focused on the future. I would do my time and get back into medicine. Greg gave me one of his inspirational books. "Stay strong," he reminded me. "The Lakins can get through anything." I had my duffel bag with me, and my Bible packed. I was as ready as I would ever be.

I left my family behind and was escorted into a back room by two sergeants and a colonel. There, I changed from my dress greens into my

ACUs, my Army combat uniform. As I did, I took a last look at my ribbons and medals. I could not help but think they had lost their luster. As a further humiliation, the colonel made sure my rank was torn off.

To be fair, the colonel and the sergeants were polite enough and were just doing their job. I even helped them put the shackles on—an eighteen-inch chain between my ankles and handcuffs attached to a heavy leather belt cinched around my waist.

The sergeants led me out the back door of the courthouse, through the snow and cold, to a waiting van. They had to lift me in, and I could only shimmy my way to my seat. It was a long drive to Walter Reed. Once there, the humiliation began in earnest. I was led into the Provost Marshal's office, which looks like one of those old police lockups you see on TV, and was promptly strip-searched.

Now I was being handled by civilian policemen employed by the Department of Defense. Maybe I am wrong, but I would guess they had failed in their military careers and were now pleased to have authority over soldiers like me. They certainly treated me like dirt. They took my shoelaces and my belt, left me with socks sopping wet from the snow, and put me in a stark, cold cinder block cell with a direct hole to the outside where the ventilating fan had once been.

They gave me just one Army blanket and two sorry bedspreads from the guesthouse. My bed was a metal slab attached to a frigid outside wall. Even the guards posted in the anteroom were cold; they were wearing fleece jackets. All I had to keep warm was a T-shirt and an ACU blouse. I did not expect four-star service, but if the prisoners at Guantanamo were treated like this, the readers of the *New York Times* would be crying over their cappuccinos.

I decided I would not eat until the guards gave me something to keep warm. Hunger strikes have worked for others, but here that gesture did not get much sympathy. I overheard one of these clowns boast, while reporting by telephone on my status, "If Lakin refuses to eat, I got a size thirteen that can take care of that." He so liked the expression, he repeated it in a second phone call.

For all the guff, I remained resolute. I was not going to let the system beat me. I did push-ups and sit-ups in my cell and read the Bible. I finally prevailed on my unfriendly custodians to give me a space heater, and they made some efforts to repair the new heating unit nearby that had not worked since renovations the year before. I was getting under their skin.

By the afternoon of day two they were ready to get rid of me. Fortunately, I got to see Pili and the kids one last time. The master sergeant who escorted me to the meeting room showed me some Army courtesy. "I am going to take the responsibility to allow you some privacy," he said, and he did just that.

What does one say to a wife and children before leaving for prison? I tried to instill in my seven-year-old son the conviction that he was now the man of the house and needed to take care of the family. I told my eleven-year-old daughter to be the best help to her mom she could be. All the while I was holding back the tears lest I set off my little one and turn this into an emotional free-for-all. Pili was incredible: hurt and sad, yet solid for the kids' sake.

It was a tender moment. I would treasure it on my drive to the airport and on my flight to Leavenworth. In fact, that memory would sustain me for the remainder of my internment.

&

15. *I Know Why You Are Here*

I never thought I would welcome a trip to the stockade at Fort Leavenworth, but after a day at Walter Reed I knew the conditions could only get better.

The journey itself I would wish on no one. The two sergeants and the full bird colonel who escorted me to Water Reed came back to take me to Leavenworth. They seemed none too happy about it. A two-day sojourn to Kansas was probably not in their Christmas travel plans. They packed me into a van and were grim throughout the ride to Reagan National and beyond. There was no joking, no small talk. I tried both unsuccessfully.

If there was a low point, it was my perp walk through Reagan National Airport. The people I passed in the busy concourses tried not to stare, but they could hardly help themselves. Shackled hand and foot, I must have looked like some desperado. As I walked, I reflected on the flags and patriotic bunting and the happy sight of returning soldiers. None of the display had lost its appeal, but I could not overlook the irony of my being chained and bound amidst it all, and for what? For asking that my commander in chief honor the Constitution.

On the upside, we got to board the commercial jet to Kansas City before the rest of the passengers. On the downside, we sat in the far back, in the seats next to the restroom that don't recline. My guardians cut me no slack. The chains remained in place, hand and foot, throughout the flight. I had no idea how hard it would be to drink orange juice while handcuffed.

When we arrived, Kansas City was as cold and blustery as D.C., but now it was around midnight. I had flown in and out of KC International many times as a medical student. Those were usually happy occasions. The airport looked much less welcoming this time.

To aggravate matters, we had a hard time finding rental car clerks at that hour. And when we found one, we had to wander through an exposed rental car lot trying to pick which of the three available vans to drive away. I had flattered myself into thinking they would have figured this part out before we got there.

For the record, Congress authorized the United States Disciplinary Barracks (USDB) at Fort Leavenworth in 1874. Prisoners built the original prison, which was completed in 1921. (They also helped build the nearby U.S. Penitentiary, which opened in 1895 as the first federal prison.) A new USDB facility came online in 2002, and it remains, in fact, the only maximum-security facility in the U.S. military. It takes a minimum five-year sentence to be sent there.

I was assigned to the Joint Regional Correctional Facility, a new 500-unit medium-security military prison across the road from the USDB. The place opened for business just two months before I got there, and they were still working out the kinks. These were many, but the stories I heard about the gang violence and worse out of the USDB made me glad I was where I was.

My initiation into prison life started off roughly. That was not by accident. The sergeants who processed me made the ordeal feel like the first day of boot camp, only more demeaning. They immediately let me who know was in charge—lots of barking orders and needless harassment.

Much of the conflict centered around the duffel bag. Half the stuff I brought—right down to little shampoo bottles—was thrown out or sent home. Then I had to repack the bag to some ever-shifting specifications. I can't complain. I only had to do it twice. The guy who followed me may still be repacking his bag.

Of course, what would a new prison experience be like without a strip search? I got another one of those. That made two in two days. Fortunately, the guards left my body cavities in peace. They then gave me some shorts and T-shirts and put me into a SHU (special housing unit) as a transitional place. Because of the holidays, the administrative process lagged.

In the Christmas spirit, the sergeant who formally processed me a day later played the Grinch. She was one tough cookie. There was no joking around with this lady. She fingerprinted me again, gave me an ID badge, threw some more of my stuff out, but then said something that gave me pause: "I know why you're here. It's my job to know the charges of all who come in here. Very interesting!"

I may have been reading too much into it, but I sensed understanding, even sympathy, on her part. I got less of the 'welcome to prison' guff than the other prisoners got. Was this due to my rank, I wondered, my respectful obedience, or maybe the issue that had put me into prison? I still don't know.

Curiously, her guard husband, a huge black weight lifter, was one of the fairest, nicest, and most respected guards in the unit.

Once assigned a cell, I was determined to stay as fit as I could, both physically and spiritually. Two or three times a day I did a full range of calisthenics including a step-up using my desk chair, pull-ups using my desk, and sit-ups on my mattress. I met with the chaplain as well and went over some Bible study questions.

Twice a day we had rec. All indoors. They said it was too cold outside, and it probably was. We took showers, played cards, cleaned cells. Only if you spend twenty-some hours by yourself each day can cell cleaning seem like recreation, but it kind of did. I hope the guys coming into the cells I cleaned appreciated it. No matter how long they were in for, they weren't likely to get a cleaner cell.

To be sure, I enjoyed the cards more than the cell cleaning, and I grew to like my fellow card players. Even though we did not discuss each other's crimes, we suddenly had a lot in common.

In time, we had official in-processing classes for new guys like me as well as for a few long-termers who had transferred from the maximum-security disciplinary barracks across the road. About a dozen of us sat around the table. We heard from the chaplain, the JAG officer, the medical people, even the commander.

During a break, one of the new guys started making jokes about the tough cookie who had processed us. The guard overseeing us heard the comments and stepped out the door to make a call. The female guard came barreling in like an unblocked linebacker, got right in the guy's face, and shouted, "You have something you want to tell me to my face? Bring it on if you do!"

The fellow could only sputter apologies. We had some tough guards there that no one wanted to cross, male and female. She was one of the toughest. Once she left, a long-termer leaned across the table and said to the wise guy, "I gotta give you lessons on how to be a good prisoner." This was the first laugh I'd had in about a week.

Unfortunately, the long-term guy soon got word he was heading back to maximum security. He didn't want to go, and he caused something of a ruckus when the MPs came to get him. My first instinct was to help the MPs; I obviously had not settled into the role of prisoner quite yet.

A few days in, I was transferred to SHU South. If nothing else, this gave me a better view of the common area. I was still getting used to the every-half-hour cell checks and the twice-a-day head counts. What with the guards talking as they saw fit throughout the night, sleep was hard to come by. On the positive side, the food was surprisingly good—chicken roast one night, pork fettuccini the next day. You'd think we were at Guantanamo after all.

I soon enough got my first reprimand—or near reprimand. It was a stupid thing. The belt the guards gave me was about a foot too long, and so I cut those extra inches off with a nail clipper. Even in prison, especially in prison, I did not want to look like a slob. I left the clipped-off end on my shelf.

During a room search, I was called from a card game by a guard. He was upset. He said I could get in a lot of trouble for altering equipment. I had to wait at parade rest while he left to discuss the issue with his supervisors. Upon his return, he said all was good, but I got the message: in prison, you are no longer your own person. Choices that make sense in the real world don't make sense in a world without real choices. This suspension of logic is among the harder things a prisoner has to adapt to.

At one point, I was called out to visit with a civilian psychologist who did assessments for the administration. He knew why I was there, or at least he thought he did. As he put it, I did not believe Obama to be born in the United States or constitutionally eligible to be president.

I corrected him. It seemed to be a minor point to him, but it wasn't to me. As I explained, I did not know where the president was born or whether he was eligible or not. The problem was that no one did. Obviously, my court-martial and imprisonment had not moved the president to produce his birth certificate. That would remain a mystery. "I think this is a question that needs to be addressed," I told the psychologist. I think he had a hard time factoring concepts like "principle" and "sacrifice" into a sanity equation.

I told him I was there to be the best inmate I could be in order to get out as early as possible. That much he got. In any case, he reviewed my offenses and said that I didn't quite meet the point criteria for "maximum security" so I would be assigned to "medium."

Close to "maximum"? I was stunned. I was hoping for "minimum" status, with some trustee-type work detail. I figured I could hold my own breaking rocks if it came to that, but in any case this was not to be a country club experience, nothing close. No reason to send for my tennis racket or golf clubs. This was the real deal, with all the indignities and abuses you might imagine. Welcome to Leavenworth.

It was many days before I had the phone codes and permission to call Pili and the kids. The guards, however, had little knowledge of how to call and even less interest in helping. So I turned for help to a guy who was reputedly the most violent inmate in the SHU. Thanks, friend! The call was short and awkward, but it boosted my spirits hugely. I was not alone, not forgotten, which was good to know with Christmas around the corner.

☙

16. Never Wanted to Be Famous

My deluxe sink toilet combo unit.

On 21 December, four days into my enforced vacation at Fort Leaven-worth, I finally received writing materials. The pen was a short, stubby plastic thing that made writing a challenge, but on the plus side, it could not be turned into a "shank" even by the most enterprising of prisoners.

There is no better way to explore my state of mind at the time than to share the contents of some of the letters I sent. This is among the first I wrote that day. I have edited it for conciseness:

> Hope all is well. Don't know how to start a letter or what to say. I hope I made a difference in a very important matter. It cost me a lot. But I now have to believe it turned out okay. There certainly are no do-overs. The important thing is for the work to carry on so we never have this situation again.

> At the time of this writing I remained isolated in the SHU in what is called "reception status."

> Reception status is mostly lock down in my cell. We now get two hours of "rec time" in the morning and afternoon. Rec time is cell door open to a common pod area with a four-seat

table, an exercise bike that does not work, a flat-screen TV that we cannot watch, and two showers. Activity is playing cards or a few board games, working out in my cell between meals, reading the rulebook, Bible, and now writing letters. Looks like the routine for the next several weeks.

After getting more integrated in January (hopefully minimum security) we may have more privileges. There will not be much use of a computer, limited phone, news, or TV. We have to order our own health and comfort supplies from a small provided list. We are allowed one order request per month and not more than $35 per month. I'm hoping they will honor my first order on credit—we have not been able to get money into our account yet—not having any communication with Pili yet.

I'm hoping to get a small radio with ear buds so I can get some news radio. Had to work hard to decide about how many batteries I could get by with vs. how many rolls of toilet paper to buy.

The trial seems long ago now. What a feeling of helplessness going through the process. I likely got the best outcome I could have—but it was painful.

After the trial I overheard someone say, "Well, he's no hero now!" Sorry, I was not in it to be a hero. Just thought I was doing the right thing. I spent enough of myself and my family's future for now. Others are going to have to continue.

Got to go now. Moving to a new cell. Phones don't look good today. They brought a phone in but no one knows how we can call out collect. Sigh…

Terry

On Friday, Christmas Eve, I was able to call Pili. Andrew answered first, but the recording of the collect operator seemed to scare him, and he hung up. I called back in a few minutes, and Pili answered. It was so sweet to hear her voice. She told me the kids were doing well, and I was greatly relieved to hear that.

She explained that our neighbors and friends in Maryland were being very generous and offering her any help she needed, which was good news. She said, too, that the Army was being nice to her, but it sounded to me as if they were having her jump through hoops to get items that I did not really need.

It snowed a little on Christmas Eve, which made it feel more like Christmas, even in prison. As my Christmas gift to the administration, I submitted eight pages of suggested improvements and typo corrections to the "Manual Guidelines of Inmates." It was a good exercise. I submitted my notes, I explained, as a "respectful and humble" submission to help them improve their manual. I meant it.

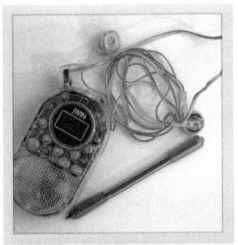

This radio and flexible pen were Terry's only means of communications during his incarceration apart from occasional phone calls. He did manage to get an upgraded radio near the end of his imprisonment.

During the afternoon that same day, I was given a rare opportunity to excel. Three of us were assigned to clean the common area for our thirty-cell wing. Then we did the same for the north wing, which included about twelve empty cells. We mopped, dusted, and mopped some more. We worked hard for about an hour and did the best we could. Then it was back to our own cells. "Rec time" was over. Here is a letter I sent on Christmas Eve:

> I just received about 15 cards and letters yesterday—all wonderful, supportive notes. I would write or call, but it has been difficult. Call privileges have to be set up well in advance. We can only have 20 people on our list, originally told "no cell numbers," and we can only modify our list once a month.

I might add here that the phrase "cell phone" has kind of an ironic ring when you are in prison. The letter continues:

> Lots of thoughts about the trial and treatment after being shackled by ankles and handcuffs strapped to leather waist-band. Not sure all that was necessary. Dirty, cold cell at Walter Reed Provost Marshal's building for 2 days and 1 night was pretty poor. I was well into a hunger strike and think that may have expedited my transfer. Not sure ankle and hand-cuffs were necessary through the airport, the plane trip either. Fellow inmate that arrived after me with a 10-month sentence for DUI and assault was escorted without cuffs. Oh well!
>
> I have not been allowed any news, TV, newspaper since being shackled after the trial. Hope the world is okay.
>
> I am not sure what others expected. Nor do I have any inkling of what is being said now. If nothing else, I am glad that it was a time for many people to converge, meet and carry on this important issue. Here's to a Merry Christmas & Happy 2011!
>
> Terry

Christmas Day started off not so merrily with two cold processed waffles, two cold sausage links, yogurt, and two hard-boiled eggs, which, thank God, even the worst cook could not quite screw up.

I followed that up with a workout in my cell. For no good reason, my neighbor got yelled at for working out in his cell. The guard told him rec time was the time to work out. But we couldn't use the outside gym because it had been declared too cold to go outside. Plus the treadmill that we'd moved in a few days before didn't work. So I decided not to work out—I would just clean the floor with my shirt while wearing it. No, cadre, they just look like push-ups!

I did a lot of Bible reading on Christmas as well. It seemed like a good day for it. Christmas dinner was little better than breakfast: cold hot dog salad without dressing—yes, hot dog salad—but good carrots. Can't really screw those up either.

As a Christmas bonus, we got to clean the whole common area again and mopped and cleaned some additional empty cells. Lest I forget, the MPs finished up our Yuletide with a lecture on how to request razor blades and toilet paper. Ho! Ho! Ho!

On Sunday, the day after Christmas, I had hoped to attend church services, but that was not yet in the cards given my transitional status. That night we had a new set of MPs, who seemed to think that if they had to stay up, so should we.

They were noisy as all get out—letting doors slam, talking loudly, dropping things, even strumming on the table. I was close to getting up and complaining, but happily, they finally quieted down. I wasn't sure complaining about anything was in my best interest.

The next morning the MPs went around waking everyone up early until the inmates reminded them that this was supposed to be a holiday sleep-in day. It took about thirty minutes for the guards to confirm with higher-ups that we could sleep in, but by that time everyone was pretty much awake.

In my newfound leisure time, I jotted down ideas for a wellness book, played gin rummy with my usual gang of four, and ate a couple of meals that were pretty tasty if you didn't mind eating without condiments and drinking a kind of mystery Kool-Aid that was pink and tasted like water.

On Tuesday the 28th, I met with some correctional guys who still were not sure whether or I not would be assigned to the maximum security facility. I did not think that likely, but in prison, even an Army prison, you never know.

I called Pili later that day, and she filled me in on the misadventures of Hawaii's new governor, Democrat Neil Abercrombie. This story is worth telling. Apparently, Abercrombie had told the *Los Angeles Times* just before Christmas, referring to Barack Obama, "Maybe I'm the only one in the country that could look you right in the eye right now and tell you, 'I was here when that baby was born.'"

A few days later, Abercrombie clarified to Mark Niesse of The Associated Press that he didn't exactly see Obama's parents with their newborn son at the hospital, but that he "remembers seeing Obama as a child with his parents at social events."

This was nonsense too. By Christmas 2010, anyone who had been following the story knew that Obama's mother, Ann Dunham, showed up in Seattle with the future president just weeks after he was born, and mother and son stayed there for a year. By the time they returned to Hawaii,

Obama Sr. had long since left for Harvard. They did not attend social events together.

My friends outside would later fill me in on this story, which would get stranger and stranger. During an interview on Minnesota's KQRS morning radio show on 20 January 2011, Mike Evans, a celebrity journalist and longtime friend of Abercrombie, shared a conversation he'd had with the governor the day before.

Evans claimed that Abercrombie had promised him that as soon as he became governor he planned to find absolute proof that Obama was born in Hawaii. On 19 January, however, Abercrombie told Evans that he had searched the relevant Hawaiian hospitals using his powers as governor and had concluded, "There is no Barack Obama birth certificate in Hawaii, absolutely no proof at all that Obama was born in Hawaii."

After Abercrombie had made such a fuss about finding the birth certificate, Evans concluded of his friend that he has "got some egg in the face." Curiously, too, when Evans asked Abercrombie when he'd first encountered the young Barack Obama, Abercrombie reportedly said, "I remember him playing in a T-Ball league." This would have been when he was roughly five or six years old.

To no one's great surprise, Evans came out a day later and said he "misspoke" during the radio interview. The problem is he "misspoke" in at least a dozen other interviews on that same day.

By this time I had begun to hear from the world outside the walls. I summed up my first two weeks in a letter to a friend:

> I'm having a great time! ☺ Can't complain too much, just trying to be the best inmate I can be. Still in the 'SHU' special housing unit. Pretty close to max custody—SHU lock up 20-22 hours a day, 1-2 hour release, 1-2 times a day to common area to shower, play games, use phone, or tasked to clean, sweep, mop units or empty cells. Have not been in outside air for 12 days now.
>
> Meals are pretty good—through the slot in the door—and we have 20 minutes to choke it down. About half way through my Bible (my first time really reading it) and another book my brother gave me before being shackled—*Inspiration*, by Dr. Wayne W. Dyer.

Book dovetails well with spirituality with God—and seems to hit home on my course of action too. Not sure if my brother intended or understood that, would like to ask him. I'm not sure he read it—as he has no free time—but I know he has read many previous Dyer Books. Pili has been the only one I am allowed to call (collect) so far. Hopefully in the next month I can get my approved phone list of numbers expanded. Even writing is limited. I was only allowed so many envelopes (10) to use. I only have 3 left after this to last until the end of the month. Only 4 pages max per envelope.

I received nearly 50 great letters and cards from people. Only allowed to keep 20 or less in my cell. They are all so great and inspirational I wish I could reply to all—but that would be impossible just for supplies. And this tiny rubber pen is hard to write with :). I will try and write to some though.

Feel free to share this with Pili, Greg, & Ducky. Save it for me for my scrapbook upon my release. Wow! Just got today's mail—big stack. Maybe a hundred letters!

I counted them and finished the letter:

Lucky guess—105 letters & NIV study Bible.

Take Care! Terry

On delivering the mail, one senior officer said, "These are from your fan club. You're famous." I told him, "I never wanted to be famous," and I was being straightforward. He replied, "Well, if I didn't work here, I would write you." I am not sure if he meant much by that, but in that situation any kind or encouraging words are valuable.

On 30 December, after two weeks alone in my cell, I finally got to move into the general population. I was assigned a second-level cell, again to myself, but that lasted for about two hours. I was at the library when the senior NCO came for me and made me move again, to the top bunk in a lower-level cell.

My roommate was a huge guy with massive arms and, happily for me, a nice disposition. He was serving three years, and the better I got to know his story, the more I became convinced that he had gotten a raw deal. In fact, after meeting several inmates who should not have been there, I began to wonder about the prosecutors and judges who sent them. What did they see when they looked in the mirror each morning?

Speaking of the library, when I first went there to work, another inmate introduced himself and asked for my autograph—for his mother! He was in one of the small pods in the SHU when I arrived. His mom, who was a big supporter, told him about my being sent to Leavenworth, and there I was in person outside the window of his pod. Small world!

Word spreads quickly in prison. When my fellow prisoners and I were being briefed after our move by the NCO of the new cellblock, he looked at me and said, "I'm not going to lie. We all know about you. You're all over the news and newspapers." Later during cards, one of the inmates, a combat warrior, asked, "What did you do, man?" He looked at me as though I were some kind of mass murderer. It took a fair amount of explaining.

On Saturday, New Year's Day—Thank you, God!—Pili and the kids arrived at the prison. I greeted them in my standard prison garb: brown pants and matching long-sleeve shirt with last name and "reg" number tags. We got to spend about a half hour together in the late afternoon in a large, sadly underused visitation room where we were assigned a table. Pili is so beautiful and so great with the kids. I cannot say enough.

Although the kids were apprehensive—they had seen prisons in cartoons and TV clips—they seemed relieved to see that I was well and being treated decently. They hugged and kissed me without prodding. It was a reassuring moment. Still, I could never forget that I was in prison. I was not allowed to hold Jack in my lap or even hug anyone for more than a moment. Jack kept trying to climb into my lap and I had to keep giving him back to Pili.

We spent several hours together that day, morning and afternoon. The kids had brought a few toys and card games to keep themselves amused. Andrew impressed me with how well he did with his math in adding up Yahtzee scores. I got to catch up on their lives and learn what they and Pili had been doing. They were troupers. They bore my absence well. I did not tell them that after each visit I was strip-searched.

After I returned to the pod, an inmate approached me about my case. He had been one of several who had made an effort to brief the new guys about how things worked in our new area. We talked about Obama's birth issue for about thirty minutes.

I also had a nice talk with my roommate, the big guy. He showed me his family album, including pictures of his sports-star sixteen-year-old son and his two pretty daughters. By this time he had already been at Leavenworth 160 days, and he had not yet received his record of trial. An inmate is supposed to get it within 120 days; he cannot apply for clemency until he gets that record.

Although I was reluctant, I shared my charges with my roommate. It started with him saying he had heard someone come up to me and ask about them. He thought that pretty rude. In prison, no one is supposed to ask why anyone is there. So I told him my story and explained that the issue was "totally constitutional." He got it. He said he could see I was not at all a racist. This was a welcome acknowledgment from anyone, but especially from a black cellmate who wore a size 57 jacket and had arms to match.

As the months went by, I got to know my roommate as a good, loving man and to see how sad it was that he would spend the next three years in the UCMJ system. Yes, everyone in prison says he is innocent, but in my estimate maybe 25 percent actually are or have been given sentences disproportionate to their crimes. My roommate's case was a tragedy of bad charges.

On Sunday morning, January 2, my roommate and I were among the twenty-five or so prisoners who attended protestant services. He played awesome drums and had a couple of voice solos. He was clearly the best singer there. The military chaplain gave a solid sermon for the New Year and served communion. All in all, it was a really good service and might make for an inspiring TV show.

My brother Greg had joined us in the afternoon for the last hour on Saturday, and I met with him again on Sunday morning after services. I told him I was reading the Bible—religiously, I guess you would say. We talked about family issues and news of the outside world. As much as I warned myself not to buck the Army system, I kept getting signs to do just that.

That evening at dinner, the sun was shining through the windows as we went through dinner line. It was the first time since being shackled and brought to Leavenworth that I had even seen, much less felt the sun. It was wonderful. From then on, every chance I got, I would time my spacing in the chow line to maximize the warm, soothing seconds in sunlight while minimizing the delay to the guys behind me—I never knew when the slightest disruption in routine would set someone off or alarm the guards.

I saw the kids and Pili again on Sunday afternoon for the last time this trip. It was hard to let them go. But on Sunday evening, as a compensation of sorts, I got to go outside. It was about thirty degrees. There were about twenty-five of us. We wore our big parkas and got frisked on the way out. I ran, the first time in a while. It felt good despite the cold. I did about two miles and walked a bunch more.

I had run the perimeter of the base in Honduras; I ran in Bosnia inside the wire, and I ran in Kandahar. But this time, instead of being the good guy inside the wire keeping the bad guys out, I was the bad guy being kept in. There were three fences and a lot of wire around me, and trucks with shotguns drove by every few minutes. It was an unsettling way to run laps.

Still, I was outside. It was dark and frosty, but it felt good. There is so much we do not appreciate until we are deprived of it—even a cold winter night.

17. A Moral and Religious People

After my first two weeks in prison, my fellow inmates began to think of me as one of them. In the beginning, I was the odd duck—"new guy, officer, in the news." Although more and more inmates and guards started calling me "sir," which they should not have done, they did so out of earned respect, not because of novelty.

My new acquaintances could see I was not fragile or standoffish. I could spar verbally as well as the next guy—a useful prison skill—and I had the wherewithal to help people with a host of problems. Guys even started asking me for advice on jobs after getting out, a good sign.

As much as I enjoyed helping educate others, prison offered me the unexpected opportunity of educating myself. Reading the Bible was a big part of that. The prison has two libraries: a traditional collection and the chaplain's library. This enabled me to begin the most intensive reading program of my life, much of it dealing with America's founding.

One book that proved particularly useful was W. Cleon Skousen's thirty-year-old classic, *The 5000 Year Leap: A Miracle That Changed the World.*

Skousen argues that the Founding Fathers shared some fundamental beliefs that enabled them to create a society more solid and more sane than any that had preceded it in the previous 5,000 years.

Among other principles, the Founders believed that all men are created equal, that all of us should look to God for enlightenment, that the social order should be based on natural law, that virtue is essential for a free people, that a limited government keeps us free, that the Constitution protects us from our rulers' frailties, that a system of checks and balances restrains power, that free markets work best, and that we should avoid debt, shun entangling alliances, and acknowledge our manifest destiny to serve as an example for other nations.

The one quote Skousen cites that I think best captures the intent of our Founding Fathers comes from John Adams: "Our Constitution was made only for a moral and religious people. It is wholly inadequate to the government of any other." With the Skousen book finished, I turned to *Basic Documents of American History: The World's Greatest Classics.*

One night I went to bed reading the Maryland Toleration Act of 1649. I may have been the first person to go to bed reading that act since 1649. What a short and fair piece of legislation that was! It established tolerance of religion, a concept fundamental to our country.

A few days later, I went to the library to follow up on some of the ideas I had been learning about. I was particularly interested in knowing more about the French observer Alexis de Tocqueville. I hoped to read his work sometime, but I thought it would be difficult to find even in the "outside" world.

But there it was staring out at me from the library shelf: *Democracy in America.* This version, a paperback published in 2010, gave the appearance of being unread. The library had more than 2,700 books, all of them numbered sequentially. This book was #1. It appeared that the library staff had picked this book first to start its inventory. As I would learn, *Democracy in America* deserved its ranking.

It is pretty amazing what de Tocqueville, a 25-year-old French noble who had spent just nine months in our young country, was able to see in 1831. Let me share one relevant example:

An American Constitution is not supposed to be immutable, as in France; nor is it susceptible of modification by the ordinary powers of society, as in England. It constitutes a detached whole, which, as it represents the will of the whole people, is no less binding on the legislator than on the private citizen, but which may be altered by the will of the people in predetermined cases, according to the established rules. In America, the Constitution may therefore vary; but as long as it exists, it is the origin of all authority, and the sole vehicle of the predominating force.

This is what our friends on the left don't get. Yes, the Constitution is a "living" document. It is subject to change, but that change must come through amendment and that can happen only "according to the established rules." Those rules don't include a judge making an exception to the Constitution for a certain presidential candidate or a president issuing an executive order contrary to the spirit of this extraordinary document.

When the Republicans took over the House of Representatives in January 2011, they elevated the Constitution to its proper place of respect by reading it aloud from the House floor. In the days afterward, I saw some pundits ridiculing this reading. Really? What was that about?

Our Founding Fathers well understood the problems of their times. The problems of our times are roughly the same as theirs. Fortunately, they created for us an instrument to deal with those problems—the Constitution, grounded in the unalienable rights endowed by our Creator.

I was going to turn de Tocqueville back in to the library after I had had it for some time. Then it just started catching me all over again. How could this man write so well and so insightfully about our government? How could he predict the weaknesses of the people and of future governments with such accuracy?

I also had the chance to reread George Washington's Farewell Address. It is an astonishingly wise document through and through, but one passage in the middle caught my attention:

It is important, likewise, that the habits of thinking in a free Country should inspire caution in those entrusted with its administration, to confine themselves within their respective

> Constitutional Spheres; avoiding in the exercise of the Powers
> of one department to encroach upon another.

You have to wonder how many people in our government have read this address. How many of them have even read the Constitution or, having read it, respect it? How many of them ever caution themselves about the reach of their power? I am not sure I want to know the answer, but it is not too late to turn the ship of state around. I am hoping that the people who read this book will take a look at Washington's Farewell Address and other documents and share them with their children.

I was glad that prison afforded me the chance to learn all of this, but I was saddened by the thought that I, like most Americans, had never learned it in school. We must have all been out sick on those days it was taught!

While reading, I would jot down the occasional thought that struck me as worth remembering. Here are a few of them:

"The creation of the Heavens and the Earth and everything in them was complete." Genesis 2:1

"So astounding are the facts in this connection, that it would seem as though the Creator, Himself, had electrically designed this planet." Nikola Tesla

"Faith is to believe that which you do not see; and the reward of this faith is to see that which you believe." Saint Augustine

"One word frees us of all the weight and pain of life. That word is Love." Sophocles

"Love is the most powerful and still most unknown energy in the world." Pierre Teilhard de Chardin

"Love is the fulfilling of the law." Saint Paul

"I am still determined to be cheerful and happy in whatever situation I may be; for I have also learned from experience that the greater part of our happiness or misery depends on our dispositions, and not on our circumstances." Martha Washington

"Success is not the key to happiness. Happiness is the key to success." Albert Schweitzer

By now I was working in the library. Unfortunately, we were not allowed to read once we got our work done; we had to keep ourselves busy for our entire shift. I took to book repair. At the rate I was going those first few weeks, all the books in the library would have had protective tape coverings in a few months. Still, book repair beat working in the kitchen or the laundry. This place was not designed for any kind of vocational training.

That was too bad. As I was coming to see, most of the inmates were good people. The lack of anything meaningful to do just aggravated their problems. Sometimes I think they acted out like schoolkids just to get attention.

Fortunately, attention was not something I lacked. I kept getting lots of mail. There is something about words on a page that e-mail cannot match. The letters were incredible! Just about every day I read a few that brought tears to my eyes. They were so touching, especially those from families I had never met thanking me for my defense of the Constitution—"for our children and us." Many retired military confirmed my interpretation of the officer's oath and thanked me for upholding it. I even received one letter from a retired Navy JAG officer who concurred with my decision.

I also received my first hate mail. Some guy thought I was an idiot and did not hesitate to say so. According to him, all I had to do was Google "Obama" and "eligibility" and I would have found out that the issue had long since been settled. Perhaps I should also have believed the two young "experts" from Factcheck.org who photographed Obama's Certification of Live Birth that was initially presented and declared it legitimate. Heck, my kids could have done that and spared me all the hassle. That is how simple life can be for people who choose to know nothing.

What continues to surprise me is how routinely obscene are the communications from our friends on the left. I may be the first soldier in history to resist deployment and not be embraced by them. Failing to understand me and my motives, they lash out and attack.

I was three weeks in prison before I got to do something we all do every day and take for granted every time we do it: I went outside before nightfall. It was pretty special to be outdoors in the early afternoon. Despite it being cold and overcast, I knew the sun was just behind the clouds. It was so nice. I got in about three miles of running and was joined for a few walking laps by one of the younger inmates. It turned out to be a pleasant interaction. I was finding that because I was an officer and a doctor, the younger guys were turning to me as a mentor. Unfortunately, too many of them had never known their fathers.

Once the newness of my environment wore off, confinement began to remind me of the movie *Groundhog Day*: same people, same issues, same journeys to the dining facility, same food day after day.

Worse, as the memory of their New Year's visit receded, I missed my family something fierce. It hurt to think of Jack wanting to cuddle on my lap or climb on my back during visitation and not being allowed lest the guards terminate the visit.

I thought I was acting normal or close to it during my blue days, but many inmate friends and several guards noticed something off and asked about me. They worried that I was not the usual smiling, cheerful Lakin. I realized I was letting many small things get to me. I was not being as thankful to the Lord as I should have been. And by not being thankful, by not being cheerful, I was letting the people around me down.

To break these spells of prison blues, I turned to my letters. They reminded me how blessed I was to have a family willing to visit. Many other inmates had no family, at least none that wanted to see them. Some inmates had never seen their children, and others lost family members while in prison.

Once I put things in perspective, and I had to do this more than once, I would snap back revitalized. I had to. I had new friends now, new obligations, new responsibilities, and yes, new opportunities to make the world at least a slightly better place.

&

18. *Love Mercy and Walk Humbly*

About halfway through my time at Leavenworth, I was offered a transfer to minimum security. It had its advantages. There would be fewer guys in the cellblock. I would have my own cell. And I could leave the cell door open until lights out.

On the downside, I would lose my cellmate, who had become a good friend, and I would miss my workout buddies and the many guys in the cellblock whom I had grown to like and respect. I decided to stay.

I told the administrative staff I wished to decline the upgrade. I reviewed all the pros and cons with several of them. "It is just not that great of an option for me," I told them. "I didn't request it." When I tried to push the issue, as much as a lowly inmate could, the senior leadership threatened me with discipline measures that could have led to removal of my good-conduct time.

So I was transferred to minimum. If you are beginning to think there is an Alice in Wonderland quality to prison, you are on the right track.

I can't claim to be an authority on prison life, but there is a difference between an Army prisoner and a civilian one. I know there are exceptions, but generally speaking, the civilian prisoner chose a life of crime and was finally caught and convicted.

The Army prisoner, on the other hand, chose to serve his country, lived a decent and disciplined life, and then was accused of doing something thoughtless or stupid or, in some cases, politically or diplomatically incorrect.

Let me give you an example. Another officer in my cellblock had been promoted to captain and got called up to active duty from reserves. The Army reimbursed him for his re-settlement costs but, several years later, after this fellow had gone to work for the Department of Homeland Security, the Army concluded that the officer had wrongly bundled up some personal bills into his reimbursement. The Army decided to make an example of him: eighteen wasted months at Leavenworth and a life ruined.

For reasons I don't understand, the incarceration strategy for the civilian and the Army guy is roughly the same. The emphasis is on punishing and isolating, not on rehabilitating. One guy I knew who was doing three and a half years had as his job mopping up and cleaning the dining hall. One day they were shorthanded behind the counter, and they assigned him to dish out food. It may not seem like a "promotion," but to this guy it was. He got to interact with people, make decisions, and assume some responsibility. When the regular guy came back, my friend was sent back to cleanup.

The next day I saw him in the cellblock and commented, "Looks like you had a short promotion and looked like you were enjoying it." He replied, "I did. I actually liked doing something that felt productive for a few minutes." This guy was smart and had been tracking for a successful career. To see an institution with great potential for rescuing and rehabbing young soldiers like this do almost nothing to help them along is discouraging.

Several books by Dr. Charles Colson confirmed my suspicion. Colson was special counsel to President Nixon and was prosecuted for his role in the Watergate scandal. Imprisoned himself, Colson became a committed evangelical leader and started Prison Fellowship Ministries and other charitable organizations. He writes that he has found many inmates incarcerated wrongly or punished too severely. I was finding the same.

To deal with my frustration, I turned to the Bible, in this case, Micah 6:8: "He has showed you, O man, what is good. And what does the Lord require of you? To act justly and to love mercy and to walk humbly with your God." This was a timely and fitting lesson.

Only over the past several years have I begun to see the need to walk with God as His humble servant. I was grateful to have had this time to strengthen my faith. I began to see the wisdom of the Bible and to understand how the Founding Fathers absorbed it and incorporated it. I pray that my children will learn these lessons sooner, faster and more thoroughly than I have, and that they will perpetuate these principles. I hope that their friends, neighbors, and fellow Americans do the same.

Rather than just gripe about the shortcomings of prison life, I decided to do something constructive. I met with the education staff several times and volunteered to teach any academic class possible. Fortunately, we were able to plan and start the facility's first math class for prisoners. After lots of bureaucratic delays—the authorities were always afraid something would go wrong—they provided me with the material and means to get started. My hope was that it would be fun for some of the inmates and would help them get ready for college-level classes when they got out.

When we finally got going, all went smoothly. We had five guys in the class. We met three nights a week. All the guys studied and did well. I enjoyed teaching. It wasn't easy, but these guys were motivated.

About this time I had started reading Frederic Bastiat. Bastiat wrote in the first half of the 19th century in France, but his book *The Law* sounds like something that might have been written last year. I found this passage relevant in the light of Congress' demand for other people's money to take care of their friends:

> When [the law] has exceeded its proper functions, it has not done so merely in some inconsequential and debatable matters. The law has gone further than this; it has acted in direct opposition to its own purpose. The law has been used to destroy its own objective: it has been applied to annihilating the justice that it was supposed to maintain; to limiting and destroying rights which its real purpose was to respect. The law has placed the collective force at the disposal of the unscrupulous who wish, without risk, to exploit the person, liberty, and

property of others. It has converted plunder into a right, in order to protect plunder, and it has converted lawful defense
into a crime, in order to punish lawful defense.

In addition to educating myself about these big themes, I was also school-
ing myself in the ways to solve the cheesy little problems prison presents.
One such problem is that the authorities don't give you nearly enough toilet paper. If you ask for more, they look at you as if you had asked for a
grindstone to sharpen your homemade shank.

So, if you can help it, you don't use the commode in your own cell. You
use the restroom everywhere else that you can—at the barbershop, the library, the medical clinic, the administrative offices, wherever. Besides, ce-
ramic and plastic beat cold stainless steel any day.

A few weeks before my exit date, the other short-termers and I were put
into a transition group. In addition to our regular duties, we would periodi-
cally be called for career-counseling sessions, résumé workshops, mock
job interviews and the like.

There were about twenty of us in this group. The rumors, of course, flew
about who did what, but everyone more or less knew what I was in for.
When Obama released what appeared to be his long-form birth certificate,
a few of my new pals asked if he did this because I was coming out. I am a
realist, I told them; I don't think so.

As eager as we all were to get out, we never knew when something might
go wrong. Most of the guards were respectful, but some were troublemak-
ers. They might decide to search a cell and find extra Q-tips or who knows
what, which would lead to various punishments. In prison, you can never
count on authorities making the kinds of rational decisions they would
make for men who control their own destinies. Here, there is always the
anxiety that comes with living in an arbitrary system.

With just a few days left, four of us were moved to the same pod where I
had spent my first few days. The transitional details did not take much effort, and we were no longer working, so we played cards to pass the time
and to ease our jitters about leaving.

One of guys leaving with us was a class clown of sorts. But as I got to
know him in those last few days, he turned out to be an OK guy. I learned
that his mother was a crackhead, and he had been headed for prison or an
early grave before the Army saved his life. He screwed up the opportunity,

but there was still hope for him. This reminded me that when you look inside people, you can almost always find goodness, and that if you choose not to look, your snap judgments can often be wrong.

Goodness, however, is not something easily found in a bureau-cracy, especially a prison bureaucracy, especially an Army prison bureaucracy. As my departure date loomed, I kept waiting for the authorities to find something wrong, and they confirmed my anxieties by doing just that.

When they asked who would pick me up, I gave them three possibilities: my brother Greg, driving up from Wichita; my friend and adviser Marco, flying in from Maryland; or my great new friends Jim and Peggy DeJarnatt, who lived just across the river in Weston, Missouri.

I made many new friends on my journey, but the DeJarnatts deserve a special note of thanks. I had not known them before I was incarcerated. I first heard of them when they sent me a Christmas card that I found very uplifting. They proved incredibly gracious. They volunteered to have Pili and the kids stay with them, and they hosted a doctor friend of mine on his visit. Though I was supposed to receive only visitors I had known before I was imprisoned, I finessed the DeJarnatts onto the list. Shhh! Don't tell anyone.

For something so crucial to them as a prisoner's departure, the authorities had no stomach for unforeseen circumstances. They gave me all kinds of grief as to who could meet and who could not and finally ruled that only Greg and Marco were eligible to meet me. Go figure.

After a thorough strip search and a complete search of my one duffel bag, a guard put me in a van and drove me to a bank in downtown Leavenworth. It was May 13, a cool, sunny spring day, and I was savoring every minute of it. Inside the bank, I withdrew the stash I had managed to save in my prison account: $25.41.

After that, the guard drove me to a nearby car park where the prison had arranged for me to meet Greg and Marco. The van pulled up alongside them. The guard checked their IDs, shook my hand, and drove away. Jim and Peggy had been waiting across the street and raced over when the van pulled away. As you can imagine, there was a whole lot of hugging going on.

After we were hugged out, Greg, Marco, and I headed to Kansas City International Airport less than a half hour away. We stayed overnight at an airport hotel. A local news affiliate team tracked me down and requested an interview that evening. I complied, even though I hate interviews. The next morning we boarded a Southwest Airlines plane for BWI. Say what you will about airplane travel, but it is a lot more enjoyable unshackled.

On the flight home, I had a couple of hours to ask myself what I had accomplished. I still don't know that answer for sure, but I know that I honored my officer's oath. That was more than enough to allow me to exit the plane with my head held high.

When we passed security at BWI, fifty or so people were waiting in the concourse with banners and balloons. Some I recognized and some I did not, but right in front and moving quickly toward me were the ones I was most eagerly looking for.

There was no missing Pili's bright, smiling face. It showed through like a beacon. The kids were jumping up and down beside her, and they all came running to grab and hug me, and here, in the free world, no one said they could not.

I was home.

19. Epilogue: Walking Righteous

(Or at Least Trying To)

Several months removed from prison now, I thought I would share what I have learned along the way. Not being the most eloquent guy on the planet, I recruited some of my friends to help me find the right words. This first quote comes from Thomas Jefferson. It speaks for itself:

> Every government degenerates when trusted to the rulers of the people alone. The people themselves, therefore, are its only safe depositories.

Few people were as extraordinary as Patrick Henry. He was one bold guy. Just nine days after taking his seat in the Virginia Legislature in 1765, he introduced a bill protesting the Stamp Act, still another British imposition on the colonists. When others wavered, he stayed the course. From day one, he was protesting corruption in government and insisting on republican principles:

> Those who expect to reap the blessings of freedom must undergo the fatigue of supporting it. It cannot be emphasized too strongly or too often that this great nation was founded, not by

religionists, but by Christians, not on religions, but on the gospel of Jesus Christ! For this very reason, peoples of other faiths have been afforded asylum, prosperity, and freedom of worship here.

Bad men cannot make good citizens. It is when a people forget God that tyrants forge their chains. A vitiated state of morals, a corrupted public conscience, is incompatible with freedom. No free government, or the blessings of liberty, can be preserved to any people but by a firm adherence to justice, moderation, temperance, frugality, and virtue; and by a frequent recurrence to fundamental principles.

Then, of course, there is Henry's most famous speech of all, which he first presented in the House of Burgesses on March 23, 1775. The question before the floor was whether Virginia should mobilize for military action against the advancing British. There can be no doubt where Henry stood on this issue:

There is no longer any room for hope. If we wish to be free— if we mean to preserve inviolate those inestimable privileges for which we have been so long contending—if we mean not basely to abandon the noble struggle in which we have been so long engaged, and which we have pledged ourselves never to abandon until the glorious object of our contest shall be obtained—we must fight! I repeat it, sir, we must fight! An appeal to arms and to the God of hosts is all that is left us!

They tell us, sir, that we are weak; unable to cope with so formidable an adversary. But when shall we be stronger? Will it be the next week, or the next year? Will it be when we are totally disarmed, and when a British guard shall be stationed in every house? Shall we gather strength by irresolution and inaction? Shall we acquire the means of effectual resistance by lying supinely on our backs and hugging the delusive phantom of hope, until our enemies shall have bound us hand and foot? Sir, we are not weak if we make a proper use of those means which the God of nature hath placed in our power. The millions of people, armed in the holy cause of liberty, and in such a country as that which we possess, are invincible by any force which our enemy can send against us.

Besides, sir, we shall not fight our battles alone. There is a just God who presides over the destinies of nations, and who will raise up friends to fight our battles for us. The battle, sir, is not to the strong alone; it is to the vigilant, the active, the brave. Besides, sir, we have no election. If we were base enough to desire it, it is now too late to retire from the contest. There is no retreat but in submission and slavery! Our chains are forged! Their clanking may be heard on the plains of Boston! The war is inevitable—and let it come! I repeat it, sir, let it come.

It is in vain, sir, to extenuate the matter. Gentlemen may cry, Peace, Peace—but there is no peace. The war is actually begun! The next gale that sweeps from the north will bring to our ears the clash of resounding arms! Our brethren are already in the field! Why stand we here idle? What is it that gentlemen wish? What would they have? Is life so dear, or peace so sweet, as to be purchased at the price of chains and slavery? Forbid it, Almighty God! I know not what course others may take; but as for me, give me liberty or give me death!

On a more peaceful note, allow me to share an excerpt from George Washington's proclamation of our first day of Thanksgiving in 1789. President Washington observed that both houses of Congress had asked him to establish a tradition to recognize the "many signal favors of Almighty God." I guess there was no ACLU back then:

Now therefore I do recommend and assign Thursday the 26th day of November next to be devoted by the People of these States to the service of that great and glorious Being, who is the beneficent Author of all the good that was, that is, or that will be – That we may then all unite in rendering unto him our sincere and humble thanks – for his kind care and protection of the People of this country previous to their becoming a Nation – for the signal and manifold mercies, and the favorable interpositions of his providence, which we experienced in the course and conclusion of the late war – for the great degree of tranquility, union, and plenty, which we have since enjoyed – for the peaceable and rational manner in which we have been enabled to establish constitutions of government for our safety and happiness, and particularly the national One now lately instituted, for the civil and religious liberty with which we are blessed, and the means we have of acquiring and diffusing useful knowledge; and in general for all the great and various favors which he hath been pleased to confer upon us.

Someone should write a book with all these great quotes, In fact, someone already has. In fact, about ten such books sit on my nightstand, and I have promised myself to read them soon. Every page I read, I am continually astounded at how wise our Founding Fathers were, how well grounded they were in their faith, and how determined they were to bequeath us the greatest and most prosperous culture that has ever existed even at the risk of their own lives.

These men were an inspiration to me during the ordeal that culminated with my court-martial and imprisonment. Some of the Founding Fathers— and other Americans, men and women, throughout history—have endured the humiliation and fear I have and much worse. What was different in my case was the specific issue.

In regard to this issue, people have asked me several very good questions for sometime now: Were you trying to unseat the president? Was taking this stand worth it? What are you going to do now?

I'll answer one question at a time.

Was I trying to unseat the president? Absolutely not. If the president was constitutionally eligible for his office, he had nothing to fear from me. My inquiry would have only strengthened him.

To be a good physician, I learned long ago, you have to be skeptical and critical. You have to take information from many sources. You have to weigh the benefits versus the risks. You have to include the patient in your decision making. You have to challenge politically correct ideas posing as the truth.

Why, I wonder, can't our political leaders do the same? Why, instead, must they embrace the conventional, ignore the obvious, and treat us like children? Can they not see that more federal government involvement leads to little but more national debt? Individuals built this country, individuals who were supported by family and friends, church and community. If they needed government, it was government closest to home that governed best. Isn't the record obvious?

It is surely not obvious to the media. Today, they write off as crazy even those congressmen and women who read the Constitution aloud on the House floor, let alone anyone who inquires into the president's constitutional eligibility. As a physician and as a citizen, I find this maddening. Rhetoric does not interest me. Accusations interest me even less. I just want the facts, ideally from the original sources.

"Facts are stubborn things," said John Adams, "and whatever may be our wishes, our inclinations, or the dictates of our passions, they cannot alter the state of facts and evidence." I could not agree more. I want to analyze the evidence, validate it, and solve the problem. There is nothing subjective about Obama's eligibility. Either he is eligible or he is not. If he is, I have yet to see the evidence to prove it.

Is this trying to unseat the president? No. This is supporting and defending the Constitution, and I swore an oath to do just that. The Constitution is surely worth defending. It is the document that allows our nation to functional lawfully, a document that has made us a very prosperous country for over 200 years. If we do not honor it, we will not succeed as a nation.

As to whether an officer in the military has the right to question civilian authority, I will leave that answer to you. I relied upon my assessment of the benefits versus the risks, including my evaluation of the possible outcomes. When you have finished my story and the essays in this book, I think you will agree that Congress, the courts, and the executive branch of government should have answered the questions I asked long before I thought to ask them.

Was taking this stand worth it? Yes, absolutely. Beyond the president's eligibility, there are many real concerns for our country now and for the next generation. If I cannot make a stand, how can I expect anyone else to? Much like the world George Orwell painted in his book *1984*, our society today is increasingly weakened by a fear of speaking out. Damn the facts; we have so much guilt over so many issues that we suppress our opinions lest we offend some group or individual.

"Thoughtcrime was not a thing that could be concealed forever," wrote Orwell in *1984*. "You might dodge successfully for a while, even for years, but sooner or later they were bound to get you." That sense of oppression seems all too close to reality now.

There is no doubt that I made some tactical errors along the way. My admission of this at the court-martial may have confused some people. I said at the time that if I had known the likely outcome of my challenge, I would not have initiated it. That is true, certainly regarding tactics. The UCMJ, I learned, was not an adequate vehicle for getting at a deeper truth. Its administrators proved incapable of doing the brave and just thing for the country. There were no Patrick Henrys among them.

I also learned that many of the military and civilian leaders I esteemed were all too human. When soldiers risk their lives, those leading them need to be bold and honest. If they cannot be, they lose my respect. I question whether I can even follow them.

Caring for the soldiers and their families has always been a privilege and honor for me, but I can no longer give my service willingly to a leadership that retreats from hard questions and surrenders its responsibility. So yes, knowing what I know now, I would not have put my trust in people incapable of honoring that trust. I would not have launched an inquiry that would provide no answers. I would not have invited a court-martial whose agents were more interested in assigning guilt than in discovering the truth.

I could not have learned any of this, however, without doing what I did. Would I have done exactly what I did over again? No. Was the process worth the pain? Yes, absolutely.

What am I going to do now? Fortunately, my ordeal has awakened me in many ways. I have, I hope, been able to scrub from my character some of the traces of relativism and self-absorption accumulated over a lifetime. I have developed a complete confidence in the Bible. I have grown even more aware of the importance of family and of country.

There is something to be said for triangles, the most structurally sound of all shapes: mind, body and soul; God, family and country; husband, wife and God; Father, Son and Holy Ghost. The more I learn and experience, the more I wonder why I did not seek or find these comforting answers long ago.

Going forward, I plan to fortify my faith in God, my joy in family, my respect for the Constitution, my knowledge of medicine, and my love of country.

Many new doors have begun to open for me as well. I have seen the military justice system from within; I could have studied it for a lifetime and learned less. I know how the prisons can be improved. I know how the prisoners can be strengthened in their faith and their self-respect. And perhaps most of all, I know how the Constitution can be brought to bear in the execution of justice. It makes no sense that soldiers are denied constitutional protections extended to common criminals.

How the Good Lord enables me to do what I hope to do remains to be seen. In the meantime, I will continue to dedicate my all to God, family and country, and I will embrace and enjoy the journey. It has certainly been interesting so far!

I could not have done it without you. *Thank you.*

Essays by Key Participants in Terry's Action

Joseph Farah: The War on Citizenship

Joseph Farah is editor and chief executive officer of WND (WND.com), the world's first and largest independent Internet news agency. He is the author or co-author of more than a dozen books and serves as publisher of WND Books.

In 2008, I initially dismissed the contention that Barack Obama might not meet the minimal constitutional eligibility requirement for being president.

Surely, I thought, the Democratic Party would not countenance the nomination of a candidate who was not clearly a "natural born citizen."

And what exactly did that phrase mean anyway?

There was plenty of politics to talk about in 2008, and few paid much attention to concerns about Obama's eligibility. In fact, all of the media's concern was over the constitutional eligibility of Obama's opponent—Sen. John McCain, a man who had spent decades in Congress and had previously run for president.

But by the end of that campaign, in which I supported neither candidate, I had become wholly persuaded that Barack Hussein Obama could not possibly be considered a "natural born citizen." And today, after participating in three years of investigative reporting on this topic, I am more convinced than ever.

While deep-seated and widespread suspicion among the American public about Obama's eligibility remains high, many in Washington and the elite media believe the issue ended with the release of what the White House purports to be his long-form, Hawaiian birth certificate.

Making that judgment, however, not only requires us to accept as legitimate the current occupant of the White House, but it also requires us to dumb down the Constitution when it comes to future presidents and vice presidents. It also requires us to overlook the blatantly fraudulent nature of the document he released in April 2011.

That is something I am adamantly unwilling to do.

First of all, I believe Obama's birth certificate is fraudulent. I also believe it is provably and demonstrably not reflective of reality. But I also believe that if it is genuine and if it is factual, it provides absolute proof Obama is not a "natural born citizen" and therefore ineligible to be president.

The Constitution has already been dumbed down in far too many ways. It's been intentional, I believe, by people and institutions that don't like operating in a nation governed by the rule of law rather than the rule of men. Think of how little American schoolchildren are taught about the Constitution—and how little of what they are taught is honest and accurate. That's where the dumbing-down process begins. But it doesn't end there. The mis-education continues through adulthood with one compromise after another. It continues as the founders' intent is obliterated by unaccountable judges and unscrupulous politicians. It continues when the Constitution is no longer perceived as the ultimate rulebook for how we govern ourselves. It continues when the establishment news media misrepresent the subject altogether.

The issue of Obama's eligibility is not a matter of where he was born. It's a matter of whether he is a "natural born citizen." Whether he was born in Hawaii or not makes little difference if his father and mother are who he claims they are—people unable to confer "natural born citizenship" on their son. Whether he was born in Hawaii or not makes little difference if his birth certificate is fraudulent—a misrepresentation of reality and not reflective of his actual legal parenthood. The Constitution doesn't say anyone born in America is eligible to become president—and it doesn't mean that. That's a deliberate media misrepresentation of what it means.

While our immediate concerns about Obama's eligibility are rightly focused on the constitutional crisis before us, how this matter is resolved will have profound ramifications on the future of our political system.

What we do in the next few years will determine whether we permanently dumb down the Constitution and our very concept of citizenship—not just "natural born citizenship."

That's what's at stake right now.

Do we want to remain a constitutional republic of limited government under the rule of law?

Or do we want to hammer what could be the final nail in the coffin of the greatest governing document in the history of the world?

Let's face it. Across the board, American citizenship is losing its meaning, being downgraded, redefined and dumbed down. When the courts interpreted the Fourteenth Amendment to mean that when any mother drops a baby in U.S. territory, no matter her own national status, the baby automatically becomes an American citizen, some cheered. I mourned.

When the American media and political establishment determined that the Constitution's "natural born citizen" eligibility requirement for the president of the United States simply meant "born in the USA," some cheered. I mourned.

More recently we learned that when foreign diplomats, clearly not under the jurisdiction of the U.S., give birth while working in the United States, their offspring are being granted U.S. birthright citizenship. Even stranger, these guest-citizens have advantages no other citizen has—diplomatic immunity, meaning they have no obligation to obey U.S. laws and cannot be prosecuted for offenses. In other words, wittingly or unwittingly, we have created a new breed of "super-citizens" who should not be regarded as citizens at all under the clear rule of law.

That's the conclusion of Jon Feere, author of a report called "Birthright Citizenship for Children of Foreign Diplomats," and, frankly, I don't know what other conclusion anyone could draw from the facts.

Even the U.S. State Department can't provide a straight answer to the simple question of whether the offspring of foreign nationals serving in their country's diplomatic corps in the U.S. are citizens by virtue of their birth on U.S. soil.

Here's what one spokesman from State told Fox News—anonymously, of course: "Persons born in the United States, including a child of foreign diplomats, are legally entitled to an official birth record issued by the Bureau of Vital Statistics of the state in which the child is born. Whether a child born in the United States to a foreign diplomat acquires U.S. citizenship at birth pursuant to the Fourteenth Amendment requires a fact-based analysis."

In other words, the State Department has no answer. It can neither confirm nor deny that foreign diplomats can attain a form of super-citizenship for their American-born offspring. It needs further review. In the meantime, we continue to diminish the essential meaning of U.S. citizenship and the rights and privileges attached to it.

The State Department does take the position that diplomatic immunity and U.S. citizenship are not compatible. Yet Feere's report documents just how easily those two seemingly irreconcilable attributes are being melded in real-life examples today.

Why?

Because the very birth certificate forms used by most states, and designed by the National Center for Health Statistics' Division of Vital Statistics, never asks about the diplomatic status of the parents. Therefore, on the basis of the birth certificate alone, there is no basis upon which the child can be denied citizenship. And, on the basis of the child's parents, there is no way he or she can be denied diplomatic immunity.

What does all this suggest?

It suggests there is widespread confusion—maybe even intentionally— within the government about what it means to be a citizen, a native-born citizen and a natural born citizen. All these terms have become synonymous in the age of Barack Obama. Members of Congress don't even have a clue as to what these terms mean. They're afraid to define these terms because of political correctness and multiculturalism and just because they will probably be called names if they try.

The result? Chaos.

The rule of men, not the rule of law.

And the men who rule don't even have to establish citizenship.

The American political and media elite have determined, for whatever reason, that the Constitution's eligibility requirements for the presidency are just not very important.

That is the only conclusion one can draw from the misinformation, disinformation and disinterest they have shown to the serious questions swirling around not only the unique case of Barack Obama but also to the definition of "natural born citizen" in future presidential elections.

It's not unprecedented that failing republics dumb down eligibility requirements for the presidency. It's not unprecedented that failing republics ignore or obscure eligibility requirements for the presidency. It's not unprecedented that failing republics make tragic mistakes in permitting non-qualified candidates to serve in the presidency.

It happened in 1932 in Germany with a candidate named Adolf Hitler.

In fact, this tragedy, which resulted in the deaths of tens of millions of innocents and the utter destruction of the German republic, is documented in the biography of Dietrich Bonhoeffer by Eric Metaxas.

We learn that on March 13, 1932, the day the German national election was being held to determine who would be president, "Nazi rowdies rode around in the backs of trucks with megaphones, stirring things up. A month earlier Hitler was found ineligible to run since he was born and reared in Austria. But this problem was strenuously shoved through a loophole, and he would run after all."

On January 30, 1933, Hitler became the chancellor of Germany.

Imagine how the course of history might have been changed had that "loophole" not been found—if the German people, political elite and media elite had held firm to their constitution that required presidents to be German-born when Hitler clearly was not.

Now, don't get me wrong. My purpose here is not to compare Obama to Hitler. Hitler is in a unique historical class of tyrants, fiends and mass murderers. There's Hitler and Josef Stalin and Mao Zedong. Together they are responsible for the deaths of more than 100 million people.

For perspective, Obama has merely contributed to the economic and moral degradation of the greatest country on earth.

I use the Hitler illustration only to demonstrate there are real-world consequences to bending the rules in constitutional republics for political expediency.

That's what happened in Germany in 1932.

It is happening again in America in the 21st century.

The media and political elite are in abject denial about the meaning of the U.S. Constitution's "natural born citizen" requirement for presidents—even more so today than in 2008.

It does not mean born in the USA.

It does not mean the child of one citizen parent.

It does not mean a guy who offers up a phony and invalid birth certificate.

It does not mean a person who claims biological parentage by a visiting foreign student.

It does not mean a person who claims an adoptive father who was a foreign national.

It does not mean a person who went to live with that adoptive father in his own country and registered for school as a citizen of Indonesia.

It does not mean a person whose very own citizenship was questioned by U.S. immigration officials in his boyhood.

It does not apply to a person whose "natural born citizenship" has never been investigated by any controlling legal authority in America.

And that's who resides in the White House today because the media and political elite don't want to do their jobs in ensuring that the Constitution prevails.

So we stumble along and define down what the Constitution says—pretending instead that it requires a presidential candidate to be born in the USA and pretending that the current occupant of the White House has demonstrated that he actually meets that criteria.

Some fifteen state legislatures were concerned enough about the Constitution that they introduced or even passed legislation requiring that future presidential candidates demonstrate eligibility before getting on the ballot. All of them claimed these legislative initiatives had nothing to do with Obama, but instead had to do with constitutional integrity. Yet, when Obama produced a document he claims is his birth certificate, these initiatives all went away.

Not only are we about to allow Obama to seek re-election as an ineligible candidate, we also are about to amend the Constitution by default.

We could only get to this point in American history through the systematic vilification of a heroic figure like Lt. Col. Terrence Lakin.

That's what the media perpetrated to discredit him, to ensure he could not get a fair military trial, to ensure that his concerns were misrepresented, to ensure that he would be punished for his sincere and heartfelt concerns for constitutional integrity

Do you remember the old concept of presumption of innocence?

We all learned in school that you were "innocent until proven guilty" in a court of law.

When I first entered the ranks of the news media, the profession actually adopted that as a standard in its news coverage of those accused.

Well, like so many other media standards, you can throw them out the window when it comes to those brave men and women who stand up for principle and the Constitution in challenging Barack Obama to prove his eligibility for office.

Lakin was tried and convicted by the media in one of the worst examples of journalistic malpractice I have ever seen in my life. And it wasn't just MSNBC, *The New York Times*, ABC, CBS and CNN. It was equally true of The Associated Press, the largest news-gathering operation in the world, and Fox News, the supposed "fair and balanced" alternative to the old guard.

Here are some of the highlights of the distortion of truth from a sample AP story posted on FoxNews.com—*before* Lakin ever had an opportunity for a hearing:

> Though officials in Hawaii verify that Obama was born there, so-called birthers claim he was born outside the United States and is ineligible to be president.

> Hawaii Health Director Dr. Chiyome Fukino issued statements last year and in October 2008 saying that she's seen vital records that prove Obama is a natural-born U.S. citizen.

> Both Fukino and the state registrar of vital statistics have verified that the Health Department holds Obama's original birth certificate.

See what I mean?

Tried and convicted in the media.

Lakin was portrayed as nothing but a "conspiracy nut" because there was no substance to his request.

Whatever happened to the presumption of innocence?

Whatever happened to fair and balanced?

Whatever happened to curiosity?

Whatever happened to the idea that the press doesn't just accept handouts from government officials as gospel truth?

I empathized with Lt. Col. Lakin because I know what it's like going against the grain of a media onslaught. But Lt. Col. Lakin did something I never was required to do. He put his career on the line. He put his reputation on the line. He put his very freedom on the line.

You would expect the media might be just a little more responsible and even-handed in a story like this. First of all, it's a total misrepresentation of Lt. Col. Lakin's view and the point of so-called "birthers" to suggest they believe Obama was foreign-born. Like millions of other Americans, Lt. Col. Lakin asked to see evidence that Obama was constitutionally eligible to be president. We're still waiting to see it.

In America, we don't leave it to appointed state officials with no constitutional law expertise—people like Hawaii Health Director Dr. Chiyome Fukino—to determine whether someone is constitutionally eligible to serve in the White House.

One has to wonder where the "compassion" of the media went when it came time to telling the story of Lt. Col. Terrence Lakin.

Likewise, Barack Obama loves to portray himself as a compassionate humanitarian.

Assuring justice and avoiding unnecessary punishment are such obsessions for him, Obama would have us believe, that he opposes detaining those participating in acts of war against the U.S. He even insisted on a civilian trial in New York for the man who confessed to masterminding the September 11 attacks.

But Obama's compassion does have its limits.

We discovered those limits in the case of Lt. Col. Terrence Lakin.

Obama let him go to prison—even though he hadn't committed any crimes, had served his country honorably in foreign wars and had impeccable reviews from his superiors.

All Lakin asked was proof of that simple requirement in the form of Obama's long-form birth certificate to be released publicly so that he and millions of other Americans in doubt as to Obama's qualifications could sleep at night knowing the Constitution still prevails as the law of the land.

Instead of complying with this request, Obama took a hard line. He actively fought all legal efforts to get him to release his birth certificate, unlike his rival in the 2008 presidential campaign, John McCain, who responded promptly when questions about his eligibility arose. Obama spent millions of dollars fighting efforts to release his birth certificate.

And then four months after Lt. Col. Lakin went to prison, Obama decided to summon what he claims is his long-form birth certificate from Hawaii and release it publicly after all.

What kind of a man does that?

Where's the pardon for Lt. Col. Lakin?

Obama has compassion for the worst kind of terrorists and murderers, but he couldn't find an ounce of compassion for Lt. Col. Terry Lakin. Does that make sense?

Would a truly compassionate man let another good person go to prison for no reason? Would a truly compassionate man let another be incarcerated for spite? If Obama had a good reason for releasing his birth certificate in April 2011, why didn't he release it in February to spare Lt. Col. Lakin a prison sentence?

If you're still not sure where you stand on the issue of Barack Obama's eligibility, ask yourself this simple question: Was Obama's behavior toward Lt. Col. Lakin the kind of behavior we expect from real Americans?

&

Miki Booth: From Near Dream to New Job: Moving Communities to Action

If anyone had told me three years ago that someday I would become a political activist and candidate for the U.S. Congress, I would have laughed in his face. Nothing could be more absurd. I hated politics. Always did and always would, I believed. In fact, three years ago I was looking forward to my husband, Fred, retiring for a second time so we could finally relax and spend time enjoying our secluded acreage and all the pets we had accumulated over the years, including a few horses.

Fred retired from the Hawai'i County Police Department a dozen or so years earlier, and we made the decision to leave the islands in search of some rural property big enough to keep horses and allow our dogs to run free. We found what we were looking for in northeastern Oklahoma, and we were on the verge of living our dream when my world was shattered by an astonishing revelation: the man running for president of the United States was a fraud.

Billed as the "Community Organizer from Hawai'i," Barack Obama enjoyed the unique distinction of coming from the fiftieth state, the island paradise of multiculturalism and Aloha, but the truth jumped out at me—Obama was a product of mainland affirmative action. He was a community organizer, not from Hawai'i really, but from Chicago.

The first I heard from candidate Obama was in 2008 when I received a request in the mail for a seventy-five-dollar donation. My first impressions of the man and the message were extremely positive. He was going to unite the country with "hope" and "change" for a better future for America. Looking at the handsome young man on the card, I had no doubt he could achieve his mission, and I set the request aside planning to send a check the next time I paid bills.

I was pleased and surprised that he was from Hawai'i—pleased that a presidential candidate was from my island home but surprised that I didn't pick up on that fact. For sure, his name and looks were not peculiar to Hawai'ian cultural heritage. Curiosity set me to find out more about this "keiki" or child of Hawai'i. I had no doubt I would discover that I had a link to him somewhere. Maybe I knew someone that he went to school with or was familiar with the beach that he might have hung out at. Even though he was clearly much younger than I, I thought for sure I would find some connection to the man who could very well be our next president.

That wasn't to be. The very first thing I found out in my research was that he attended Punahou School. Immediately that placed him above and outside my circles. Punahou, a college preparatory academy, was for the "rich haoles," the islands' elites. As I looked into Obama's background, my mild disappointment began to turn to outright alarm. It was as if I was being presented with a nicely packaged product, but like the layers of an onion, each layer I peeled back revealed something not right. The more I looked the more I was frightened of this man. His connection to radicals Bill Ayers and Rashid Khalidi and his self-confessed history of cocaine and marijuana use not only turned me against Obama the candidate but also compelled me to campaign against him by alerting others to the things I found out. That there was no counter to the disturbing facts I was uncovering convinced me Obama had an agenda, and it wasn't to unite our country.

The anti-Obama campaign I waged in Hawai'i through e-mails and phone calls left me depressed and saddened. Obama was a rock star in Hawai'i. My pleas were falling on deaf ears, but worse, I got hit with a backlash of tsunami proportions. The most hurtful rejection came from my high school classmates from Kaneohe: "Remove me from your list." "STOP SENDING ME E-MAILS." "ENOUGH ALREADY! I'm voting for him anyway." "And you want Sarah Palin? That stupid woman!" "I would never vote for a Republican—They're MURDERERS!" "John McCain will get us into another war."

I was stunned. They didn't know what I knew about Obama, and they didn't care. They also assumed that I was pro-McCain, which, after the backlash, I became. When Sarah Palin joined the team, I was elated and did my best to support the two of them. But on November 5, 2008, when they lost to a veritable ghost of extremely dubious origins, I was reduced to a meek, introverted woman, much the way I'd been before Obama arrived on the scene.

I had good reason to retreat. I suspected my phone had been tapped. During my furious e-mailing campaign leading up to the election, there were times I picked up my phone to make a call and heard tones of someone else on the line dialing. I'd had the same landline number for over eight years and never, never had that happen before. It was very unnerving, but my husband, Fred, insisted it was my imagination. Shortly thereafter, a strange thing happened that I knew wasn't my imagination. When I told Fred about it, he got upset and accused me of buying into conspiracy theories. He would later realize the conspiracy to take over the government was no theory. Still, for the time being, I kept my fears from Fred and maintained an upbeat facade around the house minus talk of politics.

I did, however, tell my growing list of contacts about the odd incident that came on the heels of the phone taps, and they believed me. They knew the power of the Democratic Party and its leader of choice. My rants against Obama were extreme, and no doubt drew the attention of his campaign machine.

Here is what happened. I was on my way to pick up mail at the post office located about two miles south of our home. Our property is set back from the state highway and nearly hidden from view. As I approached the main highway, I saw work vehicles parked across the highway in a church parking lot. I put on my blinker to turn left and made a mental note of the large utility truck and small pickups with several men standing around or leaning on their vehicles as though they were waiting for something.

I did not recognize the logo on the truck, so I knew it wasn't our local electric, water, cable or phone workers. I also noted that the men were young, good-looking and dressed sharply, though casually—definitely not work clothes. On my way back from the post office, as I crested the hill, I saw that the men were still there. Instead of turning right to return home, I put on my left turn signal, pulled up to my mailbox and checked for junk mail. As soon as my left-turn blinker went on and I started pulling toward the group of men, they jumped to attention, got into their vehicles, and sped away.

"What was that about?" I said to myself. "What odd behavior."

I collected my mail and went home. Later that day, when I thought about the incident, I got hit with a strange chill. It dawned on me that I was being monitored. My phone was being tapped, and those men had come to see if this woman, this radical anti-Obama activist, was indeed a threat to a presidential candidate.

It made sense. Everything about them was suspect. Except for the church and a flea market, the surrounding area is void of commercial property.

The highway frontage consists of long expanses of pasture and a few homes. So it was unusual to see strangers obviously waiting for something at that location. If they had been watching me, they would not have expected me to turn left and drive right up to them. They were startled, and it was I who scared them. They were burnt toast. I was onto them, or so they thought.

The incident didn't deter me and instead made me more determined than ever to stay in the fight. My contacts grew, and before long I had developed a following of citizens who recognized the truth in what I was saying. We were all flabbergasted that no one in media was even talking about our concerns.

After Obama won the election, I grew depressed and began to withdraw. Fred noticed and tried to lift my spirits. He got me to agree to give Obama a chance. Maybe it won't be so bad, he hinted, but already Obama was out with his pen, passing executive orders indifferent to Congress or the Constitution.

Obama soon proved that he was not the moderate he had advertised himself to be. People started to comment, "Whoa, I didn't sign up for this." Most, however, were still willing to give him a chance. They looked for a reason to cut him some slack, but I couldn't do that. Too many things bothered me.

Subprime mortgages, it was becoming clear, were the cause of the financial meltdown. Fannie Mae and Freddie Mac had employed a lobbying strategy to get lawmakers on their side. They strategically directed campaign contributions to the congressional representatives who were supposed to regulate their industry. In the 2008 cycle, then-senator Obama received the third-largest amount of $105,849 from Fannie and Freddie. Chris Dodd received the most at $133,900 and second-highest was John Kerry's $111,000. Hillary Clinton's take was $75,550.

There's nothing illegal about this. It's done all the time, we're told. But this is what's wrong with government. It's the cronyism, the "you scratch my back and I'll scratch yours," and if it's not illegal, it's certainly immoral.

And I remembered something else. As a lawyer, Obama represented ACORN (Association of Community Organizers for Reform Now) in a lawsuit against the state of Illinois. Along with a team of Chicago lawyers,

Obama won the 1995 suit forcing the state of Illinois to implement the "Motor Voter" bill, a law designed to make it easier for people to vote by allowing them to register at the same time they apply for a driver's license.

Millions of people register to vote this way, and the hasty, slapdash nature of it lends itself to election fraud. The capacity for runaway fraud in just such a law was not lost on ACORN, nor was it lost on Obama in his ruthless drive to win the 2008 presidential election.

Obama also instructed new community organizers in his leadership role with ACORN. He taught them the tactics of leftist icon Saul Alinsky and directed them to the preferred targets: the banks that weren't enthusiastic about making home loans to people who couldn't afford them and had almost no means of repaying them.

"Pressure them! Stir up dissatisfaction and discontent! Agitate! Agitate! Your job is getting people to move, to act, agitate to the point of conflict!" instructed Alinsky in his book *Rules for Radicals.* And under the guidance of Barack Hussein Obama they did just that. Showing up in hordes, with picket signs and bullhorns, agitators shouted and chanted and demanded the banks give loans to anyone and everyone because everybody has a right to home ownership.

It was clear to me, as it was to others: Obama had a hand in the financial collapse of 2008. There was no doubt in my mind that he had helped cause this, and now he owned the means by which to repay those who had helped him do it. It was time for me to do something more useful than mope around the house complaining.

Sometime in February 2009, I watched a news feature on FOX News about a group staging a reenactment of the Boston Tea Party. "That's what we need," I thought, "a rebellion of sorts to let Obama know we've had it and we're not going to take it anymore."

Bob Basso, a motivational speaker and longtime Hawai'i resident and radio/TV personality, had created a series of YouTube videos in the character of Thomas Paine calling for "A Second American Revolution." The videos circulated on the Internet, and people everywhere were standing up and saying, "I've had enough and I'm not going to take it anymore!"

We answered the call. We were ready for action. We were champing at the bit to tell our elected officials that they worked for us. We wanted to tell them to "STOP THE SPENDING!" and "STOP TRAMPLING ON THE

CONSTITUTION!" "WE WANT OUR COUNTRY BACK!" "BACK
TO THE IDEALS ESTABLISHED BY OUR FOUNDERS!" "NO
MORE BAILOUTS!" "WE WANT LIMITED GOVERNMENT!"
"FREE MARKET PRINCIPLES!" "OUR RIGHT TO BEAR ARMS
SHALL NOT BE INFRINGED!" "WHAT PART OF 'SHALL NOT BE
INFRINGED' DO YOU NOT UNDERSTAND?"

We had a lot to say. At least I did. I had no idea what to do, but I was
ready for action. I was angry, and I wasn't going to let Obama, House
Speaker Nancy Pelosi, and Senate Majority Leader Harry Reid dismantle
our Constitutional Republic if I had anything to do with it. I now knew
there were others just like me, and if enough of us banded together to fight
for a cause as noble as rescuing the very heart and soul of our beloved nation, I believed we could do it.

The next call to action was CNBC's Rick Santelli from the floor of the
Chicago Mercantile Exchange. Santelli called for a Tea Party during a rant
protesting government overreach into the financial sector and the automo-
tive industry. His message became an instant classic. He captured the
mood of the country. Soon there were Tea Parties springing up in towns
and cities from coast to coast. It was exciting. It was something we could
do in our own communities to make our voices heard. With tax day only
two months away, word spread calling for a national day of protest on
Wednesday, April 15.

I was a member of the Patriotic Resistance, Resistnet.com, an offshoot of
Grassfire.com, an online leader in the conservative movement. I checked
the website for listings of any upcoming events in Oklahoma. The closest
Tea Party I could find was in Tulsa, an hour and a half away, and I began
calling people I knew to see if they wanted to go. But it was a workday,
and the few people I knew had to work.

Then it hit me: I didn't need to drive all the way to Tulsa. I could plan a
Tea Party rally right in my own town. The date was set; all I had to do was
select a location and time, let people know, and they would show up with
signs and American flags and we'd all be part of a modern-day revolution.
I called the city parks and recreation office to find out if I needed a permit
for using Riverview Park. I didn't. The pavilions in the park were on a
first-come, first-served basis, so I just needed to make sure someone got
there early enough to hold our spot. The covered area of the pavilion was

somewhat small, but we could use the picnic tables provided for our sign-up sheets, petitions, and stacks of flyers and literature.

I received an e-mail from AFA, the American Family Association, announcing their T.E.A. (Taxed Enough Already) website for information and assistance for planning Tea Parties and a registration database to list scheduled events with links to websites and e-mail. "This is so great," I remember thinking. There were already hundreds of Tea Parties listed. I checked Oklahoma and found several locations throughout the state but nothing planned for Miami, so I registered my event and called it the Route 66 Tea Party. I hoped the name would draw people from Kansas and Missouri since we were so close to both states and the iconic highway tied us together.

Then I got nervous. What if I held a revolution and nobody came? I felt obligated to put together a program and find a speaker or speakers. What about music and a sound system? Would we need it? How much would that cost? What if it rains? The pavilion wouldn't be big enough for more than about twenty people because of the picnic tables. How much would it cost to put a notice in the paper? Can I really pull this off?

All of a sudden I lost my nerve. This was all waaaaaay outside my 'comfort zone,' and I wilted like a four-leaf clover in the hot sun. "I don't need to do this," I thought. "I don't even know anybody in Miami. Surely one of the leaders in the business community will answer the call. I'll go to the Tulsa rally. I know a few people in Tulsa. Alan lives there. He'll go with me unless he can't get away from work. It's at lunchtime, too, so he can at least meet me and stay for a little while, anyway. It's the least he can do for his mom."

I had caved. Gone was the determined patriot willing to step into an uncomfortable situation to fight for her country and lead others to take up signs and raise their voices to pledge their allegiance to the flag that represents our nation, a country of freedom and liberty bought and paid for by the blood of our founding fathers and the men and women of our armed forces.

I would still do my part; I just didn't want to do the planning, organizing, and shelling out the money it would take to put on an event. The rally I imagined in my mind would be pretty cool, though. I'd had enough experience as an event planner over the course of my career in the hospitality industry. It wasn't as if I didn't know what to do.

That much said, I just wanted to live a simple life. It was too much work, and even though I didn't have a job, I was needed at home and besides, I just flat out didn't want to do it. My home was my responsibility, the animals needed me, and I was comfortable in my element. They were my family, and I enjoyed the company of my pets. Why would I want to leave my comfort zone if I didn't have to?

I felt I was doing my part with the hours I spent on the computer writing and forwarding e-mails alerting and informing the other patriots in my address book who also believed that we were in trouble as a nation and that Barack Hussein Obama was part of the problem. I had a whole fourteen or fifteen people in my address book. Quality, not quantity, was my qualifier. My "signature" on every e-mail I sent was "In liberty, Miki" and under my name, "When the people fear their government, there is tyranny; when the government fears the people, there is liberty." —Thomas Jefferson

Then something happened. Pancho, a local businessman and heavy-equipment operator, came to our house to give an estimate on some bulldozing work we needed done. Pancho and Fred were talking, and I heard Pancho make a disparaging remark about government regulations. I'd never spoken to him directly before, but I interjected a question: "Pancho, what did you think of the election?"

"What a disaster that was," he answered. "We've got a socialist politician with no qualifications or experience running our country. That can't be anything but bad." He continued, "John McCain was no prize either. How about that Sarah Palin, though, don't you love her?"

I assured him I did. Fred, too.

Had I not heard Pancho's remark about government, I would have gone on thinking he was a typical Democrat, a local good ol' boy like most of the residents of Ottawa County, where we've lived since 1999. I was so encouraged to learn that he was a fellow patriot that I told him I was starting a revolution. "Dang," he said. "I was gonna do that."

I was committed. I had a partner. All the ideas I had floating around in my head for the Tea Party started swirling again.

"Hey, Pancho, can we use one of your flatbed trailers for a stage?" I asked.

He replied, "Hon, you can have anything you want."

Later that same day I received a phone call from Ray Wilson, who had seen my listing on the AFA website. He'd been thinking of putting together a rally and had actually revisited the site to post his information when he saw my listing. We discussed each other's ideas. Ray wanted to go with my plan. He runs a busy air-conditioning and heating business and didn't have the luxury of time the way I did. We exchanged e-mails and promised each other we'd stay in touch.

Others also saw the listing on the AFA website and either called or left a message on the site, which the website then forwarded to me. New contacts expanded my address book. Most of the phone calls I received were from people who wanted to attend and asked for specifics on location and time.

The next person to step up to help was Shelly Picher, an experienced activist who'd had many dealings with city hall. She was petite but would back down to no one. Shelly knew Miami and the surrounding areas like the back of her hand. She immediately went to work looking for an alternate location in case we had bad weather. She also would check with people she knew for a sound system, and she stayed in touch with me daily.

"What a dynamo!" I thought. "I'll bet city officials don't enjoy seeing her come through the door, especially if they know she's there to ask some very pointed questions."

Within a week of meeting Ray and Shelly, I scheduled a TEA Party meeting in Grove, Oklahoma, a lake community about a thirty-minute drive from Miami. We had a few friends and acquaintances there that I knew would come. I rented a small conference room in the community center and put a notice in the local paper. Shelly, always on the ball, called the local radio station with the details and they announced the meeting in their community events time slots.

About a dozen people showed up. I'd e-mailed a press release to area media and halfway expected a reporter to show up also, but none did. The meeting was successful nonetheless. Charlie Miller, a longtime friend from California and recent resident of Grove, was there. Charlie Woltz and his wife Nelda wanted to help. So did Barry Helin, a retired Marine, and Channa Morton. The others who came signed the attendance sheet and said they would see us on tax day at the park in Miami. Charlie, Nelda,

Barry, and Channa all agreed to come to my house on April 8 for a planning meeting for the April 15 event. The thirty-minute ride home on the dark, twisty highway around Grand Lake was a lonely one.

If I had known then that I would spend thousands of miles and countless lonely hours of driving in my Dodge minivan traveling to and returning from Tea Parties and related events like this one, would I have continued on as I did? In a heartbeat! Tea Party may mean different things to different people, but at the core of the movement is the firm belief that we are endowed by our creator with unalienable rights to life, liberty and the pursuit of happiness. We overwhelmingly believe the Constitution strictly limits the federal government and recognizes and protects these unalienable rights.

&

Cmdr. Charles Kerchner (Ret): An Officer's Oath Does Not Expire or Retire

Or why I came out of retirement and committed over 36 non-stop months to the Obama constitutional ineligibility issue battle

Commander Kerchner is the lead plaintiff in the Kerchner v. Obama & Congress et al. *lawsuit.*

What follows is the solemn oath of office I took upon becoming a Commissioned Officer in the United States Naval Reserve:

> I, Charles Frederick Kerchner, Jr., do solemnly swear that I will support and defend the Constitution of the United States against all enemies, foreign and domestic, that I will bear true faith and allegiance to the same; that I take this obligation freely, without any mental reservation or purpose of evasion; and that I will well and faithfully discharge the duties of the office upon which I am about to enter; So help me God.

My address and retirement remarks to the assembled unit and guests at my naval reserve center when I retired from the U.S. Naval Reserves in 1995:

> Captain Unruh, men and women of Combat Logistics Group Two Det 204, family and friends—I thank you for the kind words and honors bestowed upon me today.
>
> I came to this organization thirty-three years ago as a young man. It was 1962, the height of the Cold War, the year of the Cuban missile crisis. The closest we've ever come to global nuclear war. The Soviet Empire was poised to roll over Europe and maybe us too. I felt a calling, a sense of duty to serve my country. But as a young man I was also seeking excitement and adventure.
>
> So I joined the Naval Reserve. Because I was only seventeen years old, I had to obtain my parents' permission to enlist. They gave it willingly and with pride, so I left home and went off to serve my country.
>
> I did my duty. I also found some excitement and adventure. But, more importantly, along the way I found something else. I grew

up as a result of the experience. I became a man. I got an education in the school of the real world. I saw how people live in other countries and learned to realize how fortunate we are in this country. I found a sense of belonging and comradeship with my shipmates.

I learned leadership and honor. I gained wisdom. Via the GI Bill, the Navy even paid for a large part of my college education. I truly would not be the person I am today without the experiences I gained in the Navy.

The Cold War is over... My calling to military service is over... I have stood the watch for thirty-three years ... It is now time for me to stand aside... I now turn the watch over to you, my shipmates, who like me have volunteered to serve and defend our country.

I stand aside, but you carry on. And although we hope that the freedom from external threats this country now enjoys will last forever, we learn from the past ... that the bookmarks of world history are the names of its wars! So you... who will now have the watch... must be vigilant... and you must be prepared. Stand the watch tirelessly. Stand it well. I wish you fair winds and following seas. I stand relieved.

Thus on 30 September 1995 I ended my thirty-three years of combined active duty and reserve service with the U.S. Naval Reserves. I left the guarding of the country and Constitution from threats to its existence in the hands of the next generation and proceeded to move forward to the next phase of my life. In my civilian work I continued running my small manufacturing business founded in 1969 until I sold the business and fully retired in 2002. I was looking forward to enjoying the rest of my life as a happily retired husband, father, and grandfather who had done his duty to serve his country to the best of his ability.

Now let us fast-forward in time to early January 2008. A man named Barack Hussein Obama II appears on the political radar screen. He is being highly promoted by the mainstream media as a candidate for the presidency of the United States. As a retired military officer, I knew if elected he would also become the commander in chief of our military forces. So I began to ask myself, Who is this person, Obama? I had not heard much of anything about him prior to his running for the office of President.

I knew Obama was a new senator from Illinois, but beyond that I did not know much about him. Always interested in current events and national politics, I decided to learn more about Obama since the media were making an electoral messiah out of him. But the more I tried to learn about him, the more I found out that people didn't know much about him other than what his campaign aides were spouting and what he was spouting off his teleprompter-displayed canned speeches. The more I studied him, the more I learned we knew very little about him and that large parts of his early life were being deliberately hidden and withheld from public scrutiny.

This lack of detailed in-depth information gave me pause. I followed Obama's campaign and that of all the other candidates of the major parties in the primary season. Everyone expected Hillary Clinton to beat this newcomer for the Democratic nomination. But surprise, surprise—it increasingly became obvious that was not a sure thing. Hillary's funding started drying up, and Obama seemed to have unlimited access to money. Along the way in the primary, rumors started surfacing about Obama's radical past and associations and foreign backing. I learned of Obama's and his wife Michelle's connections to the domestic terrorist Bill Ayers, as well to Ayers's friend and fellow SDS member Michael Klonsky. These men and their respective spouses were just a few of the radical Communists, Marxists, Leninists, Maoists, Islamists, and Socialists in Obama's Chicago circle.

I started hearing that Obama would not reveal any of his early life documents such as birth records, college, travel, and medical records or the details of his adoption by his stepfather Lolo Soetoro or any other records from his life in Indonesia as an Indonesian citizen. Then all of a sudden the online digital Certification of Live Birth (COLB) image was posted on the Internet in June 2008. This was immediately suspected by digital image experts to be a forgery. Obama would not allow any controlling legal authority or forensic experts to see the alleged paper document used to make the online image. Reports surfaced that his Kenyan relatives and Kenyan media were stating he was actually born in Kenya, not Hawaii. I became even more concerned about who this Obama guy was and what he was hiding.

I began to read the website WND, since it was the only major online news site that was actively investigating Obama and his hidden life records. I heard about a new book about Obama by Dr. Jerome Corsi, *The Obama Nation—Leftist Politics and the Cult of Personality*. I bought it and read it.

Another book I read was by David Freddoso, *The Case Against Barack Obama—The Unlikely Rise and Unexplained Agenda of the Media's Favorite Candidate*. I became even more concerned that the American people were not getting the truth or the facts about Barack Obama from the mainstream media. I was also concerned that our Democrat-controlled Congress, in particular the U.S. Senate, was not investigating the natural born citizenship status of Obama in the same way they investigated the natural born citizenship status of John McCain in April 2008.

Obama was being given a free pass on his early life and the questions swirling around his true legal identity. Not only did the press give Obama a pass, they also went on the attack against anyone who challenged Obama's packaged life narrative.

I learned how, as a new U.S. senator, Obama had violated the Logan Act by interfering with an election in a foreign country by helping to raise funds for the election in Kenya for his cousin Odinga's political party. That is a felony violation of a federal law. Again, nothing was done or said about this by any controlling legal authority in the USA. Everyone seemed afraid to confront Obama about this or any other wrongdoing.

I started blogging on the Internet, asking questions and posting my opinions about Obama in late July 2008 under a pen name, as is common on the Internet. The pen name I used was Mountain Publius Goat, or just Mountain Goat, or Goat for short. I soon found out that certain questions asked about Obama on Internet sites were unwelcome and could be quickly scrubbed or deleted. There was a massive network of either paid or volunteer operatives manning the gun ports of the Internet 24/7 to counterattack challenges and ridicule those who raised hard questions about Obama's life narrative.

Sites like Wikipedia were heavily censored by Obama operatives and sympathizers. Yahoo Ask and similar sites were being monitored by Obama operatives and sympathizers, and anyone posing questions challenging Obama's life narrative were reported to the moderators by Obama operatives for picayune technicalities and exaggerated charges of violation of terms of service (TOS). These complaints often got the poster banned and the question deleted.

These "Obots" knew extremely well how to use the Internet TOS system to keep critical information about Obama off the Internet. I found out later that many of these operatives were lawyers and paralegals directly or indirectly associated with groups connected to the Obama campaign. They knew how to write complaint e-mails and letters to the moderators and/or owners of these websites to get posters challenging the Obama narrative removed and banned.

I also soon learned that the so-called fact-checking sites online such as FactCheck.org, Snopes.com, and PolitiFact.com were little more than propaganda organs for the Obama campaign. The vast majority of the usual online information sites were either willingly complicit in suppressing information that was critical of Obama or they were easily intimidated by Obama operatives into suppressing unwelcome questions.

As time went on, it became more and more obvious to me that this was all being orchestrated from the top down by the Obama machine. I believe that large amounts of money either directly, or indirectly through various cutouts, were being expended to orchestrate the massive control of information about Obama on the Internet. I believe a large amount of volunteer labor was provided as needed by organizations such as ACORN and Service Employees Internation Union and then directed by the more sophisticated top-level operatives orchestrating the Internet operation. The Obama machine controlled the major sources of information as no other political campaign in American history had done.

In August 2008 I learned that a lawyer named Philip Berg in Pennsylvania was challenging the constitutional eligibility of Obama based on charges that Obama was born in Kenya and not in the United States. Legal notice of the lawsuit was given to the Democratic Party leadership before the national convention nominated Obama. Still, no one with any controlling legal authority called for an investigation of Obama and the legal charges being leveled against him.

I started reading Attorney Berg's blog. I also started making financial contributions to his effort and tried to help him via back-channel communications. Attorney Berg's lawsuit was turned away at every level in the court system up to and including the U.S. Supreme Court on the basis that he did not have standing, that the question was not ripe yet since Obama had not won the election, and/or that it was the responsibility of Congress—not the courts—to resolve this issue.

I soon gave up on Wikipedia and similar sites in efforts to get some facts out about Obama that I had learned. I next tried blogging on Greta Van Susteren's "Greta Wire" forum. My thought was that as a lawyer she would understand that at least an investigation should be launched into the charges against Obama. While comments there were allowed, the Obots descended on her forum like a plague of locusts. One could not make any argument for common sense and try to get agreement that there should at least be an investigation of Obama without being ridiculed by teams of Obots. These Obots used a tag-team approach in these forums much like professional wrestlers. Their arguments and claims of objectivity were just about as authentic.

Around September 2008 another attorney named Leo Donofrio brought a lawsuit against the secretary of state of New Jersey charging that Obama and McCain were not "natural born Citizens" of the United States and should not be allowed on the ballot in that state. I started reading his blog and trying to help him via back-channel communications. His case also went up to the Supreme Court and was turned away on technicalities.

A similar case was filed by Cort Wrotnowski against the secretary of state of Connecticut. Leo Donofrio was assisting Mr. Wrotnowski with his case when it got to the Supreme Court. Once again the Supreme Court turned a deaf ear. No case was ever heard on the merits.

In late October and early November 2008 it became apparent to me that Google had changed its search algorithms to bury recent online articles critical of Obama's nativity story and constitutional ineligibility to be the president. At the same time, Google was pushing to the top of the search results counter stories from the Obama-friendly "fact-checking" sites, blogs, and forums putting out favorable information about Obama and attacking challengers.

Google was not unique. Instead of new news stories about the Obama eligibility issue getting placement on the first page or two, they got buried in the cellar of the Net by the search engines. Wikipedia was dominated by far-left Obot operatives, and the major search engines were largely in the tank for Obama. Obama was the left's messiah and nothing was allowed to derail the anointed one.

In California an attorney named Orly Taitz brought a lawsuit against the secretary of state of California. I contributed back-channel information and advice to her as well as donating money to help her fight the battle. Her case, too, was turned away at all levels of the federal court system, including the Supreme Court, on technicalities.

I wrote letters and sent reading materials to all the justices of the U.S. Supreme Court suggesting they reread the founding documents and stand up for their oath. If they were informed, I had hoped, they would take one of the cases being presented to them regarding Obama's constitutional eligibility.

No federal court would hear the case against Obama on the merits. The courts turned down all such cases on technical issues and claimed the issue was the responsibility of Congress. Congress said it was a legal question and up to the courts. This was the song and dance that "We the People" faced at every turn as we tried to get Obama properly vetted.

During the fall of 2008 and the rest of that year, I continued to read books about Obama including the books he claimed he wrote, *Dreams from My Father* and *The Audacity of Hope*. I kept a pocket copy of the Declaration of Independence and U.S. Constitution on me all of the time as a refresher. I decided to order a copy of other key founding documents and reference books to read.

I read the *Federalist Papers* and Emmerich de Vattel's *The Law of Nations or Principles of Natural Law*. I purchased and read *Rules for Radicals* and *Reveille for Radicals*, the key books by Obama's socialist mentor, Saul Alinsky. I read essays about the "Cloward-Piven Strategy." These detailed the far left's plan to collapse our economic system in order to force installation of a socialist government. I recommended these writings to others I was in contact with as they clearly helped me understand the motivations, intent, and plan Obama had for our republic if he won the election.

The main blog I wrote in under my pen name of Mountain Publius Goat from the end of October 2008 until January 2009 was called "Country First." A sample of some of the writings I posted in that blog I have preserved on my own website at this link: http://www.kerchner.com/protectourliberty/goatsledge/table.htm

During the last part of 2008 I was also writing letters and sending e-mails to my congressman and senators asking them to investigate Obama and the charges being made against him. Amazingly, not a single one of my elected members or the other key members of Congress that I contacted answered my letters.

I began to believe nobody cared or had the courage to stand up to Obama. Of course, the race card was being played against anyone who did challenge Obama, and this was scare enough for the more cowardly members of Congress.

In the latter part of 2008, I also tried to help with actions to get the Electoral College to vet Obama's constitutional eligibility. But I soon learned that the role of the Electoral College as a check and balance in our system of government had become inoperative. The Electoral College was designed as the first line of defense in preventing a runaway public from electing an ineligible president. This was one of the key purposes of the Electoral College as explained in the *Federalist Papers*. But at this point in our history it had been totally compromised by state laws instituted at the behest of the major political parties.

In December of 2008, after the Electoral College had failed to fulfill its constitutionally designed duty to protect the republic from the seating of an ineligible person in the office of President, I wrote letters with supporting information and data to President George W. Bush, Vice President Dick Cheney, and other officials pointing out the constitutional questions about Obama's eligibility. I received no answers from any of them, not even a form letter. And of course they did not take any action to vet Obama's true legal identity.

It was now obvious to me that our last line of defense from Obama was Congress. I thus concentrated my efforts in sending out a new round of letters, faxes, and e-mails to my elected officials and other key members of the Congress including Senator John McCain. Again I got no replies, no answers. Not even a form letter. They totally ignored my numerous attempts to get them to investigate Obama's legal identity.

I believed that no one in Washington, D.C., cared about their oath of office and what the founders and framers intended to prevent when they put the legal term of art "natural born Citizen" into the United States Constitution.

I started looking for someone to bring a lawsuit enjoining Congress itself and the leaders of both chambers as defendants if the Congress failed to properly vet Obama's constitutional eligibility at the Joint Session in early January 2009. Seeing no one willing to tackle this approach, I decided the person to bring this lawsuit had to be me. I was being called to bring forth this lawsuit against Obama and Congress whether I liked it or not and my officer's oath demanded I answer that call.

I contacted several well-known national constitutional attorneys. I either received no answer or was told they said no. I had also contacted several political action-type foundations such as The Heritage Foundation, American Conservative Union, and Judicial Watch and didn't get any response. I had contacted all the other attorneys who had or were filing lawsuits, and they were either too busy with their own suits or didn't want to take mine. I contacted local attorneys. What made my search harder was that I was looking for a *pro bono* attorney. I wanted a patriot to take this case, not a person just doing it for the money. I was willing to pay for all the court costs and out-of-pocket expenses for the proposed lawsuit.

By this time in my efforts, Congress had failed in its Twentieth Amendment duty in the Constitution to make sure that the person elected to the presidency was constitutionally qualified. They did so in record time, taking unprecedented shortcuts in the legally required order of the proceedings by not calling for the objections to each and every state's Electoral College votes.

I had gone down my list and was just about at the end of my rope in finding an attorney when I became aware of Mario Apuzzo. I called and told him that I was looking for a patriot to file a suit before Obama was sworn in. He was hesitant, given the threats being thrown around on the Internet and elsewhere toward the people who were standing up to ask these hard questions. He wanted twenty-four hours to think about it.

The next day I called him back, and he decided to take the case. At Apuzzo's request, I faxed him copies of all my letters to the various members of the Congress and the executive branch and others as evidence of who I had contacted and to which I had not received any answer or response. We worked together for the next three days via telephone and e-mail and filed our complaint at 2:50 a.m. on Inauguration Day, January 20, 2009.

I wanted the case filed before Obama was sworn in so that I was suing the president-elect, who was still a civilian not yet vested with the office, powers and protection of the presidency. My suit was filed against President-elect Obama, who had been confirmed by Congress, and the Congress itself, and several other named defendants who were complicit in confirming Obama. The political process was over at the point in time I sued.

The case proceeded through the federal court system in Apuzzo's able hands. For those who may wish to read the pleadings in *Kerchner et al. v. Obama & Congress et al.* lawsuit, you can read and get copies of the lawsuit and complaint and ultimate Petition to the U.S. Supreme Court online at:

Legal Complaint Table of Content: http://www.scribd.com/doc/19914488/

Legal Complaint/Request for Emergency Injunction:
http://www.scribd.com/doc/11317148/

Legal Filings in Federal Courts: http://www.scribd.com/my_document_collections/2344225

Petition to the U.S. Supreme Court: http://www.scribd.com/doc/38506403/

In May of 2009 I launched a national full-page advertising campaign about the Obama ineligibility issues in the print media. I focused on the *Washington Times* National Weekly edition, which has a national readership and which every member of the U.S. Congress receives each week. Copies of those ads can be seen at http://www.kerchner.com/protectourliberty/archives.htm

I initially paid for all these print media ads myself. I also started writing and contributing articles and essays to Attorney Apuzzo's blog—http://puzo1.blogspot.com. Then, in July 2009, I launched the online website ProtectOurLiberty.org to raise funds to continue the ads in the print media and to further educate the people about the issues. That website can be viewed at: http://www.protectourliberty.org .

Eventually I launched my own Word Press blog at http://cdrkerchner.wordpress.com where I continued the type of writing that I had done under my pen name of Mountain Publius Goat but now under my real name. I also did many radio and Internet news interviews with my attorney. I did everything I could to get the word out about Obama's lack of constitutional eligibility despite the mainstream media's propensity to ignore constitutionalists. The only attention we received would come when we lost our case.

In September 2010 my lawsuit reached the U.S. Supreme Court. The Petition for Writ of Certiorari was denied by the Supreme Court on November 29, 2010. Once again the court refused to address the eligibility question. As Justice Thomas said in testimony one day on the hill, "We are avoiding that issue."

The Supreme Court had the chance to adjudicate the "natural born Citizen" clause in the U.S. Constitution. Instead, it ducked the issue. The justices had painted themselves into a corner on this issue with prior cases, and they knew not what to do with my case except keep ducking.

From 14–16 December 2010, I attended the court-martial of Lt. Col. Terry Lakin at Fort Meade, Maryland, to show my full support for a comrade in arms and fellow solemn believer in our Constitution. Here is an interview report on my observations and opinion of what transpired at that court-martial: http://www.thepostemail.com/2010/12/28/cdr-charles-kerchner-speaks-out-about-the-court-martial-of-lt-col-terry-lakin/

After over three years in this fight, I am still asked by people: Why did you do this? Why are you still fighting this battle? Why don't you give up? Here is my answer to those questions. I believe in God. I believe in my country. I believe in my family, and I will fight to the death for all three of those. I took my oath, and I believe those words, and I meant those words, "so help me God." They are not just words to me.

As I observed what happened in my country during the 2008 presidential election cycle, I feared for the loss of my liberty and my unalienable rights guaranteed under the Constitution for which our forefathers fought during the American Revolution. These rights were codified into the fundamental law of the nation. This contract limited the power of the new federal government and protected our rights and liberty, my rights and liberties. I feared loss of liberty if a president were allowed to take office without constitutional vetting.

I do not trust Obama to protect me. For him the Constitution has been an obstacle in the way of his achieving even more power. If he and his progressive sycophants in Congress can ignore and usurp one part of the Constitution—Article II, Section 1, Clause 5—they will ignore and usurp other parts, such as the Bill of Rights. That is why, when I saw the other lawsuits failing, I felt I was being called forth to fight this battle: "You have to stand up, Commander Kerchner. You must live up to your oath to support and defend the Constitution. You have to stand up and fight this battle. *You must do this!*"

I answered the call when called. I did not turn away and say it was some-one else's job, as our Congress and courts have done when summoned to act by the cries from the citizenry. I have engaged the domestic enemies of our Constitution. And I will continue to live up to my oath as a commis-sioned officer to support and defend it.

The truth will be revealed. The truth and the Constitution will win in the end. But many more will need to join Lt. Col. Terry Lakin and me in this battle. A commissioned officer's oath to support and defend the Constitu-tion against all enemies foreign and domestic does not expire or retire. I will continue to fight this battle until the truth is restored and the Constitu-tion upheld. So help me God.

Dean Haskins: The Presidential Circus

On February 10, 2007, the circus came to town; but this wasn't just any circus, it was the spectacle of spectacles that forever changed our political landscape. It was also definitive proof that we no longer live in your grandfather's America. It was that Saturday when a virtually unknown and unproven freshman U.S. senator from Illinois announced his candidacy for the office of President of the United States. He was an obvious longer-than-long-shot, as Hillary Clinton was the expected Democratic Party's nomination long before the campaign even started.

What unfolded over the next several months defied any logical explanation. We witnessed much more than the election of our first black president—which, in and of itself, is something for which America should have been vastly proud. We witnessed a battlefield victory for those who had, for years, waged war upon our Constitution. What they had not anticipated, however, was a fierce counterattack waged by those citizens who recognized what they were doing.

As odd a choice as this candidate was, being unable to articulate anything of substance without a teleprompter, he did possess enough charisma to at least sell himself. What he lacked, however, was any means of properly identifying who he was and where he came from. Rather than simply showing what everyone in our country must show several times throughout our lives, he directed (through other entities, so as to provide himself with plausible deniability) that a computer-generated likeness of an abstract, devoid of any verifiable information, be posted on their websites.

At first, many of us were not entirely certain what to make of it, as we had never before been faced with a presidential candidate who went to great lengths to conceal his identity. Yes, of course, because his father was not a citizen of the United States at the time of his birth, Chester Arthur concealed his true heritage by lying about it. He then had the relevant documentation burned. But Arthur never ran for president. He assumed the office after President Garfield was assassinated and most of us weren't around in the 1880s.

Barack Obama, however, did run for president, and he did so in an age of ample information. That much said, the only information that he posted on the pro-Obama websites, the famed Certification of Live Birth, never smelled quite right.

Many of us across the nation did those things we knew we were supposed to do in our form of government: we started trying to communicate with those who would be involved in the formal election process. We sent e-mails, faxes, and certified letters from every conceivable location in the country, first to the members of the Electoral College, and next, to every member of Congress.

We made certain that we informed them, not only of the constitutional requirements for one to be president, but also detailed for them the deficiencies of Obama's scant offering of facts. We realized how the game had been rigged when we couldn't get a single elector or member of Congress to respond to us with anything but a few scripted talking points, all of which seemed to be based on the same incorrect information.

We quickly learned how masterfully the candidate used the center ring of the political circus—the spotlight shone by the national media. Normally, our ostensibly free press would have had a field day with a presidential candidate who concealed virtually every key document of his life—from birth certificate to college transcripts--while at the same time claiming that his would be the most transparent presidency in history. But not this time.

The media's first line of attack was as dirty as it was predictable. Since the half-white candidate appeared black, opposition to his candidacy was quickly met with charges of racism. This proved a potent tactic, as unfounded allegations often are, because the accused were faced with trying to prove a negative.

When race-baiting did not stop the counterattack, the media employed still another predictable defense. "Ridicule is man's most potent weapon," claimed their ideological general, Saul Alinsky. "It is almost impossible to counteract ridicule. Also it infuriates the opposition, which then reacts to your advantage."

We had come to expect ridicule from the media firmly in the Obama camp—CNN, MSNBC, ABC, CBS, and NBC. But the fear of ridicule from their media peers cowed even the purported conservative network, FOX News.

The Republicans in Congress proved no braver than the conservative media. Its members danced around this issue as if a form letter or two were sufficient to lull an exasperated citizenry. They were also the first to recognize the veritable minefields that the media had laid around its progressive poster child. To do their constitutional duty by simply verifying Obama's eligibility would have resulted in their being labeled a conspiracy theorist at best and a racist at worst, and that latter charge alone, however false, would have impeded their most important task—getting re-elected.

Since it is ultimately the duty of Congress to verify the eligibility of one for whom the Electoral College casts a winning vote, the American people were diligent in letting Washington know not only what 'we the people' expected of them, but also what their constitutional duty was. Some in Congress responded by turning for a response to Jack Maskell, the legislative attorney with the CRS (Congressional Research Service), a resource service of Congress that purports to be non-partisan. A quick perusal of the memos provided by Mr. Maskell immediately shows the CRS to be anything but.

In response to several queries from members of Congress regarding Obama's eligibility to be president, Maskell's first memo included this dishonest little tidbit:

> Many of the inquiries have questioned why then-Senator, and now President, Obama has not had to produce an original, so-called 'long' version of a 'birth certificate' from the State of Hawaii, how federal candidates are 'vetted' for qualifications generally, and have asked for an assessment of the various allegations and claims of non-eligibility status...

> Concerning the production or release of an original birth certificate, it should be noted that there is no federal law, regulation, rule, guideline, or requirement that a candidate for federal office produce his or her original birth certificate, or a certified copy of the record of live birth, to any official of the United States government; nor is there a requirement for federal candidates to publicly release such personal record or documentation. Furthermore, there is no specific federal agency or office that 'vets' candidates for federal office as to qualifications or eligibility prior to return."

Simply stated, Maskell washed his hands of this judgment and said to the citizens, "Attend to this matter yourself." The implication of his statement was that Congress ought not worry about whether it had done its job, as there is no specific statute that requires it to do so.

There need not be such an ancillary statute, however, for the Constitution itself demands that Congress verify the qualifications of one who has received the nod from the Electoral College. The Twentieth Amendment clearly includes the phrase "if the President elect shall have failed to qualify." It makes no sense to suggest that the Constitution holds Congress responsible to perform specific actions if a president-elect fails to qualify, but does not also hold Congress accountable to verify whether a president-elect does qualify.

When Congress convened to verify the Electoral College vote in January 2009, then-Vice President Cheney, in his role as President of the Senate, failed to ask if there were any objections to the Electoral College's vote. That anomaly alone should have alerted the media that all was not right, but the media had long before cast their lot with the new president.

Those citizens who requested help from their elected representatives met with condescension, if not contempt. Some examples:

> Thank you for your recent e-mail. Senator Obama meets the constitutional requirements for presidential office. Rumors pertaining to his citizenship status have been circulating on the Internet, and this information has been debunked by Snopes.com, which investigates the truth behind Internet rumors. —Sen. John Kyl , R-Arizona

Snopes.com, by the way, is nothing more than a California husband and wife clearly partial to Obama.

> Independent and official investigations as well as legal proceedings have validated President Barack Obama's eligibility to serve as President of the United States. The Health Director and Head of Vital Statistics for the state of Hawaii (an official source) has also examined and declared the authenticity of the birth certificate and most recently President Obama released his full birth certificate. If change is to take place it's likely to come in the form of an election. This is part of the reason everyone needs to make sure we vote for the people who will represent our views correctly. This is also why we must continue to talk to our friends and relatives in other states about their own elected

officials and encourage them to let their voices be heard. —Sen. Mike Enzi, R-Wyoming

The senator has an active imagination. No such investigations have ever occurred

Article II, Section 1 of the U.S. Constitution specifies the qualifications for this executive office. It states that no person except for a natural born American citizen is eligible to run for President of the United States. Also, the candidate must be at least thirty-five years of age and have resided in the United States for at least fourteen years. President Obama meets these constitutional requirements. If you were not already aware, on April 27, 2011 the White House released a copy of President Obama's long form birth certificate. He was born in Hono-lulu, Hawaii, on August 4, 1961. According to the Fourteenth Amendment, all persons born in the United States are consid-ered citizens of the United States. Under these criteria, Presi-dent Obama, a 47-year-old U.S. citizen, who has resided in the United States for longer than fourteen years, is eligible to be President. —Sen. Dianne Feinstein, D-California

The senator seems unaware that the Fourteenth Amendment includes noth-ing regarding the Article II, Section 1 mandate of "natural born Citizen." It deals only with generic citizenship.

The Constitution and federal law require, among other conditions, that only native-born U.S. citizens (or those born abroad, but only to parents who were both American citizens) may be President of the United States. In President Obama's case, some individuals have filed lawsuits in state and federal courts alleging that he has not proven that he is an American citizen, but each of those law-suits have been dismissed. This includes a recent decision by the United States Supreme Court to not review an "application for emergency stay" filed by a New Jersey resident claiming that the President is not a natural born citizen because his father was born in Kenya. Furthermore, both the Director of Hawaii's Department of Health and the state's Registrar of Vital Statistics recently con-firmed that Mr. Obama was born in Honolulu, Hawaii on August 4, 1961 and, as such, meets the constitutional citizenship require-ments for the presidency. If contrary documentation is produced and verified, this matter will necessarily be resolved by the judicial branch of our government under the Constitution. —Sen. Mike Crapo, R-Idaho

These, and many like them, are prime examples of the empty rhetoric that pervades Washington. Whenever politicians resort to citing partisan websites as authoritative sources of constitutional standards, one must immediately understand the problems with our system.

Moreover, changing one word of constitutional law can render its meaning completely ambiguous, as in Sen. Crapo's use of the term "native-born," when the Constitution clearly delineates that a president must be a "natural born Citizen." This is just further evidence of congressional indifference to the framers' intent. Article II, Section 1 clearly states that a president must be a "natural born Citizen," and the historic definition of that is "one born in this country to citizen parents." That definition was also set by the Supreme Court as binding precedent in *Minor v. Happersett* (1875).

In the midst of this indifference and evasion, one brave soldier stood up and started asking for proof that his commander in chief was actually eligible to hold his position. As this lone figure stood dauntlessly in the face of excruciating odds, one by one, the rancorous crowd fell silent, awaiting the president's response.

The president, however, in a characteristic let-them-eat-cake response, simply turned his back on the truth-seeking soldier and blocked any possibility for him to receive answers to the questions he asked. Moreover, as if the stonewalling wasn't enough of an unreasonable act by Obama, he simply turned his back as the military stripped the courageous officer of his job and his benefits—including the pension he had earned for nearly two decades of honorable service.

But wait, the president wasn't finished with his obfuscation. Rather than simply showing the requested proof, he allowed the officer to be imprisoned for five months. Surely there must have been a reason to hide such a common document from the people, for no decent human being would have ever allowed another person to lose his career and, temporarily, his freedom, over such a trivial matter.

And, therein, we should all catch a glimpse into the heart of that reason, and that is the word "decent," for the travesties endured by Terry Lakin didn't end with his personal losses. In an ironic slap in the face to him and the dumbfounded audience, while Terry did his time in a prison cell for his audacious crime of simply asking for the truth, the president cavalierly produced the very document that, had he done so a few short months earlier, would have kept Terry from enduring retribution. Or would it have? In yet another deceptive twist, it seems quite obvious that the president released an additional fake offering of proof, leaving the audience to further understand that the wrong individual in this epic showdown endured punishment and imprisonment.

As of this writing, the three-ring circus is still in full swing, although the price of admission is continually increasing. There is likely only one way for the show to be shut down, and that is for every member of the unwitting audience—those "smelly tourists" who fill the boundaries of this great land—to be willing to pay the same price that Terry paid. That is the price to which our Founding Fathers agreed, and it is incumbent upon us all to regard the gift they bequeathed to us so highly that our lives, our fortunes, and our sacred honor are but a small ransom to emancipate our constitutional republic from this circus, its calamitous captors.

&

James Bridge: An Oath Is Before God

שבע (Shaba)

"I swear seven times."

Language can be truly revealing.

Take, for example what the simple phrase "to swear an oath" actually means.

When we go to the source of the principal religions of our American people, Christianity and Judaism, we find that "to swear" is a familiar Hebrew word—*sheba*. It means "seven," and as a verb it means to "seven" *something*, or to declare seven times, or to declare a seven with intent on a future behavior or act.

The past tense of this verb is *shaba,* or swore. This word is but a tiny step away from the English word "Sabbath" or *shabat* in Hebrew, a word clearly referring to the seventh day—the Lord's Day. And the word "oath"? *Shevua*, again linked to the meaning of seven. The Sabbath, then, is *foresworn*; the Sabbath is God's and God's only. It is the day of the covenant.

So, clearly, to swear something is something that belongs to God. An oath, then, is before God. And, if nothing else, it is something said aloud with the weight of *seven times*; so should divine vengeance be visited upon the dishonorable oath-breaker, he or she is on the record volubly. So the roots of our faith reflect even in a philological sense that to swear is a thing of God.

English and German are very closely related, and what would become French had a common origin at one point. The Franks were Germanic, after all. The English word "oath" and its German counterpart, *Eid*, are truly the same word. The *Oxford English Dictionary* shows the morphology of the word from an original word, *eith, or aithe*, in the marvelously rich English tongue. The word for faith follows a similar morphology, from the origins of *feit* and *faithe*.

In the Judeo-Christian experience, and the Anglo-Germanic celebration of it, nothing could be more important than the swearing of an oath. "A man's word is his bond" is the saying.

Romans and Greeks

The pagan Romans and their Greek cousins did little without honoring God. Every first-born male was a priest in the religion of his family or tribe. Nothing of note could be done without propitiating one of his many gods, through sacrifice or through specific, sacred, secret prayer. Roman soldiers could not serve without taking an oath, or *sacramentum*. The utterance in the age of the glorious Republic was called the *praeiuratio*. In the oath, one swore before the gods to follow the command of their commanders in chief, the double presidents, or consuls. They promised also not to waver or desert their standards or colors, nor to violate Roman law.

When Roman soldiers revolted against Consul Appius Claudius in a 471 war with the Volsci, he ordered their decimation: this practice was the selection by lot of one in ten of an offending military unit. The "winners" were then put to the sword. To break one's oath, then, in their view, was a sin before the gods and left one unworthy of life itself.[5]

The ancient world of the Greeks and Romans was in fact imbued with prayers and incantations, secret verses and words that were the underpinnings of their gentile religion (gens = tribe). God was in everything. The gens were family priesthoods, handed down from patriarch to first-born son. One could move from gens to gens either through adoption or marriage, but only after the son to be adopted and the daughter to be wed were sanctified and purged of all further contact with the ritual of the family they were leaving.

All who were not first-born males were property of their father or elder brother. It was written in secret scripts that their gens would be so ordered. If father or brother were fair-minded, life was good. If not, life could be as bad as it would be for any slave. All other than the first-born priest were chattel, and the head of the family gens had the power of life and death over all of its progeny, family, and slaves.

For everything, in their world, was about God.

Those not first-born males were not always content to do father or brother's bidding. Those people left the family to lose themselves amongst the lower class of people, become itinerant merchants in the loud agoras or piazzas. By fleeing, they freed themselves of their burdensome religious

5   http://www.roman-empire.net/army/army.html

obligations to be subservient. But these people became the god-less *plebes* of the Romans, the Greek *idiots*.

The scorn visited upon these people was due to their reneging on their oath to honor their father and worship at his mantle, the home altar. They were not under the protection of a patrician; they were simply detritus, making themselves useful in finding something to do or sell that others could afford.

The Maid of Orleans

"For speaking the truth, one is sometimes hanged." —Jeanne d'Arc

When we speak of pledging before God or gods we must also examine the cost of failing to keep that word. For those who are not sure of the existence of a God, or who become uncomfortable around the word "God," they might consider making an oath to all of mankind; they might think of pledging to act against the very worth of the individual. This is the stuff of oath. One great example of such an oath-keeper was a woman of the 15th century.

This woman, dressed as a man, would lead the French against the English and drive them back across the sea. Her name was Joan of Arc. Jeanne, in French, was born in 1412. She was executed by the English in 1431 for heresy and perjury after a lengthy trial.

Her story is miraculous. Imbued with claims of revelations from saints and God, the story is steeped in drama and fact. There was indeed a Jeanne d'Arc, who did lead the French forces against the English King, Henry III.

William the Conqueror had come to England in 1066 with his band of Norman warriors, all with a piece of France in their pockets, and these Normans had wanted more than less of it. The Hundred Years War raged sporadically from 1337 to 1453, the Norman House of Anjou (Plantagenet) against the royal French line, Valois.

The Capetian line had become extinct, and the claim of the French throne was prosecuted by Edward III and his bellicose son Edward, aka the Black Prince, whose victories at Crecy and Poitiers were stunning and left the French forces suing for peace in 1360. Charles V revived the conflict in 1369, and hostilities continued for twenty years. Richard II gave way to the trouble of Richard III, and the Lancastrians mounted the throne of England. Henry IV revived the war, and his son, in an echo of Edward III and the Black Prince, sent his son Henry to bring France to England.

This ended in 1429 because of Joan of Arc. Joan had been hearing voices, one from the Archangel Saint Michael. They urged her to seek out the Dauphin of France, a reputedly profligate young man who of his own was unable to rally the French to repel their English invaders. Her voices told her that she must save France, and that she would turn the tide of the war. She was to tell her king the message she had from her saintly voices, and no one else.

On faith alone, Joan was able to convince the many gatekeepers between a common spinner peasant and a man who would be king. She was interrogated, she was examined, and in her praise of God and her clarity of an impending victory over the English, she convinced her Dauphin, Charles VII, to allow her to lead an army against the English foe. She created a banner, the Jesus Maria on it, with lilies, and with God seated on a cloud, sword in hand, with an angel kneeling by his side.

Jean would be wounded at Orleans, but the siege was lifted, and the French proved victorious on May 8, 1429. A little more than a year later Joan was captured near Compiègne in a skirmish that was without Charles VII's approval. The Bourguignons sold her to the English. Another year would pass of trial and physical abuse by her jailers. She would lose faith, and recant, and wear woman's apparel again, but in the end she appealed for forgiveness from her saints, put on the tunic and leggings of men, and awaited her fate.

When Joan was captured, she said to a soldier who demanded that she surrender, "I have given myself to another than you, and to him I will keep my oath."[6] Her voices had told her that she would be delivered, and her inquisitors showed her that they were false lights, that she would not be delivered, that she would either spend her life in prison or be killed.

She would not speak ill of her voices. Her Dauphin sent no forces to attempt her relief; he abandoned her to her fate. Still, Joan remained firm, and so she died, on May 30, 1431, burned at the stake, her last words "Jesu, Jesu."

From her testimony: "Everything I have said or done is in the hand of God, and I commit myself to Him. And I certify to you that I would do or say nothing against the Christian faith; and, if I had said or done anything,

6   http://www.jeanne-darc.info/p_multimedia/literature/0_francis_c_lowell/16_compiegne.html

or if anything were found on me which the clergy should declare to be against the Christian faith established by Our Lord, I would not uphold it, but would cast it out."

Sir Thomas More

When Henry VIII, the famed king of England, took Sir Thomas More's head from him not many years after the execution of Joan of Arc, he in no way marred More's legacy. More's great literary contemporary, Erasmus, would say after his friend's execution that More's soul was more pure than snow was white. Hapsburg Charles V told envoy Sir Thomas Eliot that he would rather have lost the finest city in his great empire than the life of Sir Thomas More.

Thomas More was close to the Crown Prince, Henry Tudor. He was one of Henry's instructors. But that didn't stop Henry from killing him, once he had become king and had set himself up as head of the English church.

More was execrated by his king and finally executed on the block on July 6, 1535. His head sat on a spike on the Tower Bridge for a month afterward. His daughter Meg took it down before it was to be tossed into the Thames. No one stopped her.

Why was Sir Thomas More martyred by King Henry VIII? More refused to swear an oath to follow Henry's ecclesiastical journey to become the new head of the English church.

Before his trouble with King Henry VIII, More had been made Archbishop of Canterbury. But while Sir Thomas More enjoyed the title in the service of his God and church, King Henry VIII had hoped he would soften therewith the heart of his aging teacher and help him find a path to a proper wedding with Anne Boleyn.

Henry wanted an heir, a male heir. He wanted a dispensation from the Pope to be rid of Catherine of Aragon so that he could marry Anne Boleyn. But Pope Clement VII denied Henry VIII the annulment he sought.

More refused to sign a letter to the Pope in support of that request in 1530. He refused to swear an oath of fealty to the new head of the English church, Henry VIII, insofar as the oath would override the authority of the Church of Rome. The Statute of Praemunire, passed in 1531, forbad appeals to the church courts, or Roman *curia*. Soon Henry's patience with More ran out, and he put his old teacher in prison in the Tower of London.

When the day came for his execution, a man named Sir Thomas Pope came to More to tell him to prepare himself. The King had no desire to hear him speak upon the scaffold and chopping block. "The King's pleasure is . . . at your execution that you do not use many words."[7] Pope, after setting down the requirements of More's beheading, began to weep, and Sir Thomas offered him this solace:

"Quiet your selfe good M. Pope, and be not discomforted, for I trust we shall one day se ech other in heaue[n], where we shal be sure to liue, and loue together in ioyfull blisse eternally."[8]

So did Sir Thomas More go to his death for his faith in his God and for honoring his oath to uphold God's law.

Outside the Promised Land

Moses wandered with his flock of liberated Jews for forty years, so Scripture reads. Moses gave the Jews the laws of God, chiseled in stone by God himself.

But Moses had a rough road to the Promised Land. First, he returned with the glow of the figure of God's presence still upon his brow to find that his fellow Hebrews had erected a Golden Calf to worship. Moses broke those two tablets over that piece of sacrilege.

Then, he realized, he'd have to climb the mountain again for another set of those ten rules:

> Thou shalt hold no God before me.
> Thou shalt make no graven images nor bow down before them.
> Thou shalt not take the name of God in vain.
> Thou shalt keep the Sabbath holy.
> Honor thy mother and father.
> Thou shalt not commit murder.
> Thou shalt not commit adultery.
> Thou shalt not steal.
> Thou shalt not bear false witness against your neighbor.
> Thou shalt not covet your neighbor's property.

---

7   http://www.luminarium.org/renascence-editions/roper1.html, The Mirrour of Vertue

8   Ibid.

These rules seem so simple, and make so much sense—yet how many of us can say we have followed them all faithfully?

God had Moses' ear; God spoke to Moses, and, eventually, to Aaron. God put those ten rules in Moses' hands, as great a figure in history as there can be—a man who was raised in the shelter of Pharaoh's great power, a baby rescued from reeds, a deliverer who had seen God not once, but many times.

He had only to obey God, and God would give him the power to liberate captive Israel, the slave people, the chattel of the powerful Pharaoh.

Moses and Aaron, at the end of the anabasis through the wilderness, were kept from the Promised Land. The Israelites were cross with Moses for leading them around in the desert. They wondered why they had even left Egypt, having forgotten the tribulation of slavery.

At the point when they were nearest to the Promised Land, they gathered before Moses to tell him these things. They wanted water, among other things. They wanted an end to the privation.

Moses and Aaron retreated to their tent, and God appeared to them as they lay prostrate on the floor. "Take your staff, and take your brother Aaron and gather your people. Speak to that rock, and water will flow out of it. You will bring water out of the rock for the community so they will have water to drink."

Moses did not speak to the rock. For some reason, he smote the rock with the staff twice, saying, "Listen, you rebels, must we bring water out of this rock?" And so the water flowed forth.

But God was cross with Moses for the reproach. God told him that because he would not honor God as holy in the presence of the Israelites, he would not be permitted to lead Israel to the Promised Land.

So the Israelites, as rebellious and cantankerous as they were, entered the land of Milk and Honey, without Moses. (Numbers 20: 1–13)

Moses had erred in his worship, his pride wounded, perhaps, by the unruly complaints of the wander-weary Jews. So he named them rebels in striking the rock, when God only wanted him to announce the miracle and watch it happen.

The message in what happened to Moses and Aaron is that the devil is in the details. An oath, like faith, is before God. What we mortals think, when we question God's word or God's basic laws, can shed light on what those laws mean to us. But when we presume through thought and through expressions of thought—through action—to have a better idea about what we should do or act, we violate there, too, the spirit of God's law.

When we pledge before God to do something, we do well to stand firm. The Maid of Orleans and the man many claim to have been the finest Englishman ever born both gave their lives for the idea that their word was key to who they were. Their actions were sacrifices to the idea of love of God, and God's word.

The great Moses could not help being human, but he offended God in God's sight. The offense was costly. But even with his legend of greatness behind him, defaulting on an oath is a thing of black and white.

An oath is before God.

Swear it seven times.

&

Vignettes of Key Participants in Terry's Cause

Numerous individuals and organizations have joined the work that Terry started. These essays provide insight into the depth of work and commitment by talented, concerned citizens from every walk of life. These essays are authored by David Mercaldo, a New York based author and supporter of Terry Lakin.

A Note about Sheriff Joe Arpaio

During 2011 and 2012 Sheriff Joe Arpaio has pursued an ongoing investigation of Obama's claims to eligibility. Contrary to the portrayal in the mainstream media, the Sherriff did not start with a mission of nullifying Obama's presidency, but rather to bring an end to the controversy. He felt, as many did, that this was likely a misunderstanding and that a simple investigation would resolve the matter. Instead, his investigative team found omissions, errors, forgery, fraud, deception, and behavior that can only be described as treasonous, deceptive, and criminal. We invite the reader to visit the official Maricopa County Sheriff's office website (www.mcso.org) and read the numerous articles at World Net Daily about the team's activities (http://www.wnd.com/?s=Joe+Arpaio).

Michael New: An American Soldier Who Refused to Be a Mercenary

On October 10, 1995, the 1/15 Battalion of the 3rd infantry Division of the U.S. Army came to attention at 0900 in Schweinfurt, Germany. All but one of the 550 soldiers was wearing a sky-blue baseball-style cap with a United Nations insignia on the front. One was wearing the olive-drab flat cap authorized to be worn with the Battle Dress Uniform. With his refusal to obey a direct order, Spc. 4 Michael New set the stage for a legal battle that has profound implications for the future of American soldiers.

Michael is living every soldier's nightmare: *what to do when orders conflict with the oath of allegiance the soldier has taken.*

In February 1993, twenty-year-old Michael New enlisted in the United States Army and took the oath of allegiance to the Constitution of the United States. His Army recruiter in Conroe, Texas, never mentioned U.N. command, foreign officers, or wearing the U.N. uniform.

Michael was and is just like every other young man with hopes and dreams of the future. He never imagined that at the age of 23 he and his case would be discussed in the halls of Congress and the Oval Office.

What happened that would make this shy young man the focus of news stories around the nation and the world?

On August 21, 1995, Michael was informed that his unit would be required to wear a blue United Nations helmet or beret and a U.N. armband or patch as part of a "peacekeeping" mission to Macedonia. Michael was told the order to wear the U.N. uniform was lawful because "The President says so, therefore it is." But no legitimate, legal or rational basis for the order was given. Eventually, a battalion briefing about the deployment offered the justification that "We wear the U.N. uniform because it looks fabulous."

"No one gave me an answer," said Michael, "and so, on October 10, the day we were supposed to be in formation in our U.N. uniforms, I showed up in my regulation U.S. Army uniform." The other 549 U.S. Army soldiers in Michael's battalion did show up in formation, wearing a United Nations emblem on their baby blue caps and U.N. patches on their right shoulders. Michael was immediately removed from the parade ground, where he was informed that he would be facing a court-martial and was read his rights under the Uniform Code of Military Justice.

After Michael was removed from formation, the remaining U.S. soldiers came to attention and saluted General Jehu Engstrom of Finland, their new commanding officer for the next six months. General Engstrom, like other U.N. officers, had taken a pledge of allegiance to the United Nations.

Thus began the chain of events that continues to send shock waves.

Michael was court-martialed and found guilty. Like Terry, his defense was restricted to arguing one issue only: disobeying an order. Like Terry, he was not allowed to bring the actual issue, *why* he had disobeyed the order, into the trial. He received a Bad Conduct Discharge (BCD) from the Army in January 1996, and has been a private citizen since.

But that was only the beginning. There have been briefs and counter briefs, appeals and appeals of the appeals, and the Supreme Court has refused to hear the case.

In his attempts to get his court-martial conviction overturned, Michael has the United States government in a quandary. If they exonerate him, then they will have to exonerate anyone who refuses to serve in the U.S. military under the United Nations. If they continue upholding his conviction, they have to admit in public that Americans are no longer free to serve their own country exclusively— an admission the government does not want to make.

Michael's case was used by the prosecution in Terry's case to establish that Terry should not have disobeyed a direct order. Yet both cases highlight the same issue: *Is an order to be followed even if is clearly in conflict with regulations or the U.S. Constitution? And if so, to what degree?* At Nuremberg, soldiers were prosecuted for committing crimes under direct orders, and we were told they should have known better.

As Terry Lakin has said, "The Constitution matters. The truth matters." Both Michael and Terry should be celebrated by every American for their bravery and principled actions.

David Mercaldo, PhD:
Voices Crying in the Wilderness

A book has life, and perhaps a soul, in that it transcends time; it lives far beyond the human who created it. You might be reading this text in the early days of its release, or you may have found it in a library or bookstore many years after its publication date. In any case, to fully appreciate the message and the mission of its authors, it is necessary to understand the condition of the country at the time the volume was written. This book will give you at least a few snapshots of the era.

The world has been a stage where the political affairs of men and women have played out over the centuries. Because of the limitations of travel and communication, much of what transpired in the past has remained in obscurity. Today, we have transcended the miles and airwaves and are privy to the most private affairs of individuals and nations. Even so, there are many secrets; and there are groups and individuals who work to keep these secrets from the scrutiny of the masses.

The news media are certainly among those groups with the power to keep from the public information that is not consistent with their agenda. They have played a significant role in shaping modern America and perhaps the world—divulging some secrets while shading, deflecting and even hiding others. Keep in mind that from the first hand-pressed, one-page "daily," political dogma has been part of the news media's mission.

The press has done a great service to society, but it does a great disservice when it withholds the truth from its readers. Is it a secret that this has become standard practice in the journalistic world? Traditionally, when the media printed or broadcast a story, people could accept it as true, but the press abandoned its initial calling to print the "unadulterated" truth a long time ago. When it is determined that information might jeopardize a protected political ideology, publishers play the game of censorship. Sometimes what has been validated as "fact" is edited and "modified" according to a different set of journalistic standards.

Today, one is justifiably tempted to refer to the "press" as the "liberal press." Many citizens are fully aware that the liberal press does not always print the truth, but many people are innocently and ignorantly trapped in their naïve trust of the media. It is sad that the base knowledge too many Americans have about Barack Hussein Obama is what they read in the newspapers and see on the news stations.

The media brought Obama to the Oval Office and are determined to keep him there, even if they must deny or "interpret" facts to do so. Remember, the mission is more important than the truth, especially when that truth is revealing and embarrassing.

We should assume that the news services throughout the country share our doubts about the document that this president has divulged as his "real birth certificate." So, why are journalists silent? Perhaps it is because they, too, feel complicit.

The errand of this book has been to share certain information about the life of Lt. Col. Terry Lakin, specifically a resolution he made to challenge the eligibility of the most powerful man on earth. His mission was never intended to be a secret, but the media have done everything in their power to obscure it.

At this writing we cannot know the impact of Terry Lakin's decision, but we can rest assured that because of it, history will at least testify to his willingness to stand and be heard.

It is equally important for the reader to appreciate that the archives of this political era will also confirm that Terry Lakin did not stand alone and that his actions were justified. While supporters did not experience the isolation and loneliness of his prison cell, they understood the significance of what he had done in an effort to expose the truth about the president of the United States. These patriots participated in their own ways to get the truth to the American people; thus, it is their story as well. Let's meet some of them.

Walter Francis Fitzpatrick III: A Republic... do or die!

There is story that when the Constitutional Convention of 1787 ended, a Philadelphia resident, Mrs. Powel, asked Benjamin Franklin, "Well, Doctor, what have we got? A republic or a monarchy?" Franklin responded, "A republic, if you can keep it."

Let's think about that question for a moment. Is there any doubt this lady knew the differences between these two forms of government? Had she not lived under the rule of a monarch? Was she not part of the ongoing conflict of many political philosophies? In 1787 the very idea of establishing a republic was fantasy. A republic ordained individual rights, privileges and opportunity. It meant emancipation from the laws and edicts of one person.

Remember, Franklin said, "A republic, if you can keep it." The responsibility to preserve the republic, from the moment the Constitution was fully signed, rested with the citizen. More than two centuries have passed since Dr. Franklin presented that challenge, and we still should be asking ourselves, "Can we keep it?"

We have lived in the comfort and safety of a strong republic; the decision to live under a monarchy is fantasy for us because no one really believes a U.S. citizen would exchange a republic for a monarchy—or any other form of government, for that matter. If given a choice, I don't think there'd be any takers; but if the political apparatus to destroy our republic was subtle and cunning, who would know? Will this generation see the death of our republic?

If our republic will survive an age of open intellectual experimentation and opportunism, where our leaders have exempted themselves from the rule of law, created flexible guidelines and fiscal entitlements to fit their selfish purposes, and claimed special immunity from parts of our Constitution, then citizens of our republic will have to consider a path they must take to protect the Union from these destructive forces. As in the first American Revolution, they must mobilize and organize. (That's even Alinsky's first rule for radicals who seek change!)

The good news is that nationwide, citizens have already convened a great national convention. They're not meeting in Philadelphia or New York this time, but in the "sacred halls" of their living rooms and offices and around their kitchen tables. They can be seen in the window of the local Starbucks where Wii fi is available. Others are also part of this great national dialogue and for their outspokenness and defiant political voice, are forced to communicate from self-imposed protective seclusion and others from prison cells.

Meet Navy Commander Walter Francis Fitzpatrick III. For two generations his family stood in the gap for U.S. citizens who cherish this republic, pledging to defend it.

Fitzpatrick's service is part of our national heritage, and he has quite a legacy. The son of a Navy commander, Walter also chose a military career, and is the recipient of numerous medals and citations. He received the Navy Commendation Medal, the Navy Achievement Medal, two National Defense Service Medals, the Armed Forces Expeditionary Medal, the Navy Expeditionary Medal, and the Humanitarian Service Medal. Commander Fitzpatrick is also a designated Naval Parachutist.

Significant academic credentials are part of his impressive résumé too. The media would lead you to believe that "conservative radicals" have not achieved academic par with liberals. The research tells a much different story, and men like Fitzpatrick are testimony to the academic excellence in the politically conservative population. He is a distinguished graduate of Villanova Preparatory School, Ojai, California (1969), holds a Bachelor of Science degree in Naval Science and a Master's degree in Business Administration and Technology Management.

This is an exceptional man, a "do something about it citizen" who cannot accept dishonesty at any station in government. He has targeted the highest level of corruption in our present federal administration and takes particular issue with the eligibility of Barack Hussein Obama to hold the highest office in the land.

Pieces of research that are available on the net (much has been removed, abridged or squelched), journals Fitzpatrick's work to uncover and expose corruption in government. He doesn't pull any punches, and his words are forceful. To Barack Hussein Obama he challenges, "You have broken in and entered the White House by force of contrivance, concealment, conceit, dissembling, and deceit. Posing as an impostor president and commander in chief, you have stripped civilian command and control over the military establishment... I accuse you and your military-political criminal assistants of TREASON. I name you and your military criminal associates as traitors. Your criminal ascension manifests a clear and present danger. You fundamentally changed our form of government..."

Walter has paid a dear price for his convictions and his outspokenness with a series of confinements in jail, loss of property through what he believes was illegal search and seizure, and a court-martial. He suffers continuous harassment from local and state officials in Tennessee, where he has uncovered corruption in the legal system as it pertains to the activities of the grand jury.

A citizen or an officer in the military has four choices when he or she uncovers corruption in government: watch it and do nothing, deny it, defend it, or fight it. Today there are literally millions of people, a massive corrupt media machine, and a protective and shielding press that blatantly defend "modification" (that's corruption) in government policy in what has become known to this generation as political correctness. For example, if the White House is challenged, it's called racism, anarchism and intellectual naïveté and ignorance. By virtue of the verdict in numerous 'court tests' that have challenged the White House, one is left to conclude that the average citizen has no standing in the courts when it comes to questioning the Obama Administration.

It's gratifying to know that Fitzpatrick, like the Founding Fathers, is not obliged to appease his oppressors or back down when threatened. Rather, he has chosen to stand firm on the rule of law, knowing, like those Founders, that it might cost him his life.

"I'd rather die for something than stand for nothing!" he says.

Commander Fitzpatrick takes his oaths seriously and he's taken several important ones in his lifetime. In his youth, as an Eagle Scout (Troop 508, Meiners Oaks, California), he pledged: "On my honor, I will do my best, to do my duty to God. On my honor, I will do my best, to do my duty to my country." As an officer in the United States Army he swore this oath: "I, Walter Francis Fitzpatrick, having been appointed a Commander in the United States Navy, do solemnly swear that I will support and defend the Constitution of the United States against all enemies, foreign and domestic; that I will bear true faith and allegiance to the same; that I take this obligation freely, without any mental reservation or purpose of evasion; and that I will well and faithfully discharge the office upon which I am about to enter. So help me God."

There was a time when people understood that a "vow" meant an unbreakable promise. Commander Fitzpatrick made a promise to that woman in Philadelphia in 1776 and today he makes it to you. On that day he stood next to Benjamin Franklin on that street in Philadelphia and echoed the challenge to her and the hundreds of millions who followed: "if you can keep it!" Do the Scriptures not testify to the heart and soul of an individual who is willing to lay down his life for a friend? Has history not taught us that freedom comes with a price?

At this writing Commander Walter Fitzpatrick has spent many months in prison with few privileges because of his actions. What further price will he pay to do his part to preserve the republic? Our republic. Your republic. Is he less intent, less courageous, less honorable, less committed, and less patriotic than the handful of men who concluded that great liberating document upon which our nation was founded with a thirty-one-word promise? "And for the support of this declaration, with a firm reliance on the protection of Divine Providence, we mutually pledge to each other our lives, our fortunes and our sacred honor."

There is an elusive and persistent force in the United States today to seize the authority of the United States Constitution. What is offered in its place is a blueprint for tyranny. With that "sacred" document governing us (for the writers confirmed their dependence on an Almighty God to guide them when they wrote it) we can continue to structure, and place righteous limitations on, the affairs of government; thus securing the continuance of our basic rights, privileges and freedom in our daily life. Without that document, our nation will vanish!

Read it once again: "And for the support of this declaration, with a firm reliance on the protection of Divine Providence, we mutually pledge to each other our lives, our fortunes and our sacred honor."

It is time to join Lieutenant Colonel Dr. Terry Lakin and Commander Walter Francis Fitzpatrick and reaffirm our allegiance to the greatest nation on the face of the earth. The question is not can you do it, but will you do it?

Daria Novak: Are we on the road to political China?

"When we no longer seek the truth, we are no longer a nation," says Daria Novak, who has been following the Lakin case with resolve to support and see him fully restored his former rank and pay. She is a resident of Connecticut and active in politics, having made a run for Congress. A world traveler, she sees the greater danger that faces America. "I lived in China, and what Terry went through reminded me of what goes on there. When I heard what happened to him in court, I was disgusted. I just couldn't believe it could happen here!"

Daria remembers her days in China, where she observed a government that told its citizens—or perhaps better stated, "subjects" —what to think and how to act. Can't happen in America? She's worried that we are on the *road to China* and we must turn back!

As never before, the U.S. is experiencing one of its greatest periods of immigration as the politically oppressed continue to come to our shores. Russian immigrants contrast the state-communist control they lived under in their homeland and the wonderful freedom the United States affords them now as citizens. Other groups, like these Russian émigrés who have lived under Communist rule, cannot comprehend the policies and executive orders of Barack Hussein Obama that are taking the country in the direction of a socialist state. Is our country on the road to being such a society? That's not the America Daria Novak wants for her family.

"I want my children to grow up and tell their children there was a time in America when we almost lost our freedom," says Daria. "I want them to know it is something they must fight to preserve!" Daria, who worked for the Reagan administration, knows well the price we have paid and will have to pay to preserve our freedom. She remembers her boss's warning:

> Freedom is never more than one generation away from extinction. We didn't pass it to our children in the bloodstream. It must be fought for, protected, and handed on for them to do the same, or one day we will spend our sunset years telling our children and our children's children what it was once like in the United States where men were free.[9]

Freedom does not come with a household guarantee. The individual citizen must be ready to pay a price for it. Daria Novak is willing to pay that price.

Ed Noonan: Terrorists got more constitutional protection than Terry did.

Across the country, in California, another voice cries out for the nation to return to its constitutional roots. State Senate Tea Party candidate Ed Noonan takes the issue of Barack Hussein Obama's birth certificate one step further. "I'm not even sure he is a *native*-born citizen!"

Ed Noonan's studies focus on the origins of this nation and the birth of its Constitution. He will not rewrite history or reinterpret the political events of the past to his liking. He deals in facts and is outraged by those who would see the rule of law superseded by what is convenient to their own political agenda. Noonan is not the kind to be apathetic, not the kind to sit back and watch the nation lose its identity at the whim of those who believe we have a "living Constitution."

"I came across the work of Phil Berg, the guy who brought suit against Obama about his alleged birth certificate. Through that initial investigation, I then found out about Terry Lakin." Ed followed the case with great interest because of his own study that showed that there have been other

---

[9] Address to the annual meeting of the Phoenix Chamber of Commerce, 30 March 1961

presidents whose "natural born" citizenship status has been called into question. "Obama was not the first," he contends.

A teacher by nature, Ed Noonan wrote letters to Terry on a regular basis but had a hidden agenda in doing so: he knew every bit of correspondence he sent would be scrutinized. "I wanted the people who screened Terry's letters to get a history lesson!" he says.

His book, *Chester Arthur—1st Bogus POTUS vs Death of America*, challenges the eligibility of other former presidents. As for Terry, Noonan states emphatically, "Terrorists got more constitutional protection than the Lieutenant Colonel did. It was as if the Constitution did not apply to him."

The challenge to Barack Hussein Obama is not a Republican or Democrat thing. It is an outcry from citizens who are tired of being fed half-truths and lies. Individuals scattered throughout the nation are conducting their own investigations about the man who has spent the last few years hiding his history.

Sarah Redd: I started out as a Democrat.

Texan Sarah Redd, who was a registered Democrat, has pried open the hatches of history and discovered many improprieties centering on the 2008 presidential election. Prior to the primaries, Sarah was in the trenches supporting Hillary Clinton, fighting off the political advances of the newcomer Illinois senator.

"I started out as a Democrat and was a member of Christians for Hillary. I learned that people who supported her were actually taken off the Democrat e-mail list. They began to force Obama down our throats."

Sarah comes from a military family, and she did not see Terry Lakin as an Army rebel. She understood military protocol and, as Terry's case emerged, followed it carefully, finally deciding to support him in any way she could. "It's not a party thing with me," says Sarah. "I believe in fighting for justice."

Sarah Redd is not going to remain silent while the stranger in the White House gets a free ride to the next election. She has written thousands of letters, e-mails and postcards to educate a public that up to now has been unaware of the truth about Obama.

Rock Peters: You can't run a country on personality.

"I love my country more than myself," says Rock Peters. "I'm a patriot because it is all about my country." Rock detests the "personality cult" that Obama has created. As he sees it, the seduction of the American people has not come as a result of what the man has done, is doing, or will do, but rather about how he *appears* to be doing something. "You can't run a country on personality," Rock tells his listeners in word and song.

Rock is a multi-talented musician, poet and political activist who won't spare the words when he speaks of his love for his country. He is not only a student of history but also a student of the here and now.

Rock's music and poetry wake up America to the forces that are coming up against our country right now. Not wanting the status quo to remain the status quo, Rock hopes to set the record straight about the president with lyrics and music that have a satirical lilt, his artistic signature. His website (www.godsaveusa.com) continues to educate people about where we are today and where we are going as a nation under the leadership of Obama. Rock is reaching out to a new generation of young people who identify with his medium and his message.

In Rock Peters' version of "The Emperor's New Clothes," found on his site, he leaves the reader with hope that somewhere, someone will finally come to realize that "Emperor Barack Hussein Obama stands naked before us with no verification as to his eligibility and suitability to lead this great nation!"

Patra Minocha: Political activism is not some sort of competitive sport.

Patra Minocha is known as a political activist, poet and songstress. Each morning she looks out the window of her suburban Nashville home and sees a landscape of mountains whose beauty defies easy description. But when Patra looks out nowadays, she sees beyond the beauty, and what she sees troubles her. The nation is divided. Our children are unaware of our exceptionality. We are at war on too many fronts. The economy is headed in a direction of no return. And a president of unproven eligibility continues to send our boys and girls onto the battlefield, where his PC rules of engagement put them in harm's way. These issues and so many more have prompted Patra to fight for what she believes in.

"Our nation needs to be uplifted spiritually to endure the horrific challenges we face on a daily basis," says Patra. Her passion to improve military morale has inspired her to create a flag, "THE HANDS OF FREEDOM/ THE HOPE OF THE FUTURE," along with poems and songs of encouragement.

A registered nurse, Patra yearns to help those who serve in the military. She constantly reaches out with her many talents to inspire faith in God and in our great land. When Lt. Col. Lakin came into her life, first through the media, then personally through an exchange of letters, she knew she had found a compatriot.

"Political activism is not some sort of competitive sport, but rather a spiritual quest and pursuit to discover truth," says Patra. She watched with anxious anticipation at the trial of Terry Lakin and saw justice go awry.

"The court-martial of Lieutenant Colonel Dr. Lakin is a constitutional travesty that would have been prevented if there had been true political transparency," says Patra. "If Congress possessed one quarter of the constitutional courage of Terry Lakin, this American republic would rise again!"

Her website (www.salutetosoldiers.com) takes the visitor on an inspirational journey into the heart of American greatness. Patra hopes that we are still a people capable of embracing the faith and vision of the Founding Fathers.

> He Is There
> by Patra
>
> He is there in the trenches,
> in the depths of despair.
> He is there when you're alone,
> when no one seems to care.
>
> He is there in the darkness,
> the hidden shadows of the night.
> He's the Sun. He's the Moon.
> He's the Stars shining bright.
>
> He's your torch through life's trials,
> Your wounded soul's guiding light;

When frights and fears overtake you,
He's the hands that hold you tight.

He is there like a Mother,
watching over her child,
Holding them close,
when their hearts cry out loud.

He was there in the beginning.
He will be there in the end.
He's your sister. He's your brother.
He's your Father. He's your friend.

There is only one Patra Minocha listed in the United States citizen directory, and you can be certain—she is indeed one of a kind!

Theresa Cao: Sometimes truth shouts from the mountaintops!

Other voices are crying out, and sometimes they can even be heard in the halls of Congress. It is January 6, 2011. A crowd is lined up and ready to enter the U.S. Capitol in Washington, D.C. Look carefully because Ms. Theresa Cao is in that line and ready to enter the House chamber. She opts for the stairs that lead to the balcony. Watch her take a seat high atop the great hall and listen along with her as members of the House read from the pages of our Constitution.

Now, keep an eye on that woman because in a moment, during the reading of Article II, Section 1, she will make history. After Article I is read, Theresa is poised for the reading of Article II. Those around her do not know that this is the reason she has come today.

Democrat Frank Pallone from New Jersey takes his place at the podium. He looks up at the waiting crowd and then down at the text, and reads: "No person except a natural born Citizen, or a Citizen of the United States, at the time of the Adoption of this Constitution, shall be eligible to the Office of President."

As that moment, the intrepid Ms. Cao rises and yells out, "Except Obama, except Obama. Help us, Jesus!" As is apparent, Theresa has her doubts about Obama and his eligibility to be president of the United States. Her words echo through the hall. Then there is the striking of the gavel and the demand for silence. As officers rush to her side and escort her from the chamber, Theresa knows she has been heard.

What she is unaware of is that in a matter of minutes her message is being published and broadcast around the world. The media, of course, jump on the story, calling into question Theresa's very sanity. They label her "crazy" and "a birther" in anticipation that her story will make for sensational reading, all the while belittling what she has done. As with most sensational stories, the press bets the whole matter will soon be forgotten.

But a voice does not have to be bold or brazen or dramatic to be heard; it just has to state the truth. Truth rebels against the passivity and silence of the masses—and it has an interesting way of erupting in the most unlikely of places, even Congress.

Sometimes truth has the voice of an innocent child, singing a hymn or reading from the Holy Scriptures. Other times truth is heard at a high school baseball game when a principal asks the crowd to bow their heads and pray for an injured player. You might see it in the face of a veteran who closes his eyes and places his hand over his heart as the Pledge of Allegiance is recited at a memorial service. And you can feel its emotion and its strength when a tear streams down the face of a mother who has given her child in service to the country.

There are times when a person is filled with an urgency to proclaim and defend his or her beliefs. Theresa Cao had come to such a point in her life. She made a decision to pay a price for telling the truth, and on that wintry day in January, in the great hall of Congress, she did exactly that, in her own way. And the world heard it!

Gordon Smith: Terry is the best-kept secret in America.

One of the most outspoken supporters of Lt. Col. Lakin is Gordon Smith of Oregon. His own military record documents twenty years in service: a ten-year stint in the Air Force and an equal amount of time in the Navy. His association with Terry Lakin has paralleled his own doubts about the eligibility of Obama to be president. Like millions of Americans who cannot and will not be conned by the media, Gordon began looking for the president's birth certificate.

"I was frustrated because I knew the media were covering up Obama's eligibility by not addressing the birth certificate issue," says Gordon. He first saw Terry on YouTube and was glad to find someone of his caliber standing up for the truth and asking the same questions he himself was asking.

Gordon was troubled right from the start of the Obama candidacy and spoke out boldly about his constitutional ineligibility. Through a series of events, he wound up on *The Barry Farber Show* on radio, where the host grilled him on the meaning of "natural born citizen."

After this first radio interview, when they were off the air, Farber kept him on the phone for over an hour and by the time that informal interview was over, Gordon was invited to become a regular guest on the show. He spoke with conviction and determination in his hope to see Terry receive satisfaction in the courts. The radio host joined forces with his guest and brought the case to his many faithful listeners.

Before the trial, Gordon worked to do everything he could to keep Terry out of jail. He wrote Terry and passed e-mail updates on to him as often as something new emerged that he thought Terry should know about. Sensing that the media were going to do a hatchet job on Terry and give Obama a free ride, Gordon began working for him virtually 24/7.

Farber's interest in the case continued, and Gordon finally got Terry on the show. During the interview, Terry explained his commitment to the rule of law. "The Constitution is more important than I am," Terry told Farber. Farber was impressed and encouraged his audience to reach out and support Terry.

Since 1960, Barry Farber has had thousands of guests on his show for various reasons; Terry's invitation was not typical. "A miscarriage of justice got Terry on *The Barry Farber Show*," says Gordon, adding, "Terry is the best-kept secret in America, and I get angry when I think of what happened to him."

The road to justice has not been easy for the retired Air Force and Navy veteran. Gordon Smith has met opposition along the way, but he believes his cause is righteous and he's willing to pay a price, even enduring the ridicule and loss of friends.

Perhaps Barry Farber said it best when he introduced Gordon to his radio listeners: "He's a proud, upright, unapologetic, so-called birther." And that he is. Whether the mainstream media admit it or not, Gordon has millions of brothers and sisters. One of them is Terry Lakin.

Rudy Davis: I see the world through the grid of my faith.

"I put a high value on truth!" says engineer and activist Rudy Davis. Terry's case certainly sobered him and brought about some interesting changes in his own life. "Before Terry," says Rudy, "I spent my life chasing the dollar."

Having served as a jury member in the *CIA Columbia Obama Sedition And Treason Trial* held at Pastor James David Manning's church, Rudy was familiar with the Obama ineligibility issue. That is where Rudy also met his wife Erin. Rudy was appalled at how the mainstream media was reporting on the Obama ineligibility issue what was happening to an honorable serviceman who had devoted so many years to his country. So Rudy not only followed the Lakin case but also tried to educate his local community on the subject. "I went to the trial and saw him get railroaded," says Rudy.

Rudy is a tough Texan who doesn't back down when he knows he's within his rights. "Hey, I am a Constitutionalist," he says. "I respect the rule of law and no one should be above the law." His detainment which was caught on video by his wife Erin in Dallas attests to his determination to exercise his freedom of speech. Rudy believes that our congressional leaders have dropped the ball and not done their jobs in vetting Obama. Terry Lakin should have never had to bear this burden.

Rudy was handcuffed by the local police in front of Dallas' Majestic Theater for handing out flyers about Terry Lakin's case during a conservative gathering which included Sarah Palin and Rick Perry. Said Rudy at the time, "If the people of America don't stand up for the truth and stand up for the Constitution and stand up for freedom, we're going to lose our right to speak out!"

"I see the world through the grid of my faith", says Rudy who is a bible believing Christian and on a mission for truth. "I see the motives of this president, and it troubles me. What we need now are righteous men and women to stand up. Without that we will lose our country!"

Brent Morehouse: Americans have been asleep.

West Coast author and activist Brent Morehouse is a student of our country's heritage and admits he never thought he would write a book about it. He has an appreciation for his country's unique history and the events that led to its founding. He also recognizes Obama's contempt for the Constitution, his disdain for the rule of law, and his disregard for the rights of a certain military officer, Lt. Col. Terry Lakin, U.S. Army.

The Californian has a keen understanding of the Constitution and natural law. Brent phrases it this way: "The concepts of natural law, while seemingly common sense, are very difficult to implement within a society because they require ceaseless vigilance from their benefactors, the citizens." Terry Lakin is one such citizen.

"Americans have been asleep," says Morehouse. He adds, "I feel responsible as a citizen for falling asleep and not holding our elected officials responsible. Our problems have existed for decades." He cites trade deficits, deficit spending and a Social Security program that is nothing more than a Ponzi scheme, all of which have gotten worse since World War II.

"The federal government is broken, and a corrupt central government cannot solve the problems of a corrupt central government," says Morehouse. "In a way, I feel it is my fault that Terry Lakin went to prison. We failed to be diligent about our elected officials."

Brent Morehouse has skillfully dissected many of the problems that face us today in a book, *Tea Party: The Awakening*. In his sixty-five-page forward, he compares the 1770s to the present. It is a masterful analysis of our beginnings and a sobering evaluation of the nation's political status.

Brent's research centers on the battle between two factions that still exist today. For over two hundred years, the Whigs (modern Tea Party) and the Tories (modern Democrats) have battled for political dominance.

"In the end, the Declaration of Independence wasn't just a victory of the Whigs over the Tories," says Brent. "It was the radical faction of the

Whigs that won over the establishment faction of the Whigs. The established Whigs had opposed independence hardly less than the Tories." In the end, says Morehouse, the establishment Whigs—read: moderate Republicans—"finally checked their consciences and threw in their lot with the Tea Partiers."

Brent is of the opinion that Terry's efforts may eventually help the moderates check their consciences. "It's for sure that Terry Lakin drew attention to the fact of where we are as a nation," he says. Brent, whose family tree dates back to the 1600s, acknowledges the problems facing us as a free society, but he is still an optimist and hopes history will repeat itself.

David Moxley: The least I can do is let Terry tell his story.

"I don't like the birther tag, but I do want the truth!" says David Moxley. He operates a web radio broadcast site out of Atlanta, Georgia—a small traditional AM station with 90 percent of its broadcast power moving through the web. The station offers a variety of programming options that range from farming to chat radio. With a half-million downloads a month, the station is well on its way to becoming an important tool in educating and informing citizens about the affairs of the nation.

"At first I thought Terry was a 'ghostbuster,'" David says. "When I learned more about him, I did the only thing I could do; I called his people and said you can come on board the station." The Terry Lakin Action Fund now broadcasts once a week on its airwaves.

David has continued to support Terry with his broadcast resources and endorsement. "The least I can do is let Terry tell his story," he says. The weekly broadcast, which follows an interview format, features individuals who work with the Terry Lakin Action Fund, including Jack Cashill, Joseph Farah, Jerome Corsi, Rev. James David Manning and many others. Hosted by Marco Ciavolino, the show updates Terry's supporters on his status and shares new information on the eligibility challenge.

"The question I ask is this," says David. "Why are 535 people afraid to raise their hands and call for Obama's real birth certificate, if he even has one?" David answers his own question. "I think they're afraid of a civil uprising."

Those who doubt Obama's eligibility are fully aware of the potential consequences if their fears prove justified. "I accept General Paul Vallely's thinking that we are so close to economic disaster, that will bring people to the streets," says David. "At that point I would hope that the people would start waking up!"

Not surprisingly, David has great admiration for Terry. "Terry Lakin took a chance. He put his life on hold and his life on the line." But he feels that people are beginning to get the message about these two men: the lieutenant colonel is telling the truth; his commander in chief is not. While the media protect Obama, David Moxley is determined "to help keep Terry's story alive."

Linda M.: I'm aghast at the ambivalence of the American people.

The matter of Barack Hussein Obama's deceitful rise to power."

Linda came upon Terry's story much the same way as millions of others. It was early on a Sunday morning when she leaned forward in her chair and focused on the computer screen. Within seconds her fingers pressed the familiar key that opened her Facebook page. Her eyes scanned the morning news, and a quick gaze at each story gave her an update on world and local affairs. She scrolled down and paused at the photo of a soldier.

Next to the thumbnail picture appeared an unfamiliar name with a few words in boldface: "QUESTIONS OBAMA'S ELIGIBILITY." The text noted that Lt. Col. Terry Lakin was being charged with a serious crime. Linda's knowledge of military affairs told her this soldier was in big trouble. But who was he and what had he done?

Her eyes fixed on the screen as she read the entire news story. Terry had questioned the authority of the United States commander in chief to issue orders for his next deployment. His question was simple: Could Barack Hussein Obama prove he was a "natural born citizen"—the basic requirement for the office of President and commander in chief? As of that date, he had not produced a valid long-form certificate of birth.

Even before Obama was elected, Linda had launched her own inquiry into the matter, searching websites and investigative news services. Her study revealed disturbing information. She learned that millions of dollars had been spent to suppress Obama's records. No candidate had ever done that before.

Linda asked the same logical questions millions of people were asking. If Barack Obama could prove his citizenship, then why wouldn't he produce a valid birth certificate? The "sympathetic press," as she called it, tried to disarm an unsuspecting public by creating a word to belittle skeptics. "Birthers" was a condescending tag that made light of the issue.

On that memorable morning, pictured before her was a man willing to sacrifice his career and his freedom for the same issue. In that moment Linda emotionally joined forces with the decorated officer and absorbed the details of the case.

When she'd finished reading, her eyes gazed upward and she cried out, "O God, Terry Lakin needs Your help. Our country needs Your help!"

As she spoke, her husband appeared. "What's for breakfast?" he asked.

"Justice!" she replied. During the next few minutes Linda shared the story. Both sat speechless. The greatest political deception in the history of the United States had been artfully perpetrated, and this Army officer was giving up his career and much more to try to uncover the truth.

"We've got to help this guy," she announced. Her husband, in full agreement, charged, "Let's do it!"

Linda began to write Terry almost every day, not realizing that he was receiving an endless stream of letters from people all over the country assuring him he had their support. She was relieved to learn that Terry was not standing alone.

From the day Linda discovered Terry Lakin, she was determined to tell every-one she met about the deceptive steps that had been taken to get Obama into office. Most people were unaware of the matter and stood in amazement that this could really happen in America. Few people knew the constitutional requirements for the office and Obama's failure to meet them.

The issue was hot. The Obama administration would surely be in jeopardy if Terry could fully present his case. Although he was unable to do so, his imprisonment added to the mounting pressure on the White House, even from Obama supporters, to present his long-suppressed birth certificate. Linda was not convinced by the copy Obama ultimately produced. "It proves nothing," she says.

Linda has spent the last year educating people about the case. With a deep respect and understanding of the United States Constitution, she has met supporters and skeptics alike with the challenge to read it for themselves.

Her ongoing study of the documents that inspired our Constitution, as well as her review of subsequent court cases that defined the term "natural born citizen," has led Linda to one definite conclusion: Barack Hussein Obama was not eligible for the highest office in our land.

Linda continues to share Terry's story and the constitutional requirements to be president with all who will listen. Her goal? She is one more citizen who will do everything in her power to defeat Barack Hussein Obama in the 2012 election.

The Reverend David Manning: Everybody in Congress knows this man is a fraud!

These are tough words coming from a tough man about the sitting president of the United States, Barack Hussein Obama. Listen to his radio broadcast, *The Manning Report,* for five minutes and you know you're dealing with a man who doesn't back down when it comes to fighting for the preservation of our country and our Constitution. The Reverend Dr. James David Manning is on the battlefield and his message is clear: Obama must go!

The reverend tells his radio audience, "Our Constitution has been trampled on—our Bill of Rights. Obama has destroyed our nation internally by destroying our courts!" From Harlem to the world, his radio broadcast is clear in its purpose.

With a riveting voice, Rev. Manning warns, chastises, criticizes, rebukes, teaches, and does a whole lot more in an attempt to wake America up, get the sands of doubt out of our eyes, and help us take back the White House.

Like never before, this president is changing the rules by which his branch of government has operated since its inception. The "executive order" is used and abused by Obama while the Congress stands by, letting him seize its power. And where are our representatives in all of this? "Congress acts as if the Constitution doesn't matter!" says the reverend.

"Why is it that so many people run away from this issue? If it is a question that needs to be raised about the most powerful man on the planet, why is it that you are slammed and criminalized or called a racist if you raise the question?"

In a speech titled "I am Terry Lakin's brother," Rev. Manning said the following: "I am prepared to publicly declare the court-martial of Lieutenant Colonel Terry Lakin an act of tyranny. The Obama administration aims to put down the brewing revolution of military officers who question his eligibility!"

Rev. Manning is also fed up with the hypocrisy of the conservative media. He cited Glenn Beck, who called those who challenge Obama's eligibility "misguided and foolish." He also challenged Bill O'Reilly of *The O'Reilly Factor*. Said the reverend, O'Reilly "swore he had seen the birth certificate and referred to the 'birthers' as kooks who did not represent mainstream America." Obviously, members of the conservative movement are "in bed with Obama too," as Rev. Manning puts it.

He feels there are too many fragmented groups all believing the same thing and that these individuals and groups must find a singular voice to reach America with the "bad news."

Rev. Manning is not a favorite of the media. He is constantly challenged about his predictions that the country will see a time of rioting and rebellion in the streets against the person and policies of Barack Hussein Obama.

He has supported Lt. Col. Terry Lakin right from the beginning and has paid a price for his support. He has been fingerprinted, interrogated, locked up in a room, intimidated, held in custody, accused of trespassing, harassed by U.S. military officers on a base, publicly humiliated, and denied his civil rights.

"I go direct; I don't cut corners. I'm not backing down. My voice is strong," he warns listeners who might wish that he were not so critical of Obama. His message is abundantly clear: James David Manning does not see Obama's eligibility as a black-and-white issue; he sees it as a right-and-wrong one!

"I'm going to keep doing what I'm doing, and Obama will not know any freedom or peace. The only way will be over my dead body!" Sounds like a man willing to give his life to get the truth out to save his country, like a certain lieutenant colonel.

The reverend was an eyewitness to the Lakin court-martial, which he sums up in four words: "unprecedented travesty of justice."

With Rev. Manning, it is a "court thing," and he is troubled by the status of the American judicial system. "Every court in America has denied the American people the opportunity of due process," he argues. "Not one American has standing before the court regarding Obama's eligibility or the constitutional right to know."

The reverend continues, "Terry Lakin was denied access to information regarding Obama's eligibility because the court's ruling is that he, too, does not have standing."

As Rev. Manning sees it, the courts have "held Obama in a form of protective custody against the truth." He blames the media for keeping this matter of Obama's ineligibility out of the public domain, where it could be fruitfully discussed. The minister pleads with his audience to do the right thing for themselves and the country. "America has to wake up, because Obama's silence about his birth certificate is rubbing off on the people!"

The day after the Lakin trial ended, Rev. Manning addressed his radio audience and laid out the facts. Terry's guilty plea to a lesser charge was met with some disappointment, but the reverend knew that Terry is an honorable man and made an honorable decision because of his respect for the military. He closed his broadcast that day with a courageous announcement to bring definition to the Lakin trial: "Terry's trial is not the end. It is only the beginning!"

Jerome R. Corsi, PhD: Can our military raise a legal question?

Our Courts Will Not Allow Our Military to Raise a Legal Question.

Terry Lakin posed a legitimate question. It was not that he was merely entitled to ask the question. It was his moral duty, under the oath he swore, to ask, "Is the president of the United States constitutionally qualified to hold the office?" A rather simple question, and Jerome Corsi was among the first to ask it.

"The American military ought to be disgraced for what they did to Terry!" says Dr. Corsi.

The author of a number of best-selling books—including *The Obama Nation, America for Sale,* and *Where's the Birth Certificate?*—Jerry has not only challenged the authenticity of the birth documents presented to the American public as official records, but also actually predicted just about every move Obama has made thus far regarding the issue of his birth certificate.

"I knew Obama was so afraid of the issue that sooner or later he was bound to release a birth certificate. I actually wanted to see if he could be tempted into releasing one. I needed him to release it, and he did. I also knew it would be a forgery."

A forgery is a likely felony. It is often defined as a "crime of high seriousness." And it doesn't get higher or more serious than a president forging a document that concerns his very eligibility to be president.

"In 2008 I said the short form was bogus," says Dr. Corsi. The reasons seem obvious. "First, it is a poorly done document. It was electronically created. There are numerous external scans that have been imported into the document. It wouldn't be acceptable in a court of law; as everybody knows, copies are not acceptable. It is not an original. He's fooling no one, and sadly, the press won't call it like it is, a forgery, and a poor one at that!"

So, just who is Jerome Corsi? You can investigate him fully, as his credentials, college records, dissertation, house mortgage and more are all available on the Internet. Oh yes, and his birth certificate, not a forgery, is carefully tucked away in his file cabinet.

"The media are not independent, as they make you believe," says Jerry. "I'd like the media to investigate Obama as hard as they've investigated me."

Dr. Corsi is a man with many critics. There are those who would seek to strip him of his Harvard PhD and revoke his law degree, accuse him of being a bigot and racist, curse him, defame him and mock his creditability as one of the nation's top political writers. What did this guy do? Jerry uncovered arguably the biggest lie told since a certain husband and wife lost their long-term lease in the Garden of Eden.

His books regularly show up on the best-selling lists, with such critiques as "Investigative reporter Dr. Jerome Corsi has surpassed himself in possibly one of the most important books in American history." Even those who are cynical yield to his message: "Even the skeptical reader will have to appreciate how conscientiously he makes his case that Barack Obama's eligibility is by no means a given."

As Dr. Corsi has discovered, if you post facts that call into question Obama's birth certificate, you are labeled a racist and an extremist. To disagree with the president's defenders is to be called mindless and a "wack job." Jerome Corsi deals with these slurs constantly, but the rude and vicious insults do little to stop him. You can't stop the truth, nor can you hide it, disguise it, alter it, bend it, shape it, deny it, or cut it in half. Truth is fact. It is reality. It is authenticity. It is certainty.

Jerry does not mince words. "It's simple," he says. "The bottom line is that Obama has taken part in a felony when he provided a poorly produced forgery as his long-form birth certificate and gave it to the nation. He lied!"

Terry Lakin is Jerome Corsi's kind of patriot. "I admire Terry. Here's a guy who put his life and career on the line. We, as a country, should admire him, a man of courage. Personally, I think we should give him a medal."

What awaits America? "Our kids are not learning American history," says Corsi. Indeed, history has been reduced to a course in "apologetics." Schools have failed to instill pride in our past, respect for our Founders, and the merits of our Constitution. These kinds of messages are lost in the left-controlled state educational curricula. The scholastic agenda from kindergarten through college and upward in our major universities has brought us to the point that half of our citizens do not know who we were, who we are and what we must be to remain a symbol of hope and a citadel of freedom to the world.

People like Terry Lakin and Jerome Corsi understand the importance of preserving the integrity of the nation. And there are others, great men and women who daily are willing to give their lives for the nation's preservation. While some have a calling to serve in our military and defend the truth, others report it.

Catherine "Kate" Vandemoer, PhD: God had a great deal to do with the Constitution.

When Terry was found guilty of the first charge brought against him, he was standing. So was Catherine Vandemoer. She is no stranger to the lieutenant colonel; she has fought for his acquittal since the beginning. She was there at all proceedings, even at briefing sessions. She prepared documentation and watched and prayed. Many who were in the courtroom that day could not believe what happened, and while the White House may have concluded that the case is closed, there are those who will not give up the fight to see this American hero fully restored. Kate is one of them. She believes this must be done in the name of justice. After all, she is a "constitutionalist" and everything about this case concerns the Constitution.

Ask this constitutionalist writer what the bottom line is with regard to Barack Hussein Obama and she will sum it up in a few words: "It all boils down to allegiance. Obama does not have allegiance to the United States!"

Dr. Kate, as she is known, was not born in this country. As a child, she listened to her schoolmates boast that when they grew up they wanted to be president. She wanted to be president too, but knew this could not happen. When a person is born in another country, she understands how they could have a "natural sympathy," as she calls it, for that other country. In matters of national security, she knows there must be no confusion of allegiance.

Dr. Kate looks at it this way: "If the Founding Fathers had thought being a 'citizen' was sufficient to be the president, the words 'natural born' would not have preceded the word 'citizen' in Article II."

From childhood, Kate pursued the American dream, earning a PhD and becoming a celebrated spokeswoman for the Constitution. She is a proud American and thankful that she grew up with American values and principles. But she also remembers the pressure from her peers and professors to hate America. Something inside her told her to hold on to the dream and not succumb to the propaganda of the "mob." Since that time, the Constitution has been her anchor.

When interviewed, Dr. Kate shares her admiration for the framers of the Constitution. "The Constitution is just 44,000 words…it's a piece of brilliance, and I feel God had a great deal to do with it!"

Listening to her in an interview or reading her captivating monographs, you are left with nothing less than "pearls of information" about the American way of life. She is fast becoming one of the most-quoted women in America. Those looking for a concise explanation of Obama's ineligibility would do well to quote her.

The legitimacy of this president and the fact that he is directing the national and international affairs of the most powerful nation on the earth is what Dr. Kate calls "the greatest crisis we have faced since our founding."

"After what they did to Terry, how can you not help but ache inside?" says Kate. She sees things a little differently from those who say our citizens are in revolt.

"The people are not rebelling against the government; the government is rebelling against the people," she says. Perhaps a prime example of this took place in a courtroom where an American officer, Lt. Col. Terry Lakin, was subject to humiliation and disgrace and treated like a criminal. Dr. Kate lays out her case:

> When the putative commander in chief tells his supporters to bring a gun to a knife fight, to 'get in peoples' faces,' calls vast swaths of the American public his enemies, pays his bloggers to threaten, intimidate, and attack, has his homeland security chief assault Americans, has his justice department free terrorists and allow voter intimidation to go unchecked, has his military court-martialled, jailed, and discredit the service of decorated army officers and enlisted personnel, and calls anyone racist who disagrees with his policies, then the source of the violence plaguing America is clear.

Terry Lakin and Kate Vandemoer are American patriots. They are part of a significant army of people who will not give in, give up or get out.

Greg Lakin, DO, JD: I believe what my brother did was an act of patriotism!

Greg Lakin remembers watching his brother in the courtroom. Above him were three pictures: one of George Washington, another of Thomas Jefferson, and the third was of Abraham Lincoln. Greg understood something the court did not: Terry was in good company that day.

That courtroom was a long way from the hometown where the Lakin brothers grew up. Greg describes his childhood as a happy time, not unlike that of the Cunningham family depicted in the classic television series *Happy Days*. Both father and mother were great sources of encouragement, and their sons were devoted to them and to each other.

The three brothers attended public schools and could be found in the First Congregational Church on Sunday mornings all dressed up in suits and ties, clutching a songbook. "We never got into smoking, drugs or alcohol, I guess because we were well rounded. In our home, education and sports were big parts of our life. We didn't know we had an option when it came to going to college. It was a typical upbringing, with all that goes into preparing us for the day we would leave home."

The three boys respected their parents. "My father was a counselor, university professor, and was also a Korean War veteran of the Marines," says Greg. "He held a EdD in psychology, so we were well managed. We grew up with a man who was a patriot and one who understood human behavior. He was an intellect, always reading, writing and talking to us about things. He was quite an example for my brothers and me."

Today, their parents remain cautious about Terry's decision, knowing what it has done to him and his family. They had envisioned the possibility that their son might be chosen as the surgeon general of the United States Army, but that is not to be.

Despite setbacks, the devotion of the Lakins to each other is a constant in the lieutenant colonel's life. He hopes that in the long run they will understand why he did what he did. The one distinct characteristic of their relationship with each other, says oldest brother Greg, is the overwhelming confidence that "no matter what happens, the Lakin brothers will land on their feet!"

But could anyone in the family have anticipated the decision the youngest Lakin boy would make to order his own court-martial? When Terry grew uncomfortable with the thought that the sitting president might not be eligible for his position, he made a written appeal to him to show his birth certificate. Greg also wrote letters to Obama.

Greg asked the president, if possible, to meet his brother Terry, even in private, to show him proof of his "natural born" citizenship status. Not one of his letters was ever answered in any way. "I was amazed that the president of the United States would not honor the request of one of his officers, a man who had served the country with honor," says Greg. The president did receive the letters because they were forwarded to higher military offices and filed.

Why did his brother take this extreme course? Greg answers it this way. "I think there are three reasons why my brother made this decision to sacrifice his career. First, I know that he has a true love for the country. Second, he was willing to sacrifice himself for his country. He knew the consequences and what could happen; still, he did it. Third, this was a military issue, and he didn't leave it to civilians."

And what good will have come out of Terry's decision? Maybe someday children in classes across the country will read about a man, like the men and women of two centuries before him, who made a decision that changed the course of the country.

"My brother and I sat with Terry in the family living room one night," says Greg. "We listened as he told us what he felt he had to do. Then we laid out our own concerns. It was a long talk and one I will never forget. When we rose, we stood together, all of us realizing that Terry's life would never be the same, that his military career would probably be ended. But when we left that room, he could be assured we would be there for him."

Terry had his fair share of battles growing up, and early on, his brothers knew to respect him. Greg remembers, "If you pushed him a little bit too far, like big brothers do, well, once in a while he'd swing back. It took a lot to get him going. Terry is not afraid. He's not that kind of guy. He did make this decision for the right reason. A person sometimes has to take a stand."

"When we were kids," Greg continues, "I remember that Terry recognized injustice and couldn't stand for it. He would get upset. He was principled even back then. What he has is that rescuer mentality. Even in school he made sure that everyone was treated fairly."

"Our dad encouraged us to make the world a better place. My brother Terry has stood up against the most powerful man in the country!"

Maybe Terry heard a sermon in that community church where he grew up about patriotism and service to mankind. Then again, maybe it was something more powerful, like the word itself: "Greater love hath no man than this; that one lay down his life for his friends."

Lt. Col. Robert A. Perrich: Terry is in a war, and I'm fighting alongside him!

"I'm standing in the middle of history," says Lt. Col. Bob Perrich. "Terry Lakin's case is of the greatest historical significance since our country's founding in 1776." One doesn't get more definitive than that.

Bob learned about Terry from a friend. Then he read an editorial in his hometown paper in which the writer took Terry to task. "I countered the story and never thought they'd print it," said Bob. "I wanted to let Terry know someone cared." At the time, Terry had yet to learn there were millions who thought the same way Bob did about Obama's treatment of an officer.

"Terry held to his convictions," says Bob. "He took the moral high ground with his oath of office. The average person doesn't know what he did."

Sharing the rank of lieutenant colonel, Robert Perrich understands what an order is and the assurance an officer must have that it has come down through a proper chain of command. He understood the concerns of Lakin and respected his decision to question his orders. "The war we are in now with this president supersedes the war I fought in Iraq," says Bob. "Terry is in a war, and I'm fighting with him!"

Three generations of the Perrich family have faithfully served our country in the military. With a family tradition of military service as his legacy, why would Robert Perrich want to get involved with what appeared at first to be an obscure case involving a stranger?

Bob wants to see a real, unedited birth certificate. "The time for hiding is over!" he says. Like Terry, he questions any and all orders that come from the pen of President Obama: ''I consider him to be a threat to the United States of America.''

Like Terry, Lt. Col. Perrich took the officer's oath. He served in the U.S. Army from 1972 to 1993 as a Senior Army Aviator. His major career contributions took place in the UH-60 Black Hawk Special Operations arena as a maintenance test pilot. He has served in the steaming jungles of Vietnam and on the blistering sands of Iraq. He knows war and the price men and women pay to engage in it. But things are different now.

"'We don't know who this guy is, or if he meets the qualifications for president or commander in chief of the armed forces. That is frightening!'" says the proud veteran. "If I were called today, I wouldn't report."

Margaret "Ducky" Hemenway: This issue is one of paramount national importance.

This is not a political issue it is a legal issue.

"An election doesn't nullify the Constitution!" says Ducky. Don't let the nickname fool you. Ducky Hemenway is a hard-hitting American intellect who early on came to Terry Lakin's defense. She knew what Terry was doing and understood why he had chosen the legal path he chose. She walked that path with him throughout the trial.

A lawyer by profession, Ducky is quite well versed in the politics of politics. A fifteen-year veteran of Capitol Hill, she has seen presidents come and go, and she has been on the cutting edge of the biggest issue pertaining to this sitting president, namely his eligibility. Of this, Ducky says, "There is a cloud over his presidency. There are no markers in Hawaii!"

In an interview with Sharon Rondeau, editor of the online news service The Post & Email, Hemenway discussed the upcoming trial of Lt. Col. Lakin and the failure of both political parties in not vetting Obama. "It leaves both parties open to attacks, because obviously the DNC is guilty for not properly insuring that this papers were in order, and the RNC is guilty of not researching the opposition candidate."

Attorney Hemenway calls the matter of Obama's birth certificate "the most important case in history." To elect Obama, the rules were broken; to maintain him in the White House, more rules have to be broken.

"We are first and foremost a nation of law, where laws are supposed to apply equitably to all Americans. This is not a political issue, it is a legal issue—and one of paramount national importance," says Ducky. Margaret Hemenway is a constitutionalist and makes no apologies for her devotion to the law of the land. She observes, "The greatest danger to our freedom is disrespect for the Constitution and a president who, by his failure to provide evidence of his eligibility for the presidency, evidently doesn't believe the rules should apply to him."

Ducky believes that if the president can ignore one law with impunity, he will ignore others. "If Obama can break a basic, fundamental rule of the Constitution, then what is to keep him from ignoring or suspending other basic rights such as the writ of habeas corpus?"

Attorney Hemenway understands the confusion about the birth requirement to hold the office of President. She brings a lifetime of research and study to our understanding of the words "natural born." From one of her legal briefs we learn:

> Mr. Obama was born into a privileged class at birth, a class of those who claim their citizenship and political rights as a function of manmade laws (soil jurisdiction, i.e., Hawaii). Mr. Obama, therefore, obtains his political rights as legal privileges of manmade law and not as natural unalienable political rights that are a function of the Laws of Nature (birth to a citizen father or parents). The U.S. Constitution authorizes only those who are born as sovereign representatives of the People, according to the authority vested only by the Laws of Nature (natural born), as the ones who can give their consent and claim to be a representative of the sovereign People. They are NOT AUTHORIZED TO QUALIFY TO BE PRESIDENT BY CONGRESS, nor even by a vote of the People. The government cannot create sovereign citizens at birth with a statute or judge's opinion any more than they can pass a statute or opinion that can alter the Laws of Gravity. Sovereign citizens are not born as a privileged political class at birth due to manmade positive laws. Sovereign citizens are created by the Laws of Nature alone.

Ducky has been maligned, threatened, verbally abused and disrespected, likely in an effort to intimate and shut her up. Those who know Ducky know that is not about to happen.

No one has defined the word "birther" more intelligently than Ducky Hemenway. The following bears reading:

> When the media call us 'birthers,' it is a direct attack on our characters by attempting to discredit the sovereign citizens as a result of their claims to a sovereign political status and to the recognition of those sovereign political rights. That is what a 'birther' is in reality... And because we dare to raise our voices and demand that our rights be recognized, as is supposed to be guaranteed by the Constitution in Article II, we are labeled 'birthers.' They could not very well call us what we really are, which is 'sovereign citizens,' because it would not look right to say that the sovereign citizens are complaining that Obama cannot represent them since he was not born as a sovereign.

Sovereign citizen or subject? If this president, with his disregard for the rule of law, continues on the path he has taken, issuing executive orders that corrode our freedoms and halt our enterprise, we will eventually be severed from our history. As Ducky understands, without the rule of law we are not a nation. Without the freedom of speech to demand that this president show his birth certificate, we will have surrendered our past, our present and our future.

Joseph Farah: We're in trouble in America! We're losing our respect for the rule of law.

Joseph Farah, the founder and editor of WND, takes the eligibility issue seriously. "It's a big deal," says Farah. "If it were proven beyond a shadow of a doubt that Obama and the White House knowingly released a document that was fraudulent, perhaps even aiding in the creation of it, would this not be the biggest political scandal in America?"

It is probably safe to say that the average U.S. citizen doesn't want to believe that the White House is really occupied by someone who does not appear to be a "natural born citizen." This widespread disbelief has been Obama's greatest protection.

Joseph Farah, who served as executive news editor at the *Los Angeles Herald Examiner* and editor of the *Sacramento Union* and is the recipient of many journalistic awards, believes he has identified the roots of confusion, apathy and "the ills of society," as he calls it, that have made this generation of Americans indifferent to the truth of Obama's eligibility.

"We're in trouble in America! We're losing our moral bearings…we're losing our respect for the rule of law."

The overarching instrument that established the rules of American law is the Constitution, and Farah believes no one can opt out of it, including the president of the United States.

"I'm obsessed with the Constitution," he declared in a speech given to the National Tea Party Convention in 2010. He is a student of history and has keen insight into the "political floundering" of the American public. He has taken an active role in educating people about the economic, social and political issues of the day, and when the presidential election of 2008 arrived, he was raring to go with an important yet unpopular message.

Before the election, the WND editor was invited to be a guest on numerous media broadcasts. He explained why 2008 would be the year in which voters needed to really examine their motives for casting their ballots. He encouraged them to vote for what they believed and not blindly follow the dictates of their preferred political party.

What information did Joseph Farah have that compelled him to tell voters to exercise caution in this particular election? The 2008 election was to be the time "to cast the ultimate protest vote," he suggested.

While we'll never know if John McCain would have fulfilled Farah's prediction, Obama has. His economic, domestic and foreign policies are proving to be fatal as forecast. What is more, Obama's lack of documented credentials has become a dominant issue. An authentic birth certificate, the basic proof of his constitutional eligibility to be president, has yet to be produced. Joseph Farah has been diligent in asking the most profound question of our times: "Mr. Obama, where is your birth certificate?"

Farah is not alone in his questioning. While the "state-controlled media," as Rush Limbaugh calls them, have blatantly covered up the truth about the birth certificate, other brave men and women have emerged to take on the challenge of flushing out the truth about Obama, not only for themselves but also for the nation.

Lt. Col. Terry Lakin is one such person. "Terry is committed to the rule of law," says Farah, who has more than befriended the lieutenant colonel. "I have a big word of 'thank you' for him. People who do brave things may not be obvious to people. Now Terry needs to inspire people to follow his lead!"

For the most part, the media have dismissed Terry. WND has not. Farah concludes, "He took a courageous stand. It doesn't matter the outcome; what he did was right."

Maj. Gen. Paul Vallely: I don't think justice for Terry will come to pass.

Retired U.S. Army major general Paul Vallely is not new to the issue of Obama's birth qualifications to be president. One need only type his name in any search engine, and in seconds the robust and handsome face of an American hero and patriot appears. Upon reading his biography, one is compelled to conclude that he has served our country and served it well, and is still serving it.

It was a close friend, Margaret "Ducky" Hemenway, who first shared information about Terry with Vallely. As a spokeswoman for the soldier, Ducky confided the details of the case, and immediately the major general made a commitment to support his fellow officer. What he discovered did not surprise him. In fact, it further motivated him to press on with his mission to fight for truth from our government, especially as it relates to the birthplace of President Obama.

Vallely continues to question Obama's eligibility. Sadly, he does not believe there is one person in Congress who will stand up and demand that Obama present his real and unedited records of birth. "They don't have the courage," he declares in no uncertain terms, and adds, "I don't think justice in the matter of his eligibility will come to pass."

Vallely has been on the cutting edge of the issue from the beginning and has tirelessly given interview after interview, sharing his passion for the truth. He founded a website, Stand Up America, and from it he continues to educate the public about important issues relating to the Obama presidency.

After Obama produced his purported birth certificate in April 2011, the major general summoned a panel of experts, including former CIA agents, to study the document. The birth certificate was declared to be a forgery by ten out of the ten panelists.

What about the legitimate role of Congress to investigate the findings regarding Obama's birth certificate? And why have they not conducted their own inquiry and examination into Obama's life?

"Our legislators do not have the courage to look at the facts or to seek the facts. Many of these want to be so politically correct that they'll let the liberal media dominate the scene," says Vallely. "They are unwilling to conduct a proper investigation."

This cowardice is obvious in the case of Terry Lakin, about which the major general adds, "He was given no opportunity for his defense. This goes against the military code for trial. It was a total kangaroo court. It shows us how far down our justice system has gone."

The major general was one of the first to formally and officially ask for Obama's resignation. "He is totally inept, dishonest and guilty of treasonous events. The people of the United States need to demand the resignation of Obama, his cabinet and certain members of Congress." Vallely assures his live audiences and radio and TV listeners and viewers that there is enough information out there for people to demand Obama's resignation and removal. "They did it with Nixon!" he reminds them.

In a radio interview with Sharon Rondeau from the online news service The Post & Email, the major general said, "We're almost to the point of no return here. There has been so much destruction to the country already that we cannot wait around until the election of 2012.

"There must be a groundswell from the people in this country at the local level to deal with the corruption in Washington. By sacrificing his career and reputation, Terry Lakin is leading the way by example. We need millions to follow and demand the truth."

Lt. Gen. Thomas McInerney: I'm proud of Terry! He did what he felt he had to do.

"The issue is not Terry Lakin," says Lt. Gen. Thomas McInerney. "The issue is the Constitution!" The decorated Air Force commander—who considers himself a constitutionalist, not a "birther"—pulls no punches when it comes to the issue of President Obama's birth certificate. "Obama has given no evidence, and there should be clear-cut evidence of his birth."

Whether it is a casual conversation or a guest appearance sitting across from Sean Hannity on Fox News, Lt. Gen. McInerney is forthright and decisive when it comes to issues regarding our national security against enemies both foreign and domestic. He believes there should be no questions about the qualifications of the person sitting in the Oval Office.

"There is still no clear evidence that Barack Obama meets the qualification of being a 'natural born' citizen," says McInerney. He was deeply troubled by this issue from the outset and confronted it by giving interviews and making guest appearances. He was hoping someone would emerge to bring Obama to task.

Enter Lt. Col. Terry Lakin. McInerney received a call from a friend, Maj. Gen. Paul Vallely, and learned about the case. Fully understanding the issue but thinking it might have been handled another way, he made the decision to support Terry.

"Congress and the courts should have done what Terry was trying to do. And where was the speaker of the house?" McInerney asks. A military officer should not have had to sacrifice his career to get to the bottom of the issue, he feels. "I'm proud of Terry! He did what he felt he had to do, and I understand his reasoning. Military officers do not take their oath lightly. The commitment to uphold the Constitution does not end after twenty or twenty-five years; it is a commitment for life. I am still under that oath."

"I knew Terry was not looking for fame or fortune. He is an honorable person." That didn't matter when it came to Terry's case. McInerney was prophetic when, even before the trial, he said in an interview with radio host Peter Boyles that he had spoken to Terry and warned him that he might not be treated fairly. He added, "Dr. Terry Lakin is not going to get a fair trial in this particular proceeding." The general had enough experience to know the forces Terry Lakin would be engaging. He was not wrong in his prediction.

McInerney compares Lakin to Alfred Dreyfus, a young French artillery officer who was accused of communicating military secrets to the Germans. In each case, the initial charges were trumped up, evidence was suppressed, and the outcome was inevitable. Dreyfus was imprisoned but eventually vindicated and reinstated in the French army. Supporters hope that history will prove to be equally just for Terry Lakin.

McInerney gave sworn testimony on behalf of Terry. It is worth reading. Here is an excerpt from that affidavit:

> I recall commanding forces that were equipped with nuclear weapons. In my command capacity I was responsible that personnel with access to these weapons had an unwavering and absolute confidence in the chain of command. . . . I cannot overstate how imperative it is to train such personnel to have confidence in the unified chain of command. Today, because of the widespread and legitimate concerns that the president is constitutionally ineligible to hold office, I fear what would happen if such a crisis occurred today.

McInerney argued that President Obama must voluntarily submit his birth records, and he appealed to the court that heard Terry's case that if the president refused to bring forth his birth certificate, then the court was under the obligation to do so in the name of justice.

Those who read the full transcript of the hearing might conclude that the lieutenant general was also on trial. The judge looked him square in the face and said that the officer did not know enough about the Uniform Code of Military Justice.

"I'm intimately familiar with the Uniform Code of Military Justice, and I had general court-martial authority," says McInerney. It appears the role of the courts has somehow expanded to interpret military policy. "Our military must have confidence in their commander in chief," he states emphatically.

Cmdr. Charles Kerchner (Ret): I've got deep roots in this country and I'm not leaving!

"I never thought I'd fight a domestic enemy. I always fought the enemy from without!" says retired Navy commander Charles F. Kerchner, Jr. At issue is the question of Obama's eligibility to be president, an issue now compounded because he sits in the Oval Office.

Cmdr. Kerchner maintains that "Congress is not listening to the people, and the news media are playing interference for Barack Hussein Obama." Kerchner is not one to stand still in light of this declaration of war on our way of life and the Constitution he swore to uphold and defend. That is why he could not stand still in the matter of Lt. Col. Terry Lakin. He was a witness at Terry's court-martial.

"I watched them destroy Terry as he sat on the stand. His own lawyer, Neil Puckett, humiliated him!" Puckett had appeared for interviews on several broadcasts. Listening to those interviews now, one has to conclude that he set Terry up, ambushing him at the trial in the name of expediency.

During the court-martial, Terry, a seventeen-year veteran of the military, a doctor to our wounded soldiers and protector of the Constitution, was brought to the point of emotional collapse. The biggest battle of his career, armed only with the oath he took as an officer to support and defend the Constitution and a valid question regarding the eligibility of the sitting president, was lost in a few hours on the courtroom floor in a mockery of justice.

The commander says, "Terry Lakin was denied access to records and those who have records pertaining to Obama's eligibility. Yet these rights are guaranteed in the Uniform Code of Military Justice."

Kerchner observes that the trial counsel and the defense counsel at a court-martial should have equal opportunity to obtain witnesses and other evidence.

Cmdr. Kerchner saw and heard things he never thought would occur in a military court. "How does a judge admit that opening such evidence could be an embarrassment to the president? How could she say, 'It's up to Congress to call for the impeachment of a sitting president'? Did the judge know something that we all suspect?" asks the Navy commander.

"People today don't know the rule of law," he says. "Others actually want to trash the Constitution. They don't know what they're doing!"

Kerchner observes that Hawaii is covering up not only for Obama but also for a long list of people who got a short-form Certification of Live Birth and took it to the mainland as proof of citizenship.

And there is more. Kerchner believes that Obama's plans for the United States are right out of the Cloward-Piven strategy playbook. The plan is to systematically destroy capitalism by pushing the government into financial crisis. He invites anyone who disbelieves this to research the people who authored the plan: Richard Andrew Cloward and Frances Fox Piven.

In a letter written in 2010 to the president of the United States, Terry opened with the following:

> Commander Kerchner reminds us of an organization, Students for a Democratic Society, a radical group that emerged in the 1960s. "Remember the students who took to the streets and showed their rebellion against Capitalism? They were told to get an education, blend into society and that their day will come. Today, they are our judges, teachers, professors, politicians and hold some of the most respected positions in society."

According to the Kerchner, "Their day has arrived!" Can the American way of life be saved? Is there any hope for it? "If Congress does not wake up, we are lost!" he warns anyone who will listen.

Kerchner started out blogging in July of 2008 and continually wrote about the president's eligibility in order to try to awaken people. Finally, after waiting for someone else to take up the banner and actually challenge the president's eligibility, he felt compelled to sue Congress and the president himself because Obama had failed the eligibility test on several accounts, including his father's citizenship.

"The courts did nothing!" says the exasperated commander.

When Terry Lakin brought his grievance to the military courts, Cmdr. Kerchner thought he would finally get satisfaction. He didn't. "We are now on the verge of losing our constitutional republic," he says. "We need two million people from the silent majority to show up in Washington and demand the removal of Barack Hussein Obama. If we are silent, we are finished as a nation!"

As for Navy commander Charles F. Kerchner Jr., he's not backing down. "I've got deep roots in this country and I'm not leaving!"

Capt. Pamela Barnett (Ret): Our freedoms are at stake at this point.

Never Vetted, Unlawful President, The Loophole in Our Democracy is the title of Pamela Barnett's tell-all, a comprehensive book that deals with the most critical issue of our time, the eligibility of Barack Hussein Obama to be president of the United States. Pamela, a retired U.S. Army captain, pulls no punches in her desire to see truth prevail. "I didn't write the book to sell," she says. "I wrote it as an historical record."

In the early months of 2008, when Obama was seeking the Democrat presidential nomination, Capt. Barnett raised her own doubts about his eligibility. She attempted to get answers to her questions by following the path that most would take when dealing with such matters: she wrote to her congressman. Pamela requested that he look into the matter of Obama's eligibility to be president in accordance with Article II, Section 1 of our Constitution. She never received an answer even though she contacted his office many times.

Like millions of other Americans who have asked to see a valid birth certificate, Pamela has been dismissed as being a "radical" and a "birther." But she is concerned about other issues as well, specifically the friendships and associations that Obama made before he took the sacred oath of office to be president.

An avid student of history and world affairs, Capt. Barnett came upon information that troubled her. One concern was a frightening association with an individual in Kenya, Raila Odinga.

Odinga ran for president of Kenya in 2007. His platform included a commitment and promise to the Muslim population that he would seek to implement Sharia law if they supported him. He lost the election, and as a result of the highly contested results, his tribal followers, egged on by him, went on a rampage in mostly Christian villages. They killed at least a thousand people and displaced more than a million. In a gesture to ensure peace in the country, President Mwai Kibaki appointed Odinga to the office of Prime Minister.

What is the association of Obama and Raila Odinga? The record shows that then-senator Obama went to Kenya and actively campaigned for Odinga. About the violence and wholesale murder of Christians, Obama remains silent. Pamela remembers watching footage of the massacre during the post-election period in Kenya. "It terrified me! And no one in the mainstream media was reporting anything about it."

In her effort to flush out the real Barack Hussein Obama, she also wrote a letter to Colin Powell informing him of the senator's alliance with Odinga. A courtesy letter stated that Powell was "concerned" but would still support Obama's candidacy.

Pamela has not given up her quest to learn the truth about Obama. A continuous stream of letters has flowed from her desk. Her book, *Unlawful President*, shows the ambivalence of the nation about his legitimacy and the organized cover-up by federal agencies, individuals and the press to protect Obama.

Capt. Barnett has specific areas of expertise she brings to the question of Obama's eligibility. She knows a great deal about security clearances because she served as an battalion intelligence officer for the U.S. Army. Pamela emphatically declares, "Under the circumstances surrounding the conduct of Barack Hussein Obama and the fact that he cannot produce valid documentation surrounding his birth, citizenship and passport, there is no way he would ever get security clearance." She adds, "He has never proven he can even legally work in this country!"

"Our freedoms are at stake at this point, and I am doing everything I can to deal with the eligibility issue and other matters," she says.

And what exactly are the "other matters"? For one thing, Pamela is suing the government. Not an easy task for anyone, but she is determined to see Obama thoroughly examined by way of a comprehensive vetting process. If he is not properly certified by the standards of the U.S. Constitution at Article II, Section 1, Obama must be charged with fraud and stand before a U.S. court. She also wishes to see the entire election process "cleaned up" and only "eligible" voters permitted to cast a vote.

For Pamela this is purely a legal matter; there is no other motivation for her actions. Her reasons for supporting Lt. Col. Terry Lakin are simple. They rest in the constitutional requirements to hold the office of President. Terry is asking for proof of Obama's eligibility. Pamela is asking for the same. Her suit against the sitting president in our White House is on behalf of every American who wants to know the truth.

Lt. Col. Terry Lakin and Capt. Pamela Barnett are obligated to the Constitution, which they have pledged to uphold and defend. For this patriot, being a plaintiff in *Barnett v. Obama* is her way of defending the Constitution.

Jim and Peggy DeJarnatt: We need to get the message out!

Now it's up to individuals who believe the Constitution is the supreme law of the land to get the message out!

"I look at Terry Lakin like a signer of the Declaration of Independence," says Jim DeJarnatt. He and his wife Peggy are by no means strangers to Terry. They met him in February 2011 after having followed the case for more than a year. To their amazement, the officer was sentenced and sent to a facility, Leavenworth, practically in their backyard.

"We couldn't believe that the person we had read so much about was going to be at our doorsteps," says Jim. When he learned this, Jim wanted to visit the military prisoner, if only to encourage him that there were people "out there" who were inspired by his courage to stand up for what he believed.

The couple sent a letter directly to Terry at Leavenworth but did not expect to get a reply. Several weeks later Terry wrote and asked that they feel free to visit. From that time on, regular visitations were made, and a deep friendship was formed. Back then, Jim and Peggy had no idea how important their relationship was to the imprisoned lieutenant colonel.

"I knew he needed us," Jim recounts. He and his wife were not aware that every time Terry had a visitor, he had to be strip-searched before returning to his cell. Not a pleasant thing, but it was a price he was willing to pay for their friendship, which he needed during his imprisonment.

Interestingly, Jim and Peggy have shared Terry's story with other soldiers, who tell them they thought the whole affair was an "Internet rumor." No, it was not a rumor, even if the administration did all that it could to suppress the story. News media outlets, including some nationally televised programs, dropped the news as fast as they picked it up. "Now it's up to individuals who believe the Constitution is the supreme law of the land to get the message out," says Jim.

During those visits Jim sensed that his new friend was undergoing some interesting changes. Terry began to have a greater sense of God in his life and to understand destiny in seeing this through for the cause of truth.

After each visit, the couple not only shook hands with Terry and hugged him, they prayed with him as well. At first, Jim remembers, he led the prayer, but in time, the officer took the lead. Yes, something was happening in the life of Terry Lakin, and Jim and Peggy DeJarnatt were witnesses to it.

Personally, Jim has been overwhelmed with the decision Terry made to get to the bottom of Obama's eligibility. "I was an airline pilot for many years. I had a great job, made enough money to support my family and secured a good pension. Knowing that Terry was willing to give up the same for what he believes has really sobered me. I don't know if I could have done it."

The two supporters have never doubted that the officer, who earned a Bronze Star, was standing in the gap for them and perhaps millions who wished they had the courage to do the same. But that is what a soldier is all about—the courage to stand alone and face an enemy. The archives of history tell us that great men and women are capable of great sacrifice. "Terry certainly has sacrificed much," Jim reminds us.

The couple chronicled the lieutenant colonel's story in their local paper, *The Platte County Citizen.* In it they testified to their first-hand experiences with "a very exceptional man." Having come to learn that the vetting process is left up to the political parties, their article included this statement: "We, as a nation, have thus far operated on the honor system of scrutinizing our candidates' constitutional eligibility." While Jim questions the system, he is equally concerned with those individuals who have the responsibility to work within specific constitutional requirements. "Maybe honor isn't as honorable as it used to be," he says.

Add the couple's love of motorcycles to the story of Lt. Col. Lakin, and you have the making of another interesting partnership. On any given weekend you might see them riding down your local boulevard on their motorcycle. They won't be alone. Riding alongside the leather-clad pair will be dozens of other cyclists, members of the Christian Motorcyclists Association. Many members have supported the couple in their efforts to partner with Terry during these difficult days. Some are military veterans.

Their mission now is to continue to get out the word about Terry. They ask people to examine their own lives in view of the sacrifices he has made for what he believes to be a serious national issue. They entreat people to read the Constitution. They see Terry as an example of true patriotism, a man who did what he had to do to defend the Constitution.

When Terry was released, the DeJarnatt family took him out to a fancy restaurant for dinner. One might think that a juicy steak would have stimulated all the senses after eating prison food for all those months, but upon returning from the men's room, Terry commented, "Wow, real porcelain!" With all the luxuries and benefits of our affluent society, Jim could see that we ought never to forget the simple pleasures of freedom.

Peggy remembers thinking how tragic it was to see Terry give up a pension, lose his rank and spend five months in prison. "Although we didn't want him to go to jail, for me it was a God thing that he was imprisoned in our backyard." What she and Jim did not know at the time was that they were a godsend to Terry.

Orly Taitz, Esq.: "I believe [Obama] is the most dangerous thing one can imagine."

There is an expression that applies to Barack Hussein Obama's birth certificate. It is attributed to President Abraham Lincoln and you probably are familiar with it: *You can fool some of the people all of the time, and all of the people some of the time, but you cannot fool all of the people all of the time.*

No one likes to be fooled at any time, and that is one of the reasons why the Congress, the press and the American people cannot and will not face the truth about this president's "natural born" citizenship status. They've been fooled and can't deal with the fact that they truly have been, as the expression goes, "hoodwinked." The birth certificate Barack Obama presented at his rather hastily called press conference in the spring of 2011 would not hold up in an impartial court of law; it is a forgery. Perhaps the press, Congress and many citizens might wish the issue would just go away so they wouldn't have to deal with the embarrassing fact that they believe and support a lie. Well, it isn't going away, because there is one voice that will not be silenced. And that is the voice of Orly Taitz.

The cover-up of Obama's true identity is extensive and reaches every level of government, including the institution most responsible for defending our rights as citizens—our court system.

Orly Taitz has been a driving force in the Constitutional Movement (often called the "birther movement") and has taken her claims and evidence into our courts. The result? Judges have rudely dismissed and ridiculed her. They have literally challenged her sanity to bring such a charge against the sitting president. But Orly Taitz knows fraud when she see it, and her training and background tell her that the worse kind of fraud—the treasonous kind—cannot be tolerated in a republic that is supposed to follow its Constitution and the rule of law.

If you visit Orly Taitz's website, you are greeted with a banner: *World's Leading Obama Eligibility Challenge Web Site.* This banner is an affirmation of the efforts of a tireless and vigilant soldier on what seems to be a never-ending mission to challenge the eligibility of Barack Hussein Obama to hold the office of President of the United States. Orly Taitz is unstoppable.

Counselor Taitz has been there since the beginning. For years, she has challenged the authenticity of the "short form" birth certificate Obama first presented to the American people. But not only that; she also recognized the fraudulent résumé of a man who came from nowhere to the U.S. Senate, then straight to the White House.

She has also followed the steady stream of Social Security, Selective Service and other documents published by the White House and has had each professionally examined. A "stream" because there have been so many! All are at best deceptive.

Orly Taitz has taken this evidence nationwide to news stations and other media outlets, to individuals and community groups. As a lawyer, she has a keen understanding of Article II, Section 1 of the Constitution, and she has challenged newscasters and networks to get the facts straight about the issue. Few, if any, understand the meaning of "natural born" citizen and that is her starting point in most interviews. Her goal has been to educate and inform. The result? As in the courts, she has been ridiculed and belittled, her reputation "vandalized" before numerous audiences both publicly and privately. The media have castigated her by being rude and condescending. Bill O'Reilly typified this attitude when he called her a "nut." (One must admit, however, that the media outlets are consistent regarding

Obama's eligibility: even the competitive news services have been mum on this lie.)

It was the inevitable consequence of her desire to see our country back on the right track that brought Terry Lakin's case to Orly Taitz's attention. She has been conscientious in supporting him because the lieutenant colonel is testimony to the ends to which some people will go to support the Constitution and save the citizenry from the path to serfdom. How interesting that sometimes one person can see things that millions of others can't—or won't—see.

As a lawyer, Taitz is cognizant of the rule of law that has historically been the anchor of our political system. As the child of Russian immigrants, she defends the laws that govern her family in their adopted country. In the land of her ancestry, the government was above the laws that governed the people. Is she now to live in a duplicate society…one that exempts the president of the United States from the basic tenets of its own Constitution? Is Barack Hussein Obama above the law?

If you've heard her speak, these are the kinds of things she reports:

> A number of homosexuals from Obama's former church have died mysteriously.

> Obama has dozens of Social Security numbers—and his passport is inaccurate.

> A person who was cooperating with the FBI in connection with Obama's passport died mysteriously, shot in the head.

> A Kenyan birth certificate with the name "Barack Obama" is authentic.

> Obama's first act as president was to donate money to Hamas, which Taitz claims will be used to build Qassam rockets.

> Obama is having the Federal Emergency Management Agency build internment camps for "anti-Obama dissidents."

> Election fraud is part of the Obama presidency.

If any of these allegations are inaccurate or erroneous by any standard, Orly Taitz stands in error and deserves the negative press she gets. If what she declares is true and accurate in part or whole…well, you be the judge. But judge her after you have done your own research, the kind that reaches beyond the five o'clock news and the front page of Time or Newsweek or the newspaper you read. And watch out for the "experts"—they have their agendas too.

Orly Taitz has faithfully uncovered details and facts about Barack Hussein Obama that deserve our scrutiny. Knowing what she knows, it is no wonder she boldly declares, *"I believe [Obama] is the most dangerous thing one can imagine, in that he represents radical communism and radical Islam. He was born and raised in radical Islam, all of his associations are with radical Islam, and he was groomed in the environment of the dirty Chicago mafia. Can there be anything scarier than that?"*

You don't sum up the life or mission of Orly Taitz in a dozen paragraphs. She is an example to Americans who question our government when it compromises the Constitution with its actions, edicts or orders. Orly Taitz is one who is willing to stand up for the truth.

So, considering her determination and political insight, let's go back to that quote of Abraham Lincoln and make this adaptation: *"You can fool some of the people, but no matter what the courts try to dodge or the press publicizes or the White House suppresses, you cannot fool Orly Taitz!"*

Miki Booth: He's shredding the Constitution.

Miki Booth is a fighter: "I want people to hear the truth, because facts have a way of changing their minds." These are the words of a wife, mother, rancher and now author of a new book, *Memoirs of a Community Organizer from Hawai'i.*

To Miki, the truth about Obama does matter, and she has become a warrior in the fight to remove him from the Oval Office. She says that her involvement in this mission started several years ago when a friend recommended that she view a video of Lt. Col. Terry Lakin. She located the website and clicked on the play button. Before her was the kind of person she had admired all her life, someone willing to stand alone and pay a price for the truth, even willing to surrender his own career for what he believed.

"'When I was done viewing the video I wanted to be a champion for him, to join his cause and lend him my support," says Miki.

Miki had already been doing her own research into President Obama. "I researched everything and anything about him," she says. "What I learned was disturbing, and ever since, I have shared the facts about Barack Hussein Obama with anyone who will listen.

Mike continues, "I find that some people want to know the truth, while others find the truth disturbing and reject it. It's not that they deny the facts as much as they don't really believe this could happen in America."

Today, Miki and her family make their home in Oklahoma, but their roots are in Hawaii. Her family relocated there from Japan when she was two years old, and she grew up as a typical *keiki,* a child of the culture, eating the traditional foods, attending the same schools and hanging out with friends on the beaches that wrap the Islands. "It was a beautiful way to grow up," she recalls, and adds that everybody knew everybody.

As a young adult, she met and married another *keiki* named Fred. Together, they set out to start a life and raise a family. From the beginning of their marriage the couple had an interest in politics, and they became aware of the accepted political practices that included a great deal of corruption.

When they moved to Oklahoma, her husband's interest in running for the office of sheriff compelled them to re-register as Democrats, the dominant party in that part of the state. They fast learned that one's record of service and career experience was not as important as who one knew. When her husband lost the election, they thought they were done with politics. They were not.

In 2008, Miki received a postcard in the mail introducing candidate Barack Hussein Obama as the choice of the Democratic Party for president. The card included an appeal for funds. Of course, she was thrilled that a fellow Hawaiian would be on the ballot, but then the issue of his real birth records came into play and Miki launched her own study.

She began by opening a small box where she kept the birth certificates of her husband and son. She compared forms and information from these birth certificates and that of the Democrat candidate, Obama.

For one thing, the number on his form was not consistent with those of other children born during that time period. At that time, the only document Obama had made public, a "short form," proved only that a person had indeed been born—somewhere. Unlike most Americans, Miki knew this. To add to her anxiety, she noted that there was no "official" raised seal on his record of live birth that would properly certify the document. Now a red flag was up and it was waving! She wanted to know the truth, and she would not rest until she uncovered it.

Miki Booth wanted to see an actual birth certificate. So did Terry Lakin. After she and Terry communicated, a friendship was forged between the two. The good news for both was that there were thousands of other people with the same unanswered questions about Obama's birth certificate.

"He's shredding the Constitution," Miki tells people when she begins to explain Obama's "fast track" vetting and his dubious birth certificate.

Terry has paid a price for his convictions, and Miki has paid a price for hers. Friends from childhood have attacked and berated her. Others belittle her zeal for the Constitution. Old schoolmates have disengaged, and other former friends will have nothing to do with her.

When asked what keeps her going, Miki's reply is profound: "I'm about getting the truth out there!" Along the way, Miki started a branch of the Tea Party and even ran for Congress.

Her book, *Memoirs of a Community Organizer from Hawai'i*, tells her story. Miki Booth says she's just an honest and dedicated American citizen who makes no apologies for her love and defense of the Constitution.

Sharon Rondeau: We need to restore the rule of law.

Sharon Rondeau is an investigator. Not a private eye, but an American gal who would not let the eligibility issues raised during the 2008 presidential election pass her by without doing some serious probing. "I began to read and research information about the two senators," says Sharon. "My first thought was that both Obama and McCain might not be eligible to hold the office of President. In fact, I couldn't believe it, because nothing like this had ever come up in my lifetime."

As Sharon learned, ask the average U.S. citizen about the constitutional qualifications to be president and he might remember the "thirty-five-year-old" age requirement. Mention the words "natural born," and many will say that means someone born on U.S. soil. Throw in the words "native born" and get ready for some very interesting explanations comparing and contrasting the phrases.

Sharon Rondeau understands the meaning and differences between the two sets of words. She knows *her* Constitution, as she calls it, because it was designed to protect the individual. When Obama became the Democratic Party candidate, Sharon's questions about his birth qualifications to be president prompted her to write the Electoral College electors in her state. She received no reply. Her questions were also brought to the attention of the Republican House Judiciary Committee. "I thought when it got to that level, it would be a slam-dunk done deal!" To her amazement, it wasn't.

Looking for the truth, Sharon commenced an intense search into the life of candidate Obama. Too many things made his U.S. citizenship suspect. She thought, if he was indeed born in Kenya, he must have had or continued to have some association, some connection with the people. And he did.

Inquiry into the 2007 presidential election in that country revealed plenty. She learned about Obama's support of an opposition party candidate who promised to bring Sharia law to the country. Type the words *Odinga and Obama* in your favorite search engine, and you're in for a surprise, much the same as Sharon experienced during those first few days of study.

"Obama was so outspoken against the Kibaki administration that he became . . . an unwelcome meddler in Kenyan political affairs," wrote Sharon. "His visit there ended with a public rebuke in which a government spokesman stated, "It is now clear that he [Obama] was speaking out of ignorance and does not understand Kenyan politics; we earlier thought he was mature in his assessment of Kenyan and African politics."

Sharon would like to see an alliance among those who question Obama's eligibility. "We need to get together," she says, "all of the individuals and groups who question Obama's eligibility." As far as the birth certificate issue is concerned, she claims to have dissected all the arguments that have been offered in his defense. "There is no defense," she declares. "He is not a 'natural born' citizen."

"We've heard of a stock market crash," Sharon said in a recent radio interview. "Well, we've had a constitutional crash. Our country has literally been derailed."

As the editor of an online news service, The Post & Email, Sharon learned about the case of Terry Lakin and knew immediately she must come to his aid. "I had dealt with the birth certificate issue, and I was waiting for someone to come forth and deal head-on with the question of Obama's legitimacy," says Sharon. "I had every confidence a high-ranking officer would get answers."

Sharon believes that it was Terry's right to be granted discovery, and it surprised her when he was not given an opportunity to present his defense. "That's un-American," she says. "The issue of Obama's birthplace didn't even come up in the trial, and that's what it was all about!"

As an editor, Sharon Rondeau sifts through thousands of news stories, documents and e-mail messages each month. An article she recently published, titled "Wrists and Ankles Shackled" and written by a Vietnam veteran, picks up the fighting sentiment of many who see the injustice in Terry Lakin's case.

> Lakin rots in prison for four months, the White House sleaze releases his birth certificate, albeit a phony one. But being phony or not isn't the point. The point is that the president, eligible or not, let an honorable man rot in prison for something that he could have prevented by releasing his birth certificate back in December 2010. The point is that our government, all of the Judicial, all of the Legislative, and the Executive, was sending a message: You, the American citizen, have no redress whatsoever. None! We will destroy America and you can't stop us."

This unflinching article ends with a caveat:

> If they can do what they did to LTC Terry Lakin, in full view of the world, what chance do you think you have, for anything? For a false charge? How are you going to fight it when they own the courts, the cops, the press? What are you going to do? It's something to think about. They got off scot-free when they kangarooed and railroaded Lakin, didn't they.

Sharon is a bearer of truth and has paid a price for her beliefs. A stream of letters hits her site daily. Many incoming communications are negative. They attack her at every level, claiming she is only a glory-seeker, ignorant of the facts. Some demand that her publication cease. This is the strategy of modern-day liberal politics: insult, rebuke, complain, mock and discredit. Kill the message by killing the messenger.

On the election in 2012, Sharon reflects, "I think what brings Obama down may not be the eligibility. It might be something else!"

Peter Boyles: We still have no answers. The questions are still enormous!

"This is Talk Radio AM 630 KHOW. Coming up next is Peter Boyles!" It's early in the morning in Denver, and people are gearing up for another day. The routines are in order, and for many, these include a morning dose of their favorite talk radio host, Peter Boyles. His listeners have come to assume that their morning talk host will uncover another story of local or national significance.

Peter has done it before. Boyles was the first to report on Ted Haggard; he came out in support of the legal defense of Bureau of Immigration and Customs Enforcement Senior Special Agent Cory Voorhis; and he was among the first to raise the issue of Barack Obama's birth certificate. The list goes on.

Peter Boyles has taken on some of the most controversial issues and people of our time. Surely he knows that one broadcast could end his career—mistaking gossip for truth, making the wrong conclusion about something or someone. Fearless? Cautious? He doesn't have to be; for him it's all about telling the truth.

Being politically correct has never been his posture, and "fiddling 'n' fudging" with the details of a story is not what has kept him on the radio for so many years. While some commentators claim "the spin stops here," with Peter Boyles, it is best said that "the bull stops here!"

The archives of his broadcasts are filled with memorable interviews. Many of them deal with complex political issues like the case of Terry Lakin. If you're a guest on his program, and the topic for your interview is, say, national security, foreign policy or immigration, you will find that first and foremost, in any political dialogue with Peter, the Constitution will dictate the parameters of the interview.

Peter's radio audience must wonder, with dozens of stories coming across his desk early each morning, how Peter chooses one or two as topics for the day. He has to speculate which are worth the time and are of interest to his listeners. But some stories just have to be told.

And what was his first reaction to the story of an unknown lieutenant colonel who questioned his orders because he wanted to know if Obama was eligible to be president?

"I took it to the people right away!" he says. "I thought, 'Good, here's someone willing to call his hand.' And yet the mainstream people made fun of the guy. I mean, in fact, locally, they did a horrible job."

This issue of Obama's birth certificate was not new to Peter. He had spent a good deal of time on the airwaves talking about it. "A crescendo was building, particularly after it became apparent with that list of suppressed documents. No one knows this guy's story, and he continues to tell a story that's not true," says Peter. "The governor of Hawaii had lied for him; I think the mainstream press lies all the time about it."

Then there are the books allegedly written by Obama. Perhaps he thought his "life story" (or shall we say stories) would suffice for a birth certificate. The discrepancies are numerous. Journalist and author Jack Cashill, who has appeared with Peter on numerous occasions, reports that as he read *Dreams from My Father*, he found Bill Ayers staring out at him in the form of his vocabulary, style, semantics and syntax. Peter agrees that there is no way Obama wrote *Dreams from My Father* by himself.

"I think there has to be a break in this story," says Boyles. "I believe the birth certificate itself is a forgery, the one that the president released in that quickly called conference."

"I continue to be intrigued by the eligibility question just simply because this birth certificate has shown up in this very bizarre press conference. Many experts have taken the birth certificate apart. We still have no answers. The questions are still enormous!"

Peter continues to assert more of his concerns. "His Connecticut Social Security number that isn't his—how did he get that? Why are all of these things being suppressed? It's because there is something there." School records, draft records, college transcripts, publications, dissertations are not available, and Peter Boyles wants to know where they are.

But isn't it a risk for a noted newscaster to deal with such sensitive issues, especially since they are dealing with the president of the United States? When asked if he had any concerns about supporting Terry Lakin, he was quick to answer. "No, the show goes free form. No man is its master. Anyone who thinks they can control a talk show should get out of the business. They can't!"

Peter has a tremendous amount of respect for Terry and for what he did. You can hear anger in his voice as he tells his audience about the treatment Terry received from his government.

"Why did Obama allow Terry Lakin's life to be destroyed when all he had to do was present the document that he presented?" asks Peter. He observes that the release of the birth certificate came as Jerome Corsi's book *Where's the Birth Certificate?* was about to be published and Donald Trump was rising in the polls and getting all the media attention. Various states were pushing to establish eligibility criteria. "The argument went mainstream," says Peter, "and at that point he releases a document that is at best questionable."

"He allowed a very good, brave man to go to the pen and lose everything," Boyles tells his listeners and adds, "I believe there are legitimate questions about this that have never been answered." Peter's commitment to Terry has been admirable. He's held fund-raisers for him, and he has faithfully updated his audience on Terry's status.

Those who have not heard the show need only go to the archives and listen to the March 16, 2010, broadcast to know what kind of person Peter Boyles is. In that interview he made mincemeat of Glenn Beck.

When questioned about the birth certificate, Beck announced to the public, "I don't know what to believe!" Well, Peter Boyles knows what he believes and fully understands why Terry Lakin questioned the commander in chief. Many people, like his friend Beck, contend there are "greater issues" than the birth certificate. But as Peter knows, everything starts and stops with that issue.

Maj. Stefan F. Cook: I Made the Decision.

Lt. Col. Stefan Cook, passed away in January of 2012. Cook, then a Major in the U.S. Army Reserves, had challenged Obama's constitutional eligibility to serve as president in July 2009. After the lawsuit was filed Cook's orders to deploy to Afghanistan were rescinded by the Army. At the time the lawsuit was filed, Maj. Cook had expressed his concern that he might be carrying out illegal orders in the event that Obama was not constitutionally qualified to issue them. He had told WorldNetDaily, "[Then] any order coming out of the presidency or his chain of command is illegal. Should I deploy, I would essentially be following an illegal [order]. If I happened to be captured by the enemy in a foreign land, I would not be privy to the Geneva Convention protections."

Like most of us, surfing the Internet has become a daily routine. The flow of information is never-ending and brings us input from all corners of the globe.

In 2008, while surfing the Net, Army Reserve Officer Stefan F. Cook stopped at some websites and received a dose of doubt about the credibility of the most powerful man on earth, the president of the United States. While Stefan is not the kind of person to question the usual orders and demands of his employers, his role in the command of U.S. troops demanded more than a cursory look at what he was viewing and hearing. As an officer in the military, he needed to make a full investigation because the lives of those in his command were at stake.

Officer Cook's investigation brought him to one of the most difficult decisions he had ever had to make, one that would change his life forever. He decided to take the president of the United States to task and demand that he prove he was legitimately entitled to hold his office. Barack Hussein Obama had never rendered any evidence concerning his "natural born" citizenship, and Officer Cook wanted to know why.

During the months preceding the 2008 election millions of others were asking the same questions. Among them was Terry Lakin. Like Terry, Cook decided to have his day in court. An early interview records this life-changing event:

> Dr. Orly Taitz has filed on my behalf a Temporary Restraining Order (TRO) in Columbus, Georgia, to prevent me from deploying to Afghanistan until such time as Barack Obama produces definitive proof that he is a "natural born" U.S. citizen. The basis for the TRO is this: It is my duty as an officer in the U.S. Army to seek clarification as to the legality of orders directed to me by someone in my chain of command (the president of the United States and commander in chief of the Armed Forces of the United States) who is not eligible to do so. Should Barack Obama be found not to be a "natural born" citizen of the U.S. and I follow such an illegal order, I could be subject to punishment under the Uniform Code of Military Justice (UCMJ) as well as should I

have the misfortune of being captured by the enemy in Afghanistan, I could be subject to prosecution for war crimes as I was conducting military operations illegally.

These are the words of Stefan F. Cook, known to his friends as "Sparky." It was no secret to him then or now that his life would never be the same after his initial court appearance. He just didn't know at the time how [much] it would change. The Army reservist paid a price for bringing the matter to the courts. He, like Terry, was left standing in an empty courtroom with no satisfaction over his request to see Mr. Obama's birth certificate.

A review of Cook's military résumé finds him a "most respected army reserve officer." His courage to stand up to the president of the United States surely cost him further promotion up the ranks that he had been assured of in the coming months. But he had to make a decision that transcended promotions, notoriety and future entitlements. He made his intentions clear in an interview.

> "I have thought long and hard on my decision to file this TRO. I realize that this action may well end my career as an Army officer. I have discussed this decision with my family, and they are understanding and supportive. This has been a gut-wrenching decision to make. For my entire career in the Army, it has been pounded into us that it is our duty to seek clarification on orders we deem to be questionable in their legality.

One has to wonder how many other men and women in the military are caught in the dilemma of what to do.

> "I was ready to be deployed to Afghanistan when it hit me: my oath I took when I was promoted to the rank of Officer. I thought, if Obama didn't have the legal authority to give orders, I would put my men in harm's way. I had to find out if he was a 'natural born' citizen before I would accept the order."

When Cook entered the court with his lawyer, Orly Taitz, he was to learn a lesson. The courts were not going to go where "no man had gone before." Simply put, the court refused to hear the case. "I had no standing because as I was ready to proceed with the case, my orders were been pulled," says Cook. The notice came in a six-word script:

"YOUR SERVICES ARE NO LONGER NEEDED."

Simply put, if Officer Cook didn't have an official order, he couldn't contest it.

"I then filed another lawsuit, one based on personal injury in the matter of an unlawful firing." The plaintiffs were listed as Barack Hussein Obama, Robert Gates and others. But the powers that be were still not going to let this officer have his day in court.

Cook also learned that the Army was going to pull his security clearance. This hit hard a man who, by virtue of his intelligence and impeccable integrity, had won his way to an education at West Point and the Air Force Academy. Upon graduation from college, Cook had worked his way up the ranks and found himself a key decision-maker for the government.

"I had succeeded in getting Guantanamo building projects funded. I was a key man in getting things done. Everybody in the Pentagon who was involved in Guantanamo knew me and what I did and could do. They left me stranded in nothing less than a debacle!"

But Sparky is a fighter. "Personally, I think they were afraid of me. They buried me in civil court."

Officer Cook chatted with Terry on several occasions. "I admire Terry because of his dedication to the cause of defeating Obama," he says.

Today he is still in the service as an "inactive reservist." Health issues and other factors have closed the curtain on his quest to get the truth out regarding Obama's ineligibility.

But truth has its own dynamics—and perhaps in some unforeseen realm, it has substance. We can only guess that it does because of its strength to withstand the darkness of doubt and reveal itself. In any case, it is so powerful that it cannot be hidden for long, even if the best schemes of men and women try to withhold it. And you can be assured of one thing: people do have a great capacity to see the truth and react accordingly. Army officers Terry Lakin and Stefan Cook are banking on this.

☙

The Art of Terry's Case

Washington Times Ads

The Chain of Command Bulletin Board

This display appears in many military facilities.

Michigan Trucks

Popping up on trucks in Ohio & Michigan.
— In our thoughts Daily!
Rick

The Emperor Has No Clothes

WHEN IT COMES TO BIRTH CERTIFICATES, THE PRESIDENT IS *NAKED!*

The Freedom Club

Timeline to Lawsuits

Eligibility Checklist

Medical Application

Eligibility for Dummies

The Websites of Terry's Case and Life

Safeguard Our Constitution

http://www.safeguardourconstitution.com

This site provided information to the public and media during Terry's initial action and trial. It remains active for researchers.

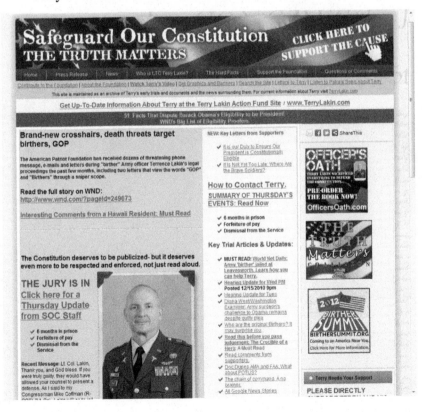

TerryLakinActionFund.com

This site was created to keep Terry's case and issue in the press.
The site carried Terry's story subsequent to his incarceration and
continues to provide information on his case and life.

OfficersOath.com

This site provides information on the book and subsequent publications.

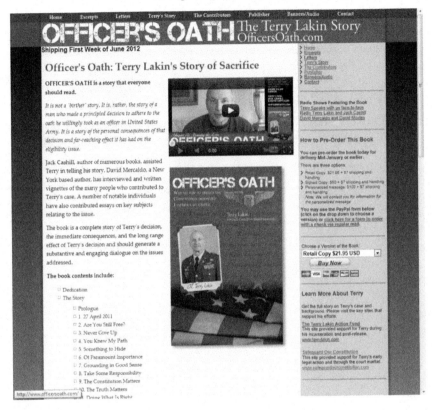

AmericasWebRadio.com

American's Web Radio approached the Trust just after Terry's incarceration. *The Terry Lakin Action Fund Radio Show,* now called, *Officer's Oath,* has provided range of interviews and insights into the eligibility issue and related topics.

HOME   PURCHASE   LISTEN ONLINE   ABOUT US   PROGRAMS   ADVERTISE   NON-PROFIT ORGANIZATIONS

Click Here to Listen to Radio Sandy Springs Online!

RSS

Officer's Oath - TLAF (Terry Lakin Action Fund) Radio Hour

Lieutenant Colonel Terrence ("Terry") Lakin most recently served as Chief of Primary Care and Flight Surgeon for the Pentagon's DiLorenzo TRICARE Health Clinic. He was also the lead Flight Surgeon charged with caring for Army Chief of Staff General Casey's pilots and air crew. LTC Lakin, selected for promotion to Colonel, is a native of Colorado, whose residency is Tennessee.

Since 2008 LTC Lakin has asked through his chain of command and his Congressional delegation for proof that President Obama is Constitutionally eligible to serve as his Commander-in-Chief. He has explained to his superiors that he cannot understand how his Oath of Office to protect and defend the Constitution does not allow military officers to pursue this proof of eligibility.

Terry has been court martialed through his pursuit of confirmation of Obama's of eligbility to act as commander of our armed services.

6 months in prison
Total forfeiture of all pay and allowances
Dismissal from the Service

All he wanted was the truth. Instead he got prison.

Terry is standing up for the nation. He needs the nation's help.

Key Eligibility Resources

These links and resources are presented only as a forum for those interested in the issues of presidential eligibility. It is not intended to be an endorsement of any particular site or position nor a specific representation of Terry's position.

- Must Read for Proponents or Skeptics:
  A Catalog of Evidence - Concerned Americans Have Good Reason to Doubt that Putative President Obama Was Born in Hawaii
  http://puzo1.blogspot.com/2010/05/catalog-of-evidence-concerned-americans.html

- Protect Our Liberty / Charles Kerchner: Commander Kerchner has lead the way in many key areas. Many great links, graphics, etc.
  http://www.protectourliberty.org
  http://cdrkerchner.wordpress.com

- Western Journalism's Landmark Report: *Clearing the Smoke on Obama's Eligibility: An Intelligence Investigator's June 10 Report*
  http://www.westernjournalism.com/exclusive-investigative-reports/clearing-the-smoke-june10/

- World Net Daily: Ongoing Coverage of the issue and regular supporter of Terry Lakin and his efforts.
  http://www.wnd.com
  List of Eligibility Resources:
  http://www.wnd.com/2012/01/the-big-list-of-eligibility-proofers

- Constitutionally Speaking: Conservative Christians for Constitutional Legislation
  http://constitutionallyspeaking.wordpress.com

- Devvy Kidd: Great article, "Military Brass Eat Their Own For Political Expediency"
  http://www.newswithviews.com/Devvy/kidd506.htm

- The Greeley Gazzette / Jack Minor: Regular Coverage of the issues and Terry Lakin's case
  http://www.greeleygazette.com

- Safeguard Our Constitution: The site that started Terry's case including the original videos and much background information.
  http://www.safeguardourconstitution.com

- Loyal to Liberty: Alan Keyes' blog full of insights and observations about everything.
  http://loyaltoliberty.com

- Birther Report: Regularly updated blog of a wide range of eligibility issues and articles.
  http://obamareleaseyourrecords.blogspot.com

- Western Journalism: A clear conservative view point.
  http://www.westernjournalism.com

- Peter Boyles on 710 KNUS Denver: Peter has been a regular commentator on this birth certificate issue with numerous hard hitting interviews and commentaries.
  http://www.710knus.com/peterboyles/

- The Birthers: Another site with many articles and links.
  http://www.birthers.org

- Patriots for America
  http://patriotsforamerica.ning.com

- AKDART: A broad collection of eligibility articles and resource from 100's of sources.
  http://www.akdart.com/obama.html

- Dr. Orly Taitz: Activist on the issue with many resources.
  http://www.orlytaitzesq.com

- Citizen Wells News: Obama eligibility, Obama news.
  http://citizenwells.wordpress.com

- The Radio Patriot: Andrea Shea King Show: Active and vocal
  spokesperson for a wide range of conservative issues.
  http://radiopatriot.wordpress.com

- drkatesview Blog: Thoughts on Our Constitutional Republic
  http://drkatesview.wordpress.com

- The Post & Email: A leading online news source for this issue and
  many others.
  http://www.thepostemail.com

- Sonoran News: Many conservative articles and wide coverage of
  Terry's case.
  http://www.sonorannews.com

General Timeline of Terry's Case

The points below outline the general timeline of Terry's case and the key issues.

- Previous to and throughout the presidential elections of 2008 former LTC Lakin became increasingly concerned about the complete absence of confirmation of Obama's compliance with the constitutional requirements for president.

- His concern came from his oath as an officer. The officer's oath is different than the enlisted man's oath. The officer's oath is to protect and defend the Constitution as is the oath of the president.

  - Officer's Oath: *I (insert name), having been appointed a (insert rank) in the U.S. Army under the conditions indicated in this document, do accept such appointment and do solemnly swear (or affirm) that I will support and defend the Constitution of the United States against all enemies, foreign and domestic, that I will bear true faith and allegiance to the same; that I take this obligation freely, without any mental reservation or purpose of evasion; and that I will well and faithfully discharge the duties of the office on which I am about to enter, so help me God.*

  - President's Oath: *I do solemnly swear (or affirm) that I will faithfully execute the office of President of the United States, and will to the best of my ability, preserve, protect and defend the Constitution of the United States.*

- For more than two years LTC Lakin pursued the issues through every standard military procedure to which had access. In every case he was ignored or stonewalled, even in procedures where responses were legally or procedurally required.

- After exhausting every avenue available to him he chose to disobey a direct order to deploy ("Missing Movement") and invite his own court martial with the hopes of forcing some evidence into the open through the normal processes of discovery. This decision was based largely on Obama's direct order to deploy troops.

- Terry produced a video outlining the reasons for his decision. http://www.terrylakinactionfund.com/terry/videos.html

- However, in the two pre-trial hearings the convening authority (equivalent of a civilian judge) stated immediately that it was her opinion that Barak Obama is the legal president and therefore all evidence to the contrary was disallowed.

- Therefore during the pre-trials and the actual court martial former LTC Lakin was not allowed to present one element of evidence in his defense. All witnesses of any type were denied. All depositions were denied. All requests for documents were denied.

- Terry produced a follow-up video discussing the pre-trial activities. http://www.terrylakinactionfund.com/terry/videos.html

- At his court martial the defense attorney simply rested (as there was no evidence to present) and worked to minimize Terry's sentence (six months instead of five years). The court also took away his pay, his pension, his benefits, his rank, and eventually formally discharged Terry from the Army.

- On May 14, 2011, Terry was released from Leavenworth and returned home to begin practicing medicine as a private physician.

- As of the date of publication not one person or organization has received or been given access to legally valid documentation of Obama's eligibility and natural born status. *However, many have been convinced that the two electronic documents are proof, though neither would be valid for common transactions or in a court of law.*